Dialectics of Chinese Labor

Studies in Political Economy of Global Labor and Work

Dialectics of Chinese Labor

Trade Unions under Market Socialism

By

Immanuel Ness

BRILL

ISSN 2667-288X
ISBN 978-90-04-76558-0
ISBN 978-90-04-76149-0 (PDF)

Library of Congress Control Number: 2026934025

Contents

Figures and Tables

Figures

Tables

Introduction: Chinese Workers under Market Socialism

For 50 years, Labor researchers and commentators have lamented that the decades-long decline in trade union representation as a worldwide phenomenon is accelerating despite the spread and growth of workers into the global South, where the majority of the world's population reside. Deindustrialization in the global North has deepened the decline of trade union membership and the societal power of trade unions, which have become less relevant in the lives of workers than at any time since the 19th century. Concomitantly, the shift and expansion of production industries to the global South have not given rise to appreciable growth in union membership. Paradoxically, robust trade unions are not emerging and existing unions are diminishing in membership and power as technological advances within workplaces have displaced workers in existing unions. Both in the North and South, workers are experiencing high levels of job insecurity. In the South, the majority of workers entering national labor markets are precarious laborers who scarcely can earn enough to survive, let alone sustain their families.

In sharp contrast to labor trends throughout most of the world, workers in China's All-China Federation of Trade Unions (ACFTU), the largest trade union federation in the world, are collectively experiencing substantial real wage growth, improvements to benefits and conditions on the job and labor rights within the workplace. Formed in 1925, the ACFTU has experienced unprecedented membership growth from 134 million members in 2005 to nearly 303 million members in 2018 (Xi 2018). Urban migrant workers comprise 140 million members of the Federation. Trade union membership is not compulsory, and all workers are covered by contractual bargaining agreements. Union dues are not paid by workers to the union; instead, unionized establishments must pay dues to fund trade union operations including organization, representation, raising grievances and public events.

The central argument of this book is that, while trade unions are declining worldwide, China's trade unions are thriving as the ACFTU supports the most unprecedented growth of organized members in history. The Chinese trade union movement is increasing exponentially and represents the most significant historical expansion in union membership ever, but this phenomenon is dismissed by Labor Studies research in the West which only considers as legitimate its own liberal democratic models of trade unionism. Trade unions in China are swept away as state propaganda or fake trade unionism without authentic labor representation. In essence, Western Labor Studies' perception of China's trade unions is nothing more than a form of cultural imperialism and anti-communism. Why must the Chinese working class adopt a model of trade unionism which benefits from the inequality of trade and pillage of the underdeveloped global South?

1   Labor and Trade Unions on the Periphery

This book specifically contrasts Western Labor Studies with the reality of labor relations found in transitional states of the global South (Lauesen 2024). At its core, Labor Studies in the West applies a model to labor movements worldwide without considering the structure of global capital accumulation and drawing identifiable distinctions among nation states. It is impossible to generalize the living conditions of the working classes worldwide and essential to recognize that workers struggle for improved living conditions within a world system and the transfer of value from the working class on the periphery to the core of the capitalist global economy.

The corollary is the formation of dynamic capitalist development with teeming working class democracy in the center and underdeveloped capitalism with anemic unions on the periphery of the world system. But, due to class polarization and the presence of revolutionary class conflict in the South, not all peripheral states surrender to the hegemony of the capitalist system.

Nation states on the periphery of the global economy are composed of three archetypes:

1.   Most peripheral states are former colonies dominated by rentier economies which are stewards of Western advanced capitalist corporations and are frequent victims of International Monetary Fund austerity programs. In most instances, but not all, peripheral economies have weak or non-existent trade unions (Afghanistan, Bangladesh, Democratic Republic of the Congo, Egypt, Ethiopia, Indonesia, Iraq, Kenya, Myanmar, Nigeria, Pakistan, Philippines, Sri Lanka, Sudan, Tanzania, Thailand, Uzbekistan, Yemen).

2.   Semi-peripheral formations, which are subservient to Western imperialism, whose economies are not fully dependent on the imperial core and have a modicum of capital and technology but where high levels of poverty are frequently rampant. Semi-peripheral societies are polarized on the basis of class, gender and other identities. Wealth is highly

stratified on the basis of class, race, religion, caste and gender. Under neoliberalism, trade unions have declined significantly and are no longer a potent societal force (Argentina, Brazil, India, Mexico, South Africa, Turkey).

3. Transitional states which resist imperialism with vigorous anti-capitalist class conflict in response to extractive and underdeveloped capitalism. Conflict often takes the form of struggle over labor and resources. These states include socialist projects (China, Cuba, Laos, North Korea and Vietnam) and states attempting to oppose imperialism (Burkina Faso, Mali, Nicaragua, Niger, Venezuela). Opposition to the imperialist core is intermittent and sustained. In transitional states, working class conflict is organized through political parties which have gained power to initiate the transition to socialism, as was the case in the Soviet Union and the People's Republic of China. Socialism does not occur instantly, above all because the revolutionary struggle only occurs on the underdeveloped periphery.

Transitional projects, including the former Soviet Union, unremittingly endeavor to advance and modernize technology and the means of production, recognizing that socialism must be accompanied by technological development. Though not always successful, only transitional states on the periphery have accomplished the transition from semifeudal and capitalist modes of production to socialism; most notably China is in an inchoate form. Before socialism can be achieved, the transitional state must acquire the capacity to develop a socialist mode of production. Socialism does not just appear without delay, and China and other socialist projects must encounter the opposition of the capitalist imperialist center.

Labor conflict does not follow a single pattern and occurs in three specific locations: the imperialist center (North America and Western Europe), the capitalist periphery (Indonesia, Mexico, South Africa) and transitional socialist states (like China and Cuba).

Successful labor movements require both a socialist political party and trade unions which are focused on mobilizing the working class: the party to develop plans to advance the interests of the working class writ large; and, according to socialist doctrine, trade unions which confine their efforts to improving the immediate conditions of the working class within a capitalist mode of production moving towards socialism. In no case have revolutionary transformations occurred immediately, an objective and standard which Western Marxists require but is impracticable and idealistic. Consequently, reformist parties tend to form in the capitalist core and revolutionary parties on the periphery of the global economy.

In the Preface to the 1892 edition of *The Condition of the English Working Class 1844*, Friedrich Engels suggests that wages and conditions for a segment of labor noticeably improved:

> That their condition has remarkably improved since 1848 there can be no doubt, and the best proof of this is in the fact that for more than fifteen years not only have their employers been with them, but they with their employers, upon exceedingly good terms. They form an aristocracy among the working-class; they have succeeded in enforcing for themselves a relatively comfortable position, and they accept it as final. (Engels 1892/1952, xv)

The emergence and expansion of the labor aristocracy may have driven the British capitalist class to capture a greater share of surplus value through advancing economic imperialism in the late 19th century. In this sense, the labor aristocracy is both cause and effect of British imperialism.

Due to the value-transfer by European colonialism and imperialism on the periphery, trade unions in the core turned into effective economistic institutions whose members profited through higher wages, and together with allied working-class parties adopted social democracy and reformism which created an aristocracy of labor from the mid-19th century to the present (Breman 2026). Eric Hobsbawm asserts that the British working class benefited significantly from imperialism in the 1860s:

> The further we progress into the imperialist era, the more difficult does it become to put one's finger on groups of workers which did not, in one way or another, draw some advantage from Britain's position, who were not able to live rather better than they would have done in a country whose bourgeoisie possessed fewer accumulated claims to profits and dividends abroad, or power to dictate the terms of trade with backward areas. Or, since there is no simple correlation between the standard of living and political moderation, on workers who could not be made to feel that their interests depended on the continuance of imperialism. (Hobsbawm 1967, 360)

The foundation of the labor aristocracy is at all times imperialist exploitation of the periphery, a pattern which expanded from 1860s Britain to Europe and North America in the 19th century through the present. Undeniably, Hobsbawm extends the labor aristocracy in Britain who benefited from imperialism to "important bodies of hitherto unprivileged and underpaid" workers (Hobsbawm 1967, 360). Echoing Lenin, Hobsbawm asserts that the labor aristocracy is unambiguously facilitated through an alignment of social-democratic political parties and trade unions with the imperialist project (Hobsbawm 1970).

2 Trade Unions and the Transitional State in the People's Republic of China

This book draws a fundamental distinction between, on the one hand, reformist social-democratic parties and trade unions and their members in the core countries, which are beneficiaries of imperialism; and, on the other hand, peripheral transitional states with communist parties and trade unions, which are striving for revolutionary transformation. Some states have revolutionary political parties and trade union federations in power (viz. Communist Party of China (CPC) and ACFTU), and others have communist parties and federations which are challenging bourgeois democratic parties for power: viz. India's Communist Party of India (Marxist) (CPI(M)) and the Centre of Indian Trade Unions (CITU); South Africa's fractured left, notably the South African Communist Party (SACP) and Economic Freedom Fighters (EFF) and independent Marxist-Leninist trade unions, including the National Union of Metalworkers of South Africa (NUMSA); and, in Brazil, fragmented left parties and unions, including the Communist Party of Brazil (PCB), the Workers Party and the splintering trade union center (Central Única dos Trabalhadores (CUT)). The former party–union alliances in core countries are beneficiaries of imperial plunder, and the latter resist economic imperialism. In that context, the CPC and ACFTU operate in partnership to advance socialism with Chinese characteristics, specifically improving the conditions of the working class as the economy advances. The character of a transitional state was powerfully set forth by Lenin in January 1922:

> Under the transitional type of proletarian state such as ours, however, the ultimate object of every action taken by the working class can only be to fortify the proletarian state and the state power of the proletarian class by combatting bureaucratic distortions, mistakes and flaws in this state, and by curbing the class appetites of the capitalists who try to evade its control, etc. Hence, the Communist Party, the Soviet government and the trade unions must never forget and must never conceal from the workers and the mass of the working people that the strike struggle in the state where the proletariat holds political power can be explained and justified only by the bureaucratic distortions of the proletarian state. ... Hence, when friction and disputes arise between individual contingents

of the working class and the individual departments and organs of the workers' state, the task of the trade unions is to facilitate the speediest and smoothest settlement of these disputes to the maximum advantage of the groups of workers they represent. … The only correct, sound and expedient method of removing friction and of settling disputes between individual contingents of the working class and the organs of the workers' state is for the trade unions to act as mediators. (Lenin 1922/1973, 187)

Without cognizance of the stark distinction between social-democratic imperialist states and socialist transitional states, it is unrealistic to compare the People's Republic of China (PRC) and the ACFTU with Western bourgeois political parties and trade unions, aside from measuring the efficacy of mobilizing workers in defense of their class interests.

3 Trade Unions in the Transitional State

In effective transitional states with the capacity to develop productive forces and advance the interests of the working class, of necessity, trade unions must serve as a transmission belt of the communist political party.

In the PRC, the trade union is a recruiting ground for cadre in the political party. The CPC views the ACFTU as the primary institution and agency for identifying and molding party members. The role of the ACFTU is to advance the line of the CPC among the working class and to prevent counterrevolutionary forces from developing. The trade union federation is decisive in ensuring discipline within the working class. The trade union is decisive for defending the revolution as any opposition would emerge through the working class. Foreign non-governmental organizations (NGOs) have used labor organizations to challenge the ACFTU, mobilizing opposition within the working class through promoting the formation of similar "worker organizations" to those currently developed in the West which are opponents to the trade unions. In the 2010s, foreign NGOs funded the development of anemic workers' centers and working-class formations as an alternative to the strong and holistic trade union model. Thus, from the 1990s to the 2010s, the West has promoted weak powerless unions which typically respond on a piecemeal basis to multinational corporations and new technological applications. These associations have opposed a centralized model of trade unionism and tried to replace them with syndicalism rather than establishing a strong voice of the working class akin to the ACFTU.

The transitional state is a peripheral nation developing a socialist mode of production. By necessity, a workers' party must retain control over the dominant state apparatus, land, finance and economy. Trade unions of the transitional state have a collective responsibility to: (1) maintain an institution to defend their workers within a hostile world-system; and (2) support the state in developing the productive forces to meet human and societal needs and move towards socialism. In the course of the history of the 20th century, sacrifices have been made by the working class to try to achieve the goals of the transitional state and make headway towards the socialist mode of production. The individual workers must make every effort to adhere to socialist state planning and programs rather than advancing their economistic self-interests. Thus, in certain phases, the working class must forego immediate demands to preserve and expand the long-term collective class interests implanted by the workers' party.

The transitional state maintains a flexible economy controlled by the state sector, collective and cooperative production and private sector markets. China has propped up a significant non-public sector of national and multinational enterprises during the "opening up" period. But the CPC has also encouraged trade union struggles in all sectors of the economy among both private and state-owned enterprises. In view of the fact that the private sector employs more than 80 percent of all workers, the ACFTU's organizing achievements and improved working conditions in the non-public economy are remarkable. Workers are participants in labor disputes, which are openly documented through the state and CPC in the *Chinese Statistical Yearbook* and *The Worker's Daily*.

However, as the CPC is in command of the economy, the political line is decided by the party without an immediate need for an antagonistic contradiction between the state and the labor movement. The CPC does not deny that labor conflict continues in the transitional state. In response, it has established an expansive labor mediation court system which this book will show typically decides on the basis of workers' interests. But investment decisions are planned by the state and "socialism with Chinese characteristics" grants it the right to prioritize immediate gains in the form of consumption over investment in future gains.

The character of the trade union struggle in a transitional state is different from the trade union struggle in societies ruled be capital. In the transitional state the capitalist sector is controlled by a planned economy, in coordination with the state-owned sector. Non-public enterprises are circumscribed by the CPC and the ACFTU.

The division of the world-system into center, periphery and transition state is also reflected in the international organization of trade unions. The ACFTU and its industrial, provincial and spatial affiliates have grown to collectively represent more than 300 million workers, or about 75 percent of 400 million workers in the PRC. The foundation of this dramatic growth is what I call holistic unionism. The two primary features of holistic unionism are the will to respond to democratic demands of workers and a formidable organization which maintains and grows the capacity to compel private and public employers to comply with workers' reasonable demands. The outcome is a significant growth of trade union membership in terms of numbers, range of industrial sectors and skill levels.

The objective of this study is to present an accurate portrait of the workers' movement in China through the lens of the ACFTU, workers and Labor research. Above all, the book seeks to avoid ridicule, trivialization and over-simplification of individual case studies based on mistaken premises leading to false conclusions. Instead, it examines Chinese workers and trade unions in historical and comparative perspective and identifies the unique constraints and dynamics of a transitional state committed to advancing the collective needs of its working class. The PRC has experienced more than 70 years of protracted challenges led principally by external forces aiming to undermine its determination to improve the standard of living for urban and rural workers. In addition to showing what the PRC and its trade union federation strive to accomplish, it is necessary to show what they do not do. Reaffirming Freeman and Medoff's valuable exploration of US trade unions (1984), this book asks: What do Chinese unions do?

4   Party–Trade Union Alliance

I claim in this book that the ACFTU has fostered the growth of holistic unionism which responds to the democratic demands of workers and then organizes them into its constituent unions, representing a large majority of China's working class, through negotiating agreements with employers and advocating for the improvement of wage and benefit standards which are supported by the state. This perspective departs from what I define as Eurocentric monolithic and intentionally immoderate assessments of the Chinese trade union movement by many Western Labor Studies scholars. These unfairly dismiss the ACFTU as a legitimate representative of the working class. Such assessments frequently function as an echo chamber through failing to account for the ACFTU's achievements in improving the wages and conditions of the Chinese working class and hold the Federation up to standards which Western unions do not meet. Over and again, the labor literature on China from left to right conforms to reinforce culturally imperialist ideals and does not consider the ACFTU on its own terms and benchmarks for success: to represent the democratic aspirations of China's working class and implement the directives of the CPC. This perspective, originating in the West, contends that the West's political institutions and organizations are far superior to all others. This interpretation's Labor Studies adherents, through disparaging the PRC, engage in unqualified cultural imperialism to denigrate all other forms of governance and labor representation as inferior and even go so far as to seek to interfere in the internal affairs of other states. However, one must ask, if Western forms of trade union organization are superior, why do their initiatives have meager results?

A second claim of this book is that the ACFTU is far more effective for the Chinese working class (even if Western standards are used as the benchmark) than Western unions are for their own members. The ACFTU outperforms all other trade unions through organizing and representing workers who have the freedom to decide if they wish to join and become members of its industrial and geographic affiliates. Moreover, the ACFTU is the driver of wage increases, benefits and insurance and is a potent force in improving working conditions in a nation state which is demonstrably committed to workplace health and safety.

The PRC is not unique in preserving a trade union alliance with a political party. Numerous such examples can be found throughout the world. Moreover, in those instances when a trade union is allied with a party holding state power, workers are not compelled to go on strike.

In Sweden, where the Social Democrats hold power, trade unions rarely strike to improve their wages and conditions as the alliances tend to reach settlements before strikes become necessary. The achievements of the CPC–ACFTU partnership in China flow from the 1949 Chinese Revolution. The ACFTU was formed in 1925 and affiliated with the CPC and remains committed to advancing the "dictatorship of the working class." If party–trade union alliances are a norm in countries with effective unions, then why shouldn't this also be true for the ACFTU in China? Detractors dismiss the ACFTU as beholden to the CPC, designating it as a "party-state," an insult to indicate that it is not a trade union in spite of the fact that the most effective trade unions are affiliated with a political party (Traub-Merz 2011). The expression is used so often that it has become a mistaken cliché which we must all follow at risk of facing exclusion. But academic scholarship should never rely upon or atrophy into a supposed absolute canon where research and debate are obstructed.

If we narrow scholarship to uninterpretable "fact," we fail to consider history, the passage of time, new events and changing practices which bear on human subjectivity and agency.

Labor Studies in the West laments the waning of trade unions in the West and worldwide yet lacks a consensus on a strategy to counter the enduring temporal decline. Research tends to focus on employer and government opposition to unions, while some thinkers celebrate the decline and many suggest that the emergence of new working-class organizations outside of existing union structures is a positive development. Yet those who revel in the decline in existing unions have no solution to staunch the regression of genuine working-class organizations dedicated to advancing members' interests. Instead, some Labor Studies scholars view the weak and practically passive trade unions as paving the way for democratic labor power in the absence of resilient and established unions. Advocates of autonomous worker uprisings and riots in response to the injustice of capitalists dismiss the value of organization. Political parties and trade unions are obsolete vestiges of past generations of workers. This book claims that it is true that new approaches to organizing workers are important as a consequence of technological change which creates new labor processes. It may also be true that a large number of existing trade unions in the West are both bureaucratic and uninspiring to a labor force which has shifted away from manufacturing towards the service sector and digital economy. But if that were the case, why in the West have so many labor initiatives sprouted up encouraging people to join unions, especially among workers outside highly socialized workplaces like factories but also including small and sporadic service establishments such as coffee shops and, increasingly, the digital economy, where workers are atomized and isolated from most of their peers?

Undeniably, a reason for the decline in the ability of trade unions on the periphery to represent workers has been their weakness in confronting neoliberalist practices which have become integrated into capitalist global supply chains. A related weakness has been their submission to conditions of foreign direct investment aimed at producing commodities and delivering natural resources at low cost. By doing so, trade unions have weakened and now lack the capacity to represent workers, let alone improve wages. Western economic imperialism condemns workers on the periphery to a subordinate position in global production. Consumers in core countries benefit from lower cost commodities resulting through the inequality of international trade (Emmanuel 1972/2025). In the postcolonial era, the value of production in the global South remains subservient to rich countries of the North, and the South's trade unions are captives to international capitalist markets which assign a lower value to the labor of Southern workers. Accordingly, Labor scholars searching for the reason why trade unions are declining in the global South even as industrialization is growing will find their answer in the depreciation of the value of production through trade. Certainly, labor unions in the South are incapable of overcoming unequal exchange of international trade which consigns workers to perpetual subordination. In contrast, under China's market socialism, wages, benefits, working conditions and ecological conditions are gradually improving. Holistic unionism is defined through the ACFTU's charge and commitment to improve the standard of living of the Chinese working class, its responsiveness to worker demands and its authority to improve wage standards and working conditions.

Labor scholar Zhang Zhongyuan contends that, despite the entry of non-public managers into the CPC, trade union organizers retain their focus on improving living standards and defending and improving the conditions of workers due to the historical legacies of revolution that "haunt would-be" class enemies. Consequently, the party and trade union are compelled to continuously deliver positive material outcomes for workers precisely because of their own first and second generational knowledge of immiserated and desperate workers. They represent a working-class stratum highly sympathetic to employees. Western critics of the PRC may identify ACFTU organizers supportive of non-public enterprises in rare instances. But organizers are occasionally supportive of employers to preserve the jobs of members. Zhang Zhongyuan contrasts ACFTU organizers who are devoted to advancing the material interests of workers qualitatively unlike "bought" union officials who are routinely found in the West or global South (Zhang 2025).

5 Research and Evidence: Applying Utopian Ideas to Historical Materialism

The analysis of the form and character of the ACFTU is derived from data available in ACFTU archives, the China University of Labor Relations, trade union university archives, interviews with trade union officials, Labor scholars, interviews with workers, ethnographic *in situ* studies with enterprise managers, workers, interview data, research on employer practices, long and all-embracing discussions with academics and students in China, and research and evaluation of NGOs in Hong Kong. This research began in 2013 and continues to the present.

This book is also based upon a study of a major 2014 strike among about 40,000 workers at a factory making athletic shoes in Dongguan, and evaluation of ethnographic work I conducted among NGO operatives embracing a range of perspectives in opposition to China and its labor movement (Ness 2015; Schmalz et al. 2016). The names of informants are confidential. Briefly, NGO operatives failed to provide convincing evidence of their claims and seemed to be in competition for foreign funding to advance a universal agenda to discredit and shame the PRC, as they do in other contexts. The US National Endowment for Democracy (NED), a US government agency, alone spends $10 million annually to disparage China (Yu 2021). The International Confederation of Free Trade Unions (ICFTU) and today's reconstituted International Trade Union Confederation (ITUC), as well as national Western trade unions, have used enormous resources, directly or through Western NGOs, to influence trade unions on the periphery towards social democracy. In Hong Kong, NGOs have attempted to build a trade union confederation in opposition to the State and have stationed labor NGOs in Hong Kong and beyond focused on unsettling the ACFTU.

To genuinely comprehend the Chinese model of trade union representation one must comprehend the goals and objectives of the Marxist Leninist model developed and advanced by V. I. Lenin in the Soviet Union and adopted by Mao Zedong based on the leadership of the CPC. In short, the CPC personifies the dictatorship of the proletariat and exercises absolute control over the political sphere; the ACFTU, as its affiliated trade union, must follow the general directives of the party.

Labor Studies literature in the West is uncompromising and one-sided in opposition to actually existing socialist projects. However, some Labor critics are silent on the question of the hegemony of the CPC over independent political perspectives. To some, the introduction of market socialism under Deng Xiaoping represented a clear-cut ideological break with the CPC under Mao Zedong. However, if one reads the literature carefully, the goals and objectives of Deng and his successors were predominantly serving the state in accordance with the principles of the 1949–76 era. Certainly, the market socialist system represents a divergence from the path towards socialism, but, according to the speeches and writings of Deng Xiaoping, the state remains committed to the path of developing and perfecting its socialist system. Labor Studies researchers share a common predisposition which is motivated by a partisanship categorically opposed to the transitory Chinese socialist state and socialism with Chinese characteristics.

By no means does this book claim that all critics are analogous, but the vast majority are disposed to use an idealistic perspective to evaluate China based on their own favorite political outlooks. Taken together, those who dare to cast a more accurate view of China based on what the state seeks to achieve and grounded in its distinct form of socialism will confront pervasive derision and ridicule from *respectable* Labor scholars in the West. Careful and attentive thinkers may come to a more nuanced conclusion which is not filled with polemical invective and animosity towards China, past and present. The meticulous work of Isabella Weber, for example, demonstrates that, in contrast to almost every other country, China did not succumb to US-led neoliberal policies. Instead, it retained control over state owned enterprises and maintained collective ownership over agriculture (Weber 2021). Taken together, China's workers also benefited from a strong and protective trade union federation which shielded them from the extreme forms of exploitation found in the periphery and former socialist states after the dissolution of the Soviet Union in 1991. Likewise, Barry Naughton contemplates how China measures up to four features of socialism without engaging in absolutes. Although his analysis ignores the concept of the principal contradiction which the state must always contemplate, at least it has a measure of rigor and an absence of bias (Naughton 2017).

6 Capitalist and Socialist Markets and the Reserve Army of Labor

Interpretation of the natural world must go beyond a historical trajectory and be repeatedly revised to reflect changes in the workers' material conditions and the new subjectivities they will respond to in their new reality. From 1978 to 2025, no working class experienced a greater transformation of its environment and material conditions than China's. Mass migration of the rural working class to urban centers permanently transformed the lived environment and the production process for 400 million workers. Marxists must recognize that the natural world is in continuous transformation as conditions are never fixed and static but change in response to the development and application to work of new technology. If workers live under capitalism or socialism, change is the common denominator. The difference is that, under capitalism, the motive force of changing relations to production is the constant pursuit of profit through the extraction of surplus value from workers.

The development of new technology under socialism is not motivated by profit but by a determination to improve working conditions and reduce the exploitation of labor and the environment. As the dominant form of production, capitalism is in continuous search of profit through investing in new instruments of production and technology to increase productivity and reduce the cost of labor, thus generating higher surplus value through extracting higher value from each worker as the pool of necessary labor declines.

If workers are more productive, individual wages may increase or decline, depending on skill and training. Conversely, surplus value can be extracted if capital is not invested in new technology through deliberately maintaining obsolete machinery and equipment and increasing the intensity of work. Instead of investing in modern productive instruments of production, capitalists can increase the exploitation of labor by lengthening the workday, withholding investment in occupational safety and disregarding government labor laws which protect workers against, for example, child labor and erratic payment of wages.

We can compare the rickshaw puller to the development of the auto-rickshaw and then the automobile, and platform technology through which the worker directly engages in work and transactions with the consumer, without the employer as intermediary. Business strategies established on the intentional non-subsumption of capital and superexploitation of labor generate surplus value up until the point when the reserve army of labor is depleted. Contrary to the capitalist market, where surplus value is the solitary goal of the capitalist, market socialism invests in new technology to improve the working conditions of labor. However, the socialist market can also generate a reserve army of labor. But the difference is that the state controls the contradictions of the market through directly intervening in it to defend workers. Certainly, a reserve army of labor is likely to emerge under market socialism. But the decisive difference is that the state takes responsibility for the well-being of workers through interceding and defending those who are displaced and exposed to the market economy. The socialist state is compelled to protect and secure the prosperity of displaced workers before they become precarious.

The trade union is the intermediary between the market and workers. In the Chinese socialist market economy, the trade union is charged by the CPC to defend workers' rights. Modern Chinese market socialism operates in accordance with the policy under which the trade union must become a transmission belt to advance the maturing working-class state, a model theorized and carried out by Lenin.

One of the greatest and most serious dangers confronting the numerically small CPC (which, as the vanguard of the working class, is guiding a vast country in the process of transition to socialism, for the time being without the direct support of the more advanced countries) is isolation from the masses: the danger that the vanguard may run too far ahead and fail to "straighten out the line," fail to maintain firm contact with the whole army of labor, that is, with the overwhelming majority of workers and peasants.

Just as the very best factory, with the very best motors and first-class machines, will be forced to remain idle if the transmission belts from the motors to the machines are damaged, so our work of socialist construction must meet with inevitable disaster if the trade unions—the transmission belts from the Communist Party to the masses—are badly fitted or function badly. It is not sufficient to explain, to reiterate and corroborate this truth; it must be backed up organizationally by the whole structure of the trade unions and by their everyday activities. (Lenin 1922/1973, 192)

It is essential for the trade union (not some other organization or party within or outside the state) to abide by the CPC to defend and improve worker rights and conditions. This salience of the trade union is decisive in defending workers as it is expected to carry out the objectives of the working class which sustain the socialist system. Fundamentally, under market socialism, the state apparatus restrains the harsh effects of unemployment and redundancy through safeguarding the working class. In China, it is the party and the union which bear the exclusive responsibility of responding to the democratic demands of the working class, not an external body which may or may not consider worker interests paramount. Unlike capitalist systems, the state's charge is to continuously promote the upgrading of technology and to make certain that the conditions of all workers are improved. Market forces are weakened by the socialist state, which prevents the unpredictability of the market.

To be sure, workers engage in democratic protest and appeals to the state as a means of struggle. The state is not challenged by workers' democracy as it stands for the interests of the working class, which openly demands improvement in its material conditions within primarily private workplaces through the ACFTU, the subjective agency representing its class interests under market socialism. Accordingly, the state does not need to be prompted by external forces to defend workers. The economic churning of the urban economy has posed new challenges to workers confronting manufacturing, new technology, displacement and the emergence of a vast urban economy composed of new forms of employment. The ACFTU is prepared to adjust its organizing strategies based on its experiences of the urban economy. The Federation is now prepared for the new economic forms in technology and the rise of the digital economy. Decisively, China is still a rural country with a rural population of about 500 million. While rural workers have greater flexibility under market socialism, all workers in urban and rural regions can always return to their own plots of land. The Chinese state continues to own all property under market socialism. The safety valve of the rural economy confers on all workers a right to live on and work the land. Xinyu Lu emphasizes the preservation of socialism in China through the state's continued formal ownership of all property (Lu 2024).

7   Chapter Outlines

Chapter 2 compares Western trade unions and the legacies of trade unions designed by European colonial authorities which endured following independence to the Chinese model of trade unions. The chapter evaluates the Chinese trade union movement using both Western metrics and the distinct goals and objectives of the CPC. A principal claim of the book is that the Western trade union model is failing the working classes of the global South as it has always been dominated by the imperialist model, which is rooted in the unequal exchange of trade and constrains workers' capacity to achieve their democratic and socialist aspirations. On the periphery, an upper stratum of workers may benefit but most are relegated to subordinate and marginal status and excluded by existing unions, most notably in South Asia.

Chapter 3 examines the central features of the ACFTU and the distortions about it advanced by Western scholars. The investigation provides concrete evidence that the ACFTU is a responsible trade union which operates within the Chinese socialist state.

Chapter 4 compares the ACFTU to trade unions worldwide over the past 50 years and demonstrates that not only is it true to its calling of advancing the interests of the Chinese working class, but it also scores far better than any other trade union on the basis of meeting their material needs and improving their working conditions.

Chapter 5 focuses on China's rural–urban migrant workers as the foundation of the country's growing economic prosperity under market socialism and the successful, tripartite state, party and trade union initiatives to absorb hundreds of millions of workers into the urban economy. China's internal migration from rural to urban areas is the largest population transfer in human history. In a span of 40 years, the country's population voluntarily moved to urban areas. Migration from rural areas to the cities in China did not result in the development of urban slums and underserved settlements that are present throughout South Asia, Southeast Asia and Latin America.

Chinese migrant workers are commonly identified as "floating workers," as it is impossible to fully economically integrate them as residents in destination cities, even though they are indispensable to the economic vitality of the nation. This chapter contends that most critics neglect or ignore the formidable challenge to the state of incorporating the masses into urban areas through granting official resident status to workers and their families. More accurately, the PRC's rapid pace of integrating migrant workers and their families into urban life is unparalleled among nations, especially considering the vast size of the population. Urban migration is growing more rapidly than the high rates anticipated by the state. To be sure, incorporating hundreds of millions of people into urban zones is a formidable task which is not without complications. Seeking doctrinal purity without allowance for error, Western opponents seek out examples of organizational imperfection and focus on adversities, temporary setbacks, aberrations and those who are inevitably passed over.

Labor migration in the West was predominantly interstate migration from Europe to colonial outposts, which displaced Indigenous people. In China, urban migration has given rise to economic growth and prosperity. Internal migration to urban regions is most prominent in China but is also a formative demographic phenomenon throughout the developing world. If Chinese urban workers are mobilizing into trade unions at an exceptional rate, why are urban workers in comparable countries not joining unions?

Even in a planned economy, inescapably, China's market socialism will produce job loss through the development of new technology and higher productivity.

Chapter 6 examines the emergence of the digital economy as a leading source of employment for China's urban working class. The ACFTU must persistently study and revise its organizing strategy to the realities of new labor markets, notably the digital economy. Urbanization and the loss of industrial jobs have given rise to the expansion of jobs in the digital economy, a labor market which requires the ACFTU and its constituent unions to launch new organizing campaigns throughout China. The formidable task of organizing digital workers into the ACFTU is incomplete and ongoing, but the Federation has become a model for labor organizing worldwide.

Chapter 7 examines the unique nature of the Chinese labor movement, which represents the transforming nature of the working class in what I call *holistic unionism*. The ACFTU responds to the working class's demands through bottom-up democratic unionism and has the capacity to advance their demands through its top-down capacity to respond through a strong and effective union and political party. To comprehend the significance of the ACFTU's proficiency to represent the democratic aspirations of the working class both practically and theoretically, one must measure the political and class unity within the political apparatus of the Chinese Communist state.

Chapter 8 challenges the prevailing literature in the West on the Chinese labor movement. Taken together, the literature is dismissive of the CPC and the ACFTU. To evaluate the merits of the ACFTU, research must study the objectives of the trade union federation and measure its success or failure on the basis of its ability to measure up to the goals. Categorically, the ACFTU is driven by its charge by the CPC to enable the working class to advance its material conditions, labor process and environment. The ACFTU affiliation with a party is unexceptional as many trade unions across the world, especially in transitional states, maintain a similar relationship. But the party–labor alliance does not conform to the Western Labor Studies literature, which stipulates that trade unions must organize in capitalist states. However, in the Chinese transitional state, the party–trade union alliance is required to modernize and develop while meeting the needs of the working class. Over the past 50 years or so, this alliance has served the working class well. However, Western Labor scholars expect immediate results when their own trade unions are in a state of inertia and declining precipitously.

In Chapter 9, the Conclusion, I assess socialism with Chinese characteristics through the lens of the working class and its trade union representative. To do so, one must understand how the trade union movement determinedly adapts its organizing to the new contradictions which workers encounter in urban areas and in new economic forms of work. In this way, I show how workers' democratic demands strengthen the ACFTU and its affiliates to meet the objectives of a forward moving union dedicated to the working class. As new material conditions transform the work process, the ACFTU is striving to reflect the new subjectivities of workers across China.

Even if the ACFTU were compared to Western trade unions, it would be seen to be faring well. Worker membership, which is non-compulsory, has grown significantly over the past 25 years as labor unions have encountered new developmental challenges. Thus, while the ACFTU is continuously challenged by technological change and the emergence of new labor markets, using both the transitional state and Western metric, the Federation is nothing less than a remarkably effective representative of the Chinese working class.

This book will show how the ACFTU is meeting the challenge of organizing urban migrant workers as well as workers entering new forms of employment in the digital and logistics sectors. The ACFTU responds to the democratic demands of the working class and is charged by the CPC to organize and represent workers to improve their wages and conditions. As China's developing economy modernizes, and the working class enters new forms of work with high technology, workers in private enterprises seek to increase their wages and improve their quality of life while often encountering difficult working conditions. The ACFTU has exhibited the capacity to respond to labor demands and to request that technology companies which have expanded with new forms of employment should now directly hire workers and improve wages, benefits and working conditions.

Workers and Labor under Capitalism and Socialism

Do what you feel in your heart to be right—for you'll be criticized anyway. You'll be damned if you do, and damned if you don't. (Eleanor Roosevelt 1933)

This book challenges the dominant perspective that working class representation based on Western models of trade unionism and cooperatives are the most successful paradigm for improving the conditions of workers. In contrast, this book asserts that the Western model of trade union representation has only opposed employers in specific moments of upsurge and then exclusively to reduce the intensity of social movements to improve wages and working conditions. As this model was discredited under neoliberalism and the 50-year decline of trade unionism in the West, labor organizations in the global South have declined at a steeper rate at a time when wages are declining, and labor exploitation has reached its highest form. Yet, despite the mostly dismal record of trade unions over the past half-century, Labor researchers remain committed to the Western bourgeois democratic form as the ideal model for the entire world, at a time when the global working class is larger than ever.

In sharp contrast to the Western model of trade unionism, which has declined and withered over the past 50 years, the All-China Federation of Trade Unions (ACFTU) has experienced significant success as it has organized into its affiliates approximately 75 percent of all 402 million workers in China. The ACFTU has organized in all sectors of the Chinese socialist market economy: from state owned enterprises to foreign multinationals and private (non-public) enterprises which have emerged over the past 20 years in response to the entry of hundreds of millions of workers into the digital economy. In the past decade, as China has increasingly focused on developing a modern service economy, technology and digital information services, major firms have turned to using platform economy workers. Industrial modernization continuously drives the ACFTU to focus on new organizing in manufacturing as well as new employment forms composed of workers who are not directly hired by technology companies and are not unionized. Over the past decade, the ACFTU has achieved significant success in responding to the democratic aspirations of workers to join trade unions through organizing them into trade unions. This book examines the multifarious mechanisms of organizing in a range of economic sectors and compares them to unions worldwide which have not had the success of the ACFTU. The book also challenges the Western Labor researchers who have a uniformly derisive perspective on the ACFTU and espouse the transformation of the Chinese market socialist economy, which is designed to benefit the working class, into a fully Western bourgeois democratic model where individual interests take precedence over the collective material subjectivity of the working class. While the Chinese opening up, known as market socialism, has displaced workers and paved the way for the world's largest migration in history, the Chinese state and the ACFTU have unremittingly strived to protect workers from exploitation. Certainly, there are exceptions to every practice, even if they are advanced for the common good. From the origins of the People's Republic of China (PRC) in 1949, the Communist Party of China (CPC) has endeavored to improve and modernize the material conditions of the working class and masses. The opening up and introduction and expansion of market socialism have ended poverty and transformed China into a modern economy under the leadership of the CPC.

In 2015, General Secretary Xi Jinping cautioned trade unions to serve as a responsive transmission belt to advance working class interests to advance socialism with Chinese characteristics. The work of the trade unions, Communist Youth League, Women's Federation and other mass organizations is to advance socialism. To do so, he said:

> Trade unions, the Communist Youth League, the Women's Federation, and other mass organizations must persist in emancipating their minds, reforming and innovating, forging ahead with determination, and working diligently. They must earnestly maintain and enhance the political, progressive, and mass character of the Party's mass organization work and its organizations, organize and mobilize … to channel their pursuit of a better life into a powerful force … to achieve … the Chinese Dream of the great rejuvenation of the Chinese nation. (Jian 2015)

Xi added that the mass character of trade unions was their fundamental characteristic, and trade unions were obligated to advance the interests of the working class. A crucial necessity:

> They should prioritize the masses in their work and activities, allowing them to play the leading role, rather than being treated as supporting characters or spectators. We must pay more attention to, care for, and show concern for the ordinary people, visiting thousands of homes, understanding their concerns, and building close ties with them. We must frequently engage in face-to-face, hand-in-hand, and heart-to-heart contact with the masses to foster genuine affection for them. We must vigorously strengthen organizations, especially

> grassroots organizations, and accelerate the development of organizations in new areas and among new social classes. Mass organizations and their cadres, especially those in leading bodies, must reach out to the grassroots and the masses, striving to be loyal practitioners of the purpose of serving the people wholeheartedly, refine adherents of the Party's mass line, and experts in the Party's mass work. (Jian 2015)

General Secretary Xi's speech, just three years after taking office, was a clarion call to the ACFTU to consistently respond to the material subjective demands of common workers, a declaration which was adopted by the federation. In the ensuing years, the ACFTU has overcome significant hurdles to respond to technological modernization and the renovation of the labor market, which poses new demands to organize and improve the conditions of workers. The ACFTU does not rest on its past laurels and formulates new strategies for organization which have had significant success adjusting to change through new models of organizing workers. Contrary to detractors, the ACFTU responds to worker demands and takes responsibility for improving worker conditions in the private and public sectors. In sum, the ACFTU represents a holistic union which both listens to workers and responds vigorously to challenges. The measure of a successful trade union is not just numbers but performance. For Lenin, rank-and-file activism and spontaneity without organization are insufficient to build sustained working-class power. As a holistic union, the ACFTU must have the capacity to advance workers' interests through organizational and numerical effectiveness. Even the ACFTU concedes that it must assess itself and regroup to meet the changing demands of the workforce, which takes time and practice.

Almost all the Labor Studies literature discounts and maligns the ACFTU because it does not operate in the image of Western unions. It decries the ACFTU as ineffective when workers take militant action and repressive when workers do not strike. The positions advanced by detractors are advanced by schools of thought from the reactionary right to the ultraleft. They seek to undermine China, which unifies all currents through social imperialism.

Repeatedly, even if their analysis does not denigrate China's labor movement, adversaries routinely apply a double binding critique: If there is labor peace, then the Chinese state is deemed authoritarian; if labor conflict and strikes are widespread, then there is pervasive opposition to the Chinese labor movement. In this way, the ACFTU is "placed in a Catch-22, 'damned if you do, damned if you don't' contradiction whereby it is impossible to satisfy Western labor studies critics" (Bateson 2020).

Opponents of Chinese socialism reflexively reject any positive attributes of the Chinese state which cannot be reformed to resemble Western liberal democracies; democracies which they consider to be the optimal form of government. Their critique ignores and dismisses factual evidence drawn from genuine events and organizations which impact on the Chinese working class. If ACFTU advances working conditions and wages, Western critics will search for shortcomings and even failure. Thus, if local unions negotiate wage increases, opponents may criticize the shortage of rank-and-file participation in collective bargaining. If trade union members go on strike, China will be criticized as incapable of representing workers and negotiating contracts with management. If workers do not go on strike, the state will be deemed authoritarian, heavy handed or aloof.

Western critics want nothing short of transforming the socialist state into a capitalist liberal democracy or a communist utopia. They disparage the ACFTU for restricting strikes to "cellular" local and municipal conflict. Instead, they give the impression that the only means to improve conditions is through the formation of a national labor movement which seeks to overthrow the socialist state. In other words, they want nothing short of removing the CPC and the "party-state" as the representative of worker interests. The ACFTU is ridiculed as an extension of the state which prevents workers from democratic and local action, a position refuted even by Western-funded NGOs which are critical of the PRC.

Not all critics are opponents of socialist China but appear from among supporters of the pre-1978 opening up. These historical works provide valid evidence within a specific temporal era but require modification through new evaluations and altering our previous thinking. Mao Zedong (Tse-Tung) asserts that we must update our evaluations of the material world based on our cognition and the emergence of the discovery of knowledge rather than remain stationary in response to the introduction of explanations based on factual evidence and understandings which have been obscured by strictly enforced prevailing interpretations. In *Where Do Correct Ideas Come From?* Mao Zedong stresses that sufficient perceptual comprehension is required before revising our conceptual knowledge, representing the first stage of cognition "from objective matter to subjective consciousness from existence to ideas" followed by bringing ideas back to existence. But in social struggle the advanced class may be defeated since they do not have the power "as the forces of reaction are temporarily defeated but they are bound to triumph sooner or later." Mao continues: "Often, correct knowledge can be arrived at only after many repetitions of the process leading from matter to consciousness and then back to matter, that is, leading from practice to knowledge and then back to practice" (Mao Zedong/Mao Tse-Tung 1963/2001, 17).

So, while some perspectives rest on truths and honest assessments which may have been correct in a specific period, as policies and activities change with the passage of time and the acquisition of new knowledge we must reassess our prior perceptions. This book calls attention to the development of the ACFTU over the past 25 years and calls for an examination and reevaluation through studying the dominant currents occurring over this interval, especially the second half of the past quarter century under the leadership of Xi Jinping from 2012 to the present.

1　The Decline and Fall of Western Trade Unionism

How do we rescue workers in the South from the application of the Western imposed liberal and false leftist constructs of trade unions which have also served to undermine communist and socialist oriented unions from waging militant demands and even seeking state power? How are unions challenging capitalism, neoliberalism, imperialism and attendant unequal exchange which impoverish most of the working class in the global South? What are the best practices of trade unionism and why do Western scholars oppose them? This book focuses on the Chinese labor movement and counters inaccurate and dismissive Western perspectives which seek to diminish the significance of workers and class struggle under socialism.

The first claim of this book to be elaborated in Chapter 3 is that Western imperialist models of trade unionism throughout the world have catastrophically failed to stem the onslaught of neoliberal capitalist restructuring and outsourcing. Western unions reached an apogee in the 20th century through consolidating labor upsurge among the industrial working classes in Europe and North America. However, since about 1980, industrial unions of the West have failed workers and declined as a democratic source of representation in public and private workplaces.

The Western model of trade unions has been fatal to the Southern working class. In the post-Second World War independence era, Western unions (inherited by emergent states through maintaining the colonial models of trade unions which defended a thin layer of privileged workers while excluding most workers) produced deep inequality within and between states. Unions in the South have maintained the identical turgid system of representation and collective bargaining which failed in the North. In impoverished newly independent countries, the vast majority of workers had no union representation, lacked job security and worked under destituting and precarious conditions. Since the 1980s, the rise of neoliberalism and the shift of production industries to Asia, Africa and Latin America, wealthy countries have become beneficiaries of the near absence of trade unions and the failure to organize. Unequal exchange in trade has depressed the value of commodities produced in poor countries, giving rise to the shift in global production to the South. By extension, it has also increased the extraction of relative and absolute surplus value and devalued the price of natural resources by blocking most countries from acquiring the technology to refine and fabricate their own products for trade with rich countries.

2 Marginal Gains for a Minority of Workers

The second claim of this book is that the Western archetype of labor–management relations has not palpably improved the wage conditions of workers in poor countries but has contained and restricted the militancy of workers and resulted in marginal gains for a minority of organized public and private employees. Most workers lack access to labor representation and are prevented from forming new unions. Over 50 years of neoliberal capitalism since the 1970s, trade unions have declined in both the West and worldwide, reducing living standards and working-class social organization in workplaces. The Western model of unionism which had proliferated throughout the world as a result of cultural imperialism has not staunched the decline of wages and working conditions. In the West, the decline in unions has depressed wages and unraveled local social organization, contributing to working-class individualism, isolation and the rise of right-wing populism. In the West, as unions declined, per capita GDP broadly increased along with inequality in rich countries. Yet, a labor aristocracy became ascendant as most workers benefited from economic imperialism and the extraction of surplus labor from poor countries through the unequal exchange of trade, reducing the cost of most commodities.

In most of the global South outside China, a small percentage of workers are union members. Those few unions which exist are holdovers from the colonial era and are mostly weak and ineffective in representing precarious workers, who are commonly jobless. Almost all existing trade unions in poor countries are ineffectual legacies of colonial era labor regimes. After independence, these exclusionary trade unions, frequently in the public sector, were often disinclined to advance the broader demands for workers and peasants. Since the 1970s, remaining trade union membership has eroded with the direction of most foreign direct investment (FDI) to those countries with low rates of unionization. To accommodate capital investment, labor unions typically engage in the labor–management models inherited from the metropoles. In the capitalist West, trade unions and their members were beneficiaries of consumption generated by unequal exchange through trade with poor countries (Breman 1996).

The Western labor–management model imposed on the South failed to mobilize most workers into unions but typically represented a fraction of the working class in the public and private sectors. Most Western enthusiasts supporting labor representation assert that workers are obstructed from organizing into trade unions by management opposition and anti-labor government regulations. Admittedly, capitalist states of the South regard trade unions as inimical to generating FDI and appealing to multinational corporations. Even if most workers may ordinarily support union representation, employers and the state caution that unions deter foreign investment. Even in Nordic social-democracies, trade union density has declined since the 2000s to accommodate capital (Kollmeyer 2021; Visser 2024). Western trade unions strive to demonstrate that they are actively fighting for all workers' rights, when most unions are in fact just consolidating the militancy of organized labor, comprising a small segment of the working class organized in past generations.

3   Socialist and Communist Contexts for Worker Empowerment

The third claim of this book is that the most successful working-class organizations over the past 75 years emerged in socialist states with communist political parties linked to trade union federations. Notably, in the first 25 years of the 21st century, the most effective membership representation and organizing can be found in the PRC, where more workers are represented than in any other state and outnumber those found in the two major international federations of unions combined. We recognize that this claim is anathema to almost all Western trade unionists and diverges from the abundant Labor scholarship viewing Chinese unions as lacking autonomy from a "party-state" which denies workers basic labor rights. However, if one examines Chinese unions, they provide far more safeguards to workers, negotiate collective bargaining agreements, protest against employers and frequently go on strike to improve wages and conditions. Local labor leaders at grassroots unions and non-public enterprises are democratically elected by rank-and-file members considerably more often than in Western unions (Ness 2015). From about 1995 to 2015, Chinese wages began to appreciably rise as a result of FDI and multinational relocation of production from higher wage regions. As a consequence of rising wage demands, Chinese workers began job actions at multinational and private enterprises. From 2005 to 2015, foreign private investment in private sector enterprises incited a rise in labor unrest for higher wages and improved conditions. Even today, foreign capital and multinational corporations seek to rein in union organizing in new sectors of the economy; viz technology, EVs, digital platform economy, including workers employed in logistics, ride hailing, food delivery and transportation. Digital workers employed in the private sector are organizing to improve their wages and conditions even if many are still exploited by their employers in much the same way as in the rest of the world. Yet, the rate of digital workers' union membership in China is far higher than in any other nation: some 24 percent of workers were identified as union members in a recent study (Tu & Wang 2024).

Most importantly, as this book argues, the Chinese state seeks to ensure that all workers are mobilized into trade unions. Of course, not all trade unions are equally effective in representing their members. But, in contrast to critics in the West, we assert that the right to join and become a member of a union is a form of industrial democracy and social right which rarely occurs elsewhere (Andreas 2019). Naysayers and opponents claim that China has no unions, because all are ultimately affiliated with the All-China Federation of Trade Unions (ACFTU). However, it is also true that many other countries have only one peak labor federation. Critics will charge that ACFTU is an arm of the CPC, yet it is also true that many unions in other parts of the world are affiliates of political parties in power.

In India, the Bharatiya Mazdoor Sangh federation (BMS), or Indian Workers' Union, is an affiliate of the Bharata Janata Party, India's ruling party, in much the same way as ACFTU is associated with the CPC in China. In India, sketchy government statistics exhibit that less than 5 percent of workers are organized into unions; even as trade union centers claim to have more members than they have in reality (Kumar & Jha 2025). India has several other central trade union federations affiliated with political parties: for example, the Centre of Indian Trade Unions (CITU) is associated with the Communist Party of India (Marxist). Likewise, from 1994 to 2024, South Africa has been dominated by a tripartite alliance linking the African National Congress (ANC), South African Communist Party (SACP) and Confederation of South African Trade Unions (COSATU). In China, ACFTU is affiliated with the CPC, which gained power in 1949. By its very nature, ACFTU is a peak labor federation, just as distinct national unions exist in many other countries. Concomitantly, in countries with weak labor movements, major independent federations are present. In still other cases, major unions have split from a political party: for example, the National Union of Metalworkers of South Africa (NUMSA), a militant industrial union in South Africa, split with COSATU and formed a new federation, the South African Federation of Trade Unions. All in all, divisions dilute the power of labor federations.

The International Trade Union Confederation (ITUC), the neoliberal pro-capitalist federation of the West, considers itself the model of "democratic unionism," even if many workers in these Western-oriented trade unions do not participate in the union activity. It simply represents a clearing house of unions which are committed to capitalism and labor–management collective bargaining, despite members and non-members being in dire need of representation. Its leaders view themselves as democratic on the grounds that they are elected by members, but most ITUC national federations do not have free elections where union leaders are chosen by the rank and file. For example, the American Federation of Teachers (AFT), the largest national union, selects its leadership through mostly handpicked delegates who are functionaries in line with the AFT's policies, including its neocon foreign policy supportive of US war and intervention. Workers have scant capacity to elect even local leadership, unlike communist unions in China where local committees form to determine tactics and strategy and are supported by the state in bargaining with management. In the West, notably the US, trade unions represent a small share of the labor force.

At the dawn of neoliberal capitalism in the 1980s, the new trade unions emerging in the global South and even the West to defend the new industrial or service sector workers were viewed by Labor scholars as fonts of democracy and the model of class struggle unionism (Chun 2011; Seidman 1994; Silver 2003). Yet, these unions operated within the constraints of labor–management relations established by capital and the state, under which class conflict was contained and limited by collective bargaining agreements and deunionization. Western Marxists viewed the objective of new union formations in Brazil, South Africa and Korea as recognizing workers' legitimate representatives who would reach collective bargaining agreements with emerging and expanding industrial corporations. The ideal was to establish labor regimes which would reflect those in the advanced economies, where trade unions were in decline as capital moved to the South to extract surplus profits through the international division of labor. In contrast to the industrial economies of the North, workers in the South acceded to lower wages through unequal exchange achieved under the inequality of trade between core and peripheral countries.

David Harvey explained wage inequality between workers in core and peripheral countries as a spatial fix in which capital relocated to regions with lower wages to capture higher levels of surplus value than could be achieved in the original location. His observation of the spatial fix did not recognize imperialism as a guiding force for the relocation of capital to new low-wage regions on the periphery. In his most highly cited article, he asserts that:

> capitalism has to fix space (in immoveable structures of transport and communication nets, as well as in built environments of factories, roads, houses, water supplies, and other physical infrastructures) in order to overcome space

> (achieve a liberty of movement through low transport and communication costs). This leads to one of the central contradictions of capital: that it has to build a fixed space (or "landscape") necessary for its own functioning at a certain point in its history only to have to destroy that space (and devalue much of the capital invested therein) at a later point in order to make way for a new "spatial fix" (openings for fresh accumulation in new spaces and territories) at a later point in its history. (Harvey 2001, 25)

The legacy of imperialism is fully absent from Harvey's analysis, where footloose capital will just flow to its lowest level without distinguishing the shift in production to low-wage countries in the South.

The objective was rarely, if ever, to advance union democracy or industrial rights; workers advanced their class rights in the global South with only a mixed record of effectiveness. Imposing the dominant trade unions in the South significantly reveals the particular nature of the nation state, be that the ubiquitous form of neoliberal capitalism, and less so, social democracy or socialism. It is not the nature of trade unions which determines labor conditions but the nature of the state. Yet, while Southern workers could not obtain workplace democracy, social democracies of Western Europe strived for these rights, which were undermined by neoliberalism in the 1980s (Dukes & Streeck 2023). This book argues that only in China do all workers have the right to union membership. The right to a union does not require class conflict, but the nature of the union is a function of the social organization of the enterprise or workplace.

4 Workers' Rights and Power under Actually Existing Socialism

This book's fourth and most significant claim is that workers under actually existing socialist states (AES), specifically China, hold far more political and democratic rights and economic power at the workplace. For over 75 years, Labor Studies scholars have repudiated AES and dismissed socialist countries as inauthentic representatives of the working class. However, the status of workers under socialism does not always require conflict as it does in capitalist states. To be sure, cynics may argue that workers in multinational corporations and contractors do not have equivalent rights to those in Chinese state-owned enterprises (SOEs). However, under Chinese socialism, workers engage in class conflict in opposition to multinational and domestic private corporations within the contours of a socialist state which stands up for them in labor disputes and strikes.

Fundamentals of labor–management relations in capitalist states are not applicable to China's AES. Consequently, measures applied to assess Western labor are often not relevant to most trade unions and workers in China.

1. *Union density.* In China, all those defined as workers are members of a trade union on a local, city, provincial, industrial and national basis. In the West, union density is essential for measuring the strength of a union. Over the last 50–60 years, on the whole, union density has declined throughout the world, with the exception of China and Cuba. In 2025, the PRC estimated that 300 million out of 402 million workers were registered members of the ACFTU and its industrial, provincial, municipal, district and street level affiliate unions, a union density rate of 75 percent (see Figure 1).

2. *Expansive labor courts.* Chinese labor courts almost always support workers in disputes with management. The Chinese state has significantly increased the number of labor courts to mediate, arbitrate and adjudicate labor–management disputes. With the assistance of the ACFTU, workers have won 95 percent of cases brought against employers.

3. *Strikes and on-the-job actions.* Chinese workers go on strike just as workers do in the West. However, most Western scholars deride such strikes as ineffective despite the fact that external Western monitors consider them to merit attention. Even the now defunct China Labour Bulletin (CLB), a Western-funded NGO in Hong Kong, documents strike activity throughout China, in many cases without accuracy. However, unlike most countries, the Chinese state typically supports striking workers over management in the private sector as well as the burgeoning public sector, where strikes typically do not occur, especially if the trade union at the local level is well organized. Similar to elsewhere, the organization of the trade union at the local level matters both in achieving good contracts and avoiding strikes.

4. *The ACFTU is not a monolithic organization.* The ACFTU is composed of a national center and unions on the provincial, municipal, district and street levels. Trade unions on all levels are directed by the ACFTU to support worker rights and facilitate organizing into unions. Where workers are contractors who are not legally employed by firms, the ACFTU and its constituent unions pressure private companies to sign legal contracts with workers. While the state controls the leading heights of the PRC economy, the private sector employs 80 percent of all workers, most of whom are legally protected through Chinese labor laws and are members of the ACFTU and its affiliates (Xinhua 2025a). Disposable income has grown along with the ACFTU (see Figure 2).

5. Leading Western labor economists have examined the differences between trade unions which are systematically organized and effective, for instance

among SOEs, and those which have yet to effectively emerge, typically in the private sector. They have also looked at cases in which workers and management have sought harmonious labor relations with employers to avoid conflict (Booth et al. 2022; Freeman & Li 2013; Xi et al. 2021). However, the primary dynamic in China is the migration of several hundred migrant workers from rural to urban areas, a significant challenge to workers and the ACFTU, perhaps the first time in contemporary history when a union federation has absorbed such a vast number of workers. Those who expect the migration unionization to occur without complications, conflict and obstacles are unrealistic and utopian. Yet, some scholars' serious misunderstanding of supposed union futility in China and beyond is based on the expectation that trade unions will instantaneously respond to technological applications in the economy which often marginalize workers; for instance, the critique of the ACFTU for not responding directly to digitization and logistics. This book argues that it is unreasonable to expect such a response when the innovations in question have been established for less than a decade (Zhang et al. 2023). All the same, as noted, China has been at the forefront in addressing digital workers' exploitation and has the highest union density rate of any country (Tu & Wang 2024; Zhou 2020).

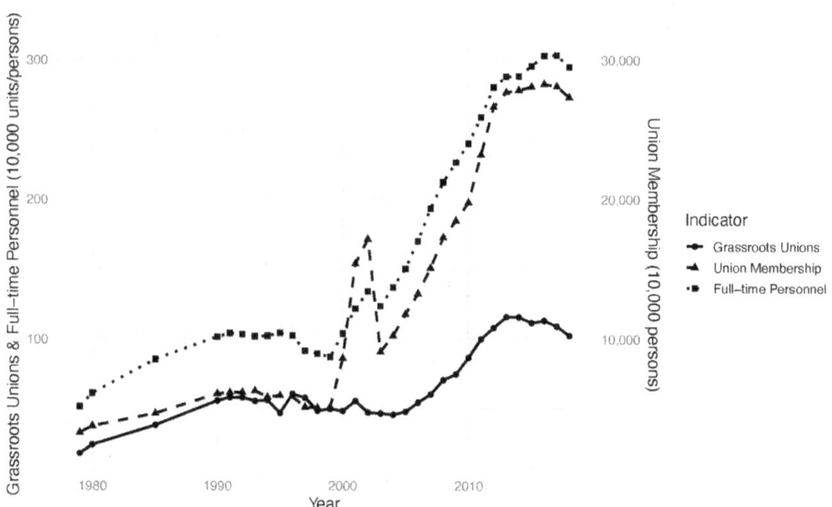

FIGURE 1   Trade unions in China, 1979–2018 (Source: National Bureau of Statistics (2024) China statistical yearbook, 2024, 24–23 statistics of trade unions by region, 2023. Beijing: National Bureau of Statistics of China. https://www.stats.gov.cn/sj/ndsj /2024/indexeh.htm)

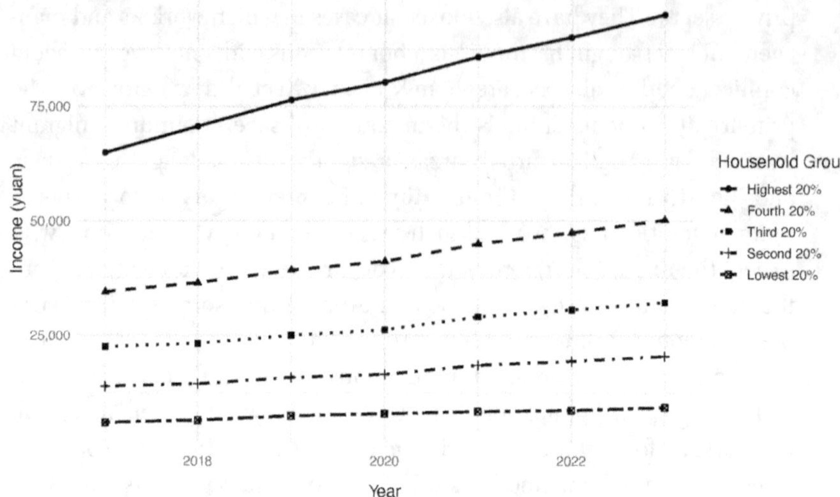

FIGURE 2   Nationwide disposable income by quintile. The income quintile refers to the five equal partitions of all sun'eyed households, who are ranked from low to high based on per capita disposable income level. The 20 percent with lowest income are classified as low-income group (Lowest 20%), and the other four levels are lower-middle-income group (Second 20%), middle-income group (Third 20%), higher-middle-income group (Fourth 20%) and high-income group (Highest 20%). (Source: Derived from China Statistical Yearbook. 2024. 6-2 Nationwide Per Capita Disposable income of Households by Income Quintile (Beijing: National Bureau of Statistics of China. https://www.stats.gov.cn/sj/ndsj/2024/indexeh.htm)

Must the working class across countries consistently engage in direct action in order to grow and achieve strength? Labor unions do have agency of various forms in relation to capital and the state. In most instances, capital is ascendant, but in socialist states, labor forms the primary force. In this context, we must differentiate between the forms of struggle required to achieve the goals of the working class. Under socialism, workers are not struggling against the state as an agent of capital, but *with* the state *against* capital. Thus, what gains would workers achieve if they were to engage in unrest against a socialist state which is committed to equality? In this sense, this book contends that socialism in practice has purchase and that genuine AES in the past, present and future are organized to defend the interests of the working class, even in market economies. This book charts out a new course for acknowledging the genuine interest in advancing the interests of the working class under socialist states while subordinating the capitalist class.

5 How and Why State/Party Unions Protect the Rights of Workers

This book parts company with the ubiquitous narrative of trade unions advanced by Labor Studies researchers that Western trade union models represent the superlative organizational form for improving the wages and working conditions of unorganized labor through collective bargaining, while reducing societal poverty through advocating social programs. Labor unions have undoubtedly been important actors in improving the wages and conditions of workers in Western Europe, North America and other advanced industrial regions in the 20th century, both in the workplace and through building social programs. But the emergence of neoliberal capitalism in the 1970s and the enduring Western "democratic" models of trade union representation have further undermined rank-and-file democracy and diminished labor's organizational capacity to mobilize and represent the working class in the workplace.

On the contrary, Western models of trade union representation, which consolidated from the 1920s to the 1950s, restrict rank-and-file self-activity, reduce pride in assembly line production and contribute to working-class cynicism and even contempt for US unions and manufacturers (Aronowitz 1973; Braverman 1974; Burawoy 1982; Davis 1986). In response and without appreciable success, a plethora of solutions has been proffered by trade union leaders, Labor Studies scholars and labor activists to revive unions as an agency for achieving upward mobility. Of particular significance, the trade union model that requires workers to hold state-sanctioned elections for recognition by management and then to negotiate collective bargaining agreements for the right to improve labor conditions has been replicated throughout most post-colonial states of the global South and applied as a model for worker democracy and working-class upward mobility (Gold 2014; Teelucksingh 2015). Whilst scholars have examined the importance of tripartite systems of state, capital and labor participation, there is remarkably little recognition of the path development of trade unions maintaining colonial unions into post-colonial eras.

Through examining the All-China Federation of Trade Unions, this book rebuts the very premise that the Western model of trade unionism is the only vehicle for achieving workers' upward mobility. Instead of striving to better the conditions of the privileged few and organizing new workers, this book argues that contemporary Western models of working-class organization founded in the early 20th century are incomplete since they do not provide the organizational opportunity for all workers to join unions and mobilize their own to challenge capital and the state.

This book asserts that the Western model of unionism is inadequate and doomed as it tends to represent only one segment of the working class. Moreover, trade unions have been in decline in capitalist states over the past 50 years. If conditions are improved for privileged workers while neglecting low wage ones, only a small portion will have the opportunity to realize gains. Only a small share of unionized workers in advanced capitalist countries that are decisive for the accumulation of capital will typically prevail, benefiting only a small segment of workers at home and abroad. In the global South, most of the world's working class is excluded from high wage jobs and condemned to work under precarious conditions as contract laborers lacking union representation. Western trade union models have historically improved a segment of labor which often lacks a working-class ideology and often has also even aspired to protect wage gains by keeping dispossessed workers' wages down. Engels (1892/1952), Lenin (1916/1964), Emmanuel (1972/2025), Edwards (1978) and other socialist theorists have noticed the disturbing tendency for the outsourcing of production to low wage regions. Meanwhile, unorganized labor is typically restricted from forming trade unions to better its wages and conditions. Put baldly, since the 1850s, trade unions have helped form a privileged class of workers whose interest is in maintaining and enlarging inequality within and between countries. Strictly speaking, most workers organized into existing trade unions represent an aristocracy of labor which is subordinate to and unified with capital's pursuit of surplus value. In effect, labor unions and a segment of workers in imperialist countries are bribed through the accumulation of super-profits invested in poor countries and establish a parasitic relation to them. H.W. Edwards goes even further, asserting that imperialist expropriation has permitted advanced capitalist states to develop welfare states for their working classes (Edwards 1978; Lenin 1916/1964). Emmanuel (1972/2025) asserts that the inequality of trade engenders an economic conservatism among imperialist countries of Europe and North America.

In this way, the global working class is also segmented between, on the one hand, a privileged minority of workers in the global North aligned with the capitalist class; and, on the other hand, the majority of workers, whose class interests diverge from maintaining the status quo. Today, the pursuit of profit overlaps the global capitalist economy. In unison, owners and workers are taught to believe in the capitalist system, which only benefits capitalist classes and a segment of the working class. Paradoxically, in *The German Ideology*, Karl Marx underscores a dynamic which mitigates against working-class solidarity:

> The ruling ideas are nothing more than the ideal expression of the dominant material relations, the dominant material relations grasped as ideas; hence of the relations which make the one class the ruling one, therefore, the ideas of its dominance. The individuals composing the ruling class possess among other things consciousness and therefore think. Insofar, therefore, as they rule as a class and determine the extent and compass of an historical epoch, it is self-evident that they do this in its whole range, hence among other things rule also as thinkers, as producers of ideas, and regulate the production and distribution of the ideas of their age. (Marx with Engels 1932/1998, 67)

Interclass solidarity, expressed through support for capital accumulation and rising nationalism, is the veneer which overlays the international division of global labor and the dominant international ideology. In fact, the ruling class dominates by the diffusion of the ideas of capital, expressed in the 2020s through increased nationalism. Following the dissolution of the Soviet Union in 1991, the dominant view was that capital was ascendant and unbounded by national interests. This book rejects the perspective that the hegemony of the US was articulated through neoliberal capitalism and freedom of international movement of capital. Instead, it maintains that neoliberalism has always been a means to protect and expand the dominance of affluent imperialist states at the core of the world's economy, disguising this fact behind the false assertion that global capitalism is a constant, independent international variable (Harvey 2005; Robinson 2014).

The Labor Studies literature derides communist unions as undemocratic since they do not hold elections but are dominated by autocratic leaders. But in fact, communist unions do have democratic elections and are more likely to challenge capital. By virtue of the socialist character of the trade union, it is presupposed that disciplined institutional actions that reflect the interests of workers are far more important than electoral contests. The competence of the leadership is far more important than the individual leader, a concept advanced by V. I. Lenin in *What Is to Be Done?* which should be de rigueur reading for those seeking to build effective trade unions and political parties:

> The worst sin we commit is that we degrade our political and organizational tasks to the level of the immediate, "palpable", "concrete" interests of the everyday economic struggle; yet they keep singing to us the same refrain: Lend the economic struggle itself a political character! We repeat: this kind of thing displays as much "sense for the realities of life" as was displayed by the hero in the popular fable who cried out to a passing funeral procession, "Many happy returns of the day!". (Lenin 1902/1969, 67)

Liberal capitalist societies supposedly allow workers to freely decide the most suitable trade unions to represent their economic interests in opposition to employers in the private and public sectors of the economy. However, Western trade unions fail to pursue blanket membership across society but have typically represented workers in specific economic labor markets. In the US, the Teamsters represent truckers, the United Food and Commercial Workers International Union represent food and commercial workers, the United Auto Workers represent auto workers. Even in the public sector, where union density tends to be highest, the majority of workers are unorganized, and workers are trapped in jobs with few prospects of upgrading their wages and conditions. In 2025, despite the significant uptick in labor mobilization, only 5.9 percent of all private sector workers and 32.9 percent of public sector workers were union members (BLS 2026). In almost every country, the share of unionized workers has declined from 2000 to the present, and most workers are unrepresented and must fend for themselves. Consequently, most workers are mired in low wage jobs with few prospects of collective progress.

This book argues that the most effective trade unions must possess three primary features: (1) bottom-up democracy; (2) efficacy to advance the interests of the working class, including mobilization, organizing and a state which supports the improvement of labor conditions; (3) trade unions must be linked to a strong political party which has unwavering devotion to improving the conditions and standard of living of the working class. The trade union succeeds if the Communist Party of China, the governing working-class based political party, is centered on developing the productive forces of the economy through research and technological advancement driven by the concomitant responsibility to advancing class interests to ensure prioritization of the working class and masses.

1.   Genuine working-class democracy is found within the weave of the democratic aspirations of workers within workplaces and communities rather than liberal bourgeois democratic competition for leadership among the ruling class. In this way, workers at the shopfloor and workplace place bottom-up demands on the union to improve conditions. Decisively, the trade union must be motivated by improving the interests of workers and have the organizational capacity to substantively respond to their demands.

2.   Trade union efficacy in furthering workers' interests consists of the ability to recognize the subjective demands of workers and formulate strategies which challenge management to respond to the material needs of their members and all workers: a form of top-down unionism. Ongoing confrontation with employers is not always necessary if the trade union

has the capacity and authority to effectively advance the will of the workers through new policies. Western Labor Studies scholars wrongly contend that antagonism to management is an obligatory prerequisite to building a strong union (Taylor & Li 2007). But this perspective is fixed in the spectacle of a work stoppage or strike which may or may not be necessary. It fails to recognize that trade unions' success is contingent on their ability to tangibly improve the material conditions of workers. The top-down approach is a reaction to bottom-up democratic demands. Collectively, they representative what I call a holistic trade union, which is both democratic and efficacious.

3. Socialist and communist trade unions are almost always affiliated with left political parties. If the working class based political parties gain power, they are far more effective in charging their trade union affiliate to establish a holistic organization capable of advancing their members' interests.

4. Socialist and communist unions in both capitalist and socialist states are far more effective in improving workers' material interests than Western trade union models that advance economistic demands of a small segment of workers who are in their organizations. Western trade union models deem democracy to involve a choice for workers about whether or not to join unions in the face of fierce opposition from management and the state, which is often also the employer. The Western notion that socialist unions are not democracy and that union democracy is a matter of individual worker choice of selecting leadership is a false dichotomy. In socialist trade unions like China's ACFTU, local leadership is selected through democratic elections. This historical record of trade unions in the West is that they are *always* subservient to the capitalist state, and any effort to form opposing forces will be crushed by trade unions and the state. Trade union history in the US illustrates that communist and radical organizations will be crushed and dismantled. The Congress of Industrial Organizations (CIO) actively participated in the breakup of the United Electrical Workers in 1949 in response to its communist influence (Sears 2019; Young 2017). Today, the UE has survived and remains a prototype of a socialist and democratic union committed to working-class militancy and international solidarity while many US and Western models of trade unionism have declined into service organizations with dwindling membership.

This book challenges three central claims about labor unions and particularly criticizes the dominant Western models of trade unionism in which the state is viewed as neutral in labor–management disputes. In so doing, it summons concepts considered anathema by "enlightened" Western leftists, who are accustomed to a coercive state operating in the interests of expanding capital accumulation. This book responds by making three assertions:

1. *Western trade unions in capitalist countries are exclusionary and less democratic.* Today's Western European and North American unions originated in the supposedly ethical worldview set out by the International Labour Organization (ILO). Theoretically, this gives voice to workers as it strengthens the power of capital. For many Western leftists, voice is established inside the labor organization but not in relation to capital. The ILO was founded in 1919 by nine countries, led by the US and its racist and collaborationist leader Samuel Gomers of the American Federation of Labor. Other founders were Belgium, Cuba (at that time a US semi-colony), Czechoslovakia, France, Italy, Japan, Poland and the United Kingdom: positively unrepresentative of the global working class (ILO 2023). This book contrasts unions in the International Trade Union Confederation (ITUC), a legacy of colonial unions, with unions in the World Federation of Trade Unions (WFTU), a federation which formed and expanded globally under the Soviet Union. Both were strengthened in the 2000s. The ITUC and WFTU federations represent workers in countries throughout the world. In some cases, trade unions are affiliated with both federations. However, the primary difference is between ITUC's support for liberal models of capitalism which are advanced by the ruling classes, and WFTU's espousal of a socialist model for trade unions. Certainly, trade unions in each country may contrast, the most substantial distinction being what ITUC considers interunion competition as the primary form of democracy while WFTU prefers compulsory membership. Undeniably, membership is advantageous for workers who are union members. Crucially, the Western models countervail the notion of equality confirmed by citizenship. ITUC and its Labor Studies acolytes do not give all workers the right of citizenship. Socialist democracy must confer on all workers membership of trade unions. In bourgeois electoral democracies, most citizens vote in elections, but all are theoretically granted rights with the option to participate. Authentic democracy must grant these same rights for workers to join trade unions and construct organizations of their choice.

2. *ACFTU is more democratic than almost all Western unions.* China confers the human right of trade union representation on all its citizens. From liberals to Marxists, the vast majority of Westerners who study Chinese labor view unions there as undemocratic and impotent extensions of the CPC. To a fault, anyone reading the literature on Chinese labor will

find a doctrinaire position that Chinese workers are highly exploited, oppressed and without a voice. The perception of Chinese unions as authoritarian and undemocratic has been repeated so many times that it has become an article of faith. Challenging this concept is a taboo, risking exclusion from the field of Western Labor Studies. In contrast, this book asserts that the dominant Western perspective is false and that, in fact, ACFTU is far more democratic than almost all Western unions. Admittedly, ACFTU unions are not equivalent and range from being highly democratic to inert. However, every union has the potential to mobilize members to take collective action. For too many scholars of Chinese labor, time stands still, and reforms and transformation of ACFTU are considered irrelevant or lack independence of action in response to working-class demands. Even those Labor scholars who acknowledge that the labor rights of Chinese workers have expanded assert that they are only available to educated and privileged workers (Franceschini et al. 2022; Gallagher 2017; Lee, 2007; Pringle 2011).

3. *The beneficiary of low wage labor is the aristocracy of labor in rich states.* Western labor unions are unable to halt the decline of trade unions as working-class mobilization primarily occurs in manufacturing industries, which have largely relocated to the global South. Ever since the 1980s, strong and robust labor unions have only formed in industrializing states, including Brazil, China, India, South Africa and South Korea (Silver 2003). The beneficiary of low wage labor is the aristocracy of labor in rich states, which thrives on inequality between the global North and global South.

Canonical Western Labor Studies literature since the 1970s has been dominated by labor historians and social scientists who are fixated on the decline of trade unions in the US, Canada and Western Europe, due to anti-union government policies and the state's partiality to capitalist development over working-class democratic rights. Likewise, advocates of union democracy who find fault in the rise of bureaucratic, entrenched and corrupt unions, racism, sexism, xenophobia and absence of "social movement unionism" all also criticize the rise of neoliberalism and its assault on unions (Cowie 2010; Cowie et al. 2003; Fletcher & Gapasin 2009; Galenson 1994; Gerstle 2022; Greenhouse 2020; Hyman 2001; Lichtenstein 2013; McAlevey 2016; Moody 1988; 2017; Sugrue 2014).

All explanations of trade union decline view the Western models of trade union organization as unassailable or, as unions are in decline, some advocate new models for social movement or class struggle unionism, monikers which are consistently restated by proponents of union renewal (Burns 2022; McAlevey 2020). Unquestionably, bureaucratization, corruption, racism, sexism and lack of democracy have contributed to the decline of unions in the West, but not all scholars examine, as the author of this book will do, the nature of the Western capitalist state and its exclusion of workers.

But the Western models of unionism typically exclude most workers from membership, a condition applied in capitalist states; while socialist states at least allow workers to mobilize labor in their existing unions to transform the lives of workers in state and private enterprises (Herod 1998, 197–217). Whilst the state is essential to understanding the diverse nature of working-class organizations throughout the world, a critique of the Western liberal model of labor unions is absent. Decisively, all critiques of Western unionism reject socialist forms of inclusive representation and broader organization, viz WFTU and ACFTU. In fact, both have prodigious historical legacies and are actively engaged in organizing class struggle organizations (Ness 2021). Contrary to the position of liberal and left proponents of Western trade unions and labor federations, the premise of this book is that contemporary labor unions, including new forms of worker organization (NFWO), whilst contributing to piecemeal gains, oppose economic equality and the eradication of poverty and do not contribute to national economic development and prosperity.

This book will uncover evidence that union models linked to socialist parties in single and multiparty states contribute to the improvement of the immediate needs of workers, enable the organization of militant rank-and-file trade unions and present a persuasive counterhegemonic model to the Western social-democratic and liberal models of trade unionism.

6   Globalism, the State and Workers' Power

As globalization challenges labor unions seeking to improve wages and working conditions for organized and unorganized workers, the global industrial workforce has expanded. It now comprises a larger share of labor than at any time since the foundation and spread across the world of capitalism from Western Europe. Trade unions have declined in the global North and the global South as neoliberalism and globalization have forced states and firms to reject organizations formed to defend workers.

This book makes a striking and unique contribution to prevailing perspectives on union democracy advanced in the Labor Studies literature. Its argument is both counterintuitive and heretical to the widespread established unions which the Western models of trade union democracy regard as the superlative paradigm to which all other trade union organizations must adhere if they are to be considered legitimate. According to this paradigm, successful labor representation emerges from competition for the hearts and minds of workers by unions vying for the right to represent them in collective bargaining with management. I argue that this Western model of representation distinguishes workers as individual customers in a free market who choose from among unions which promise them the best deal. I propose that this liberal model of labor representation is in reality a form of free market capitalism which fails to confer on workers the right of union membership. In most cases, trade unions are prevented from forming by the state and capital. If a state and party bestow upon labor the canonical right of union membership as a prerogative, workers can form the unions of their choice on a local and industrial level. If workers are denied this right, they are likely to be repressed in the workplace. The position of Labor Studies and advocates of Western models is that a field of unions should compete for workers and hypothetically represent their interests, but in this system, they can also be crushed by the state and management. If union membership were instead conferred as a right of citizenship, as it is in China, members could decide to mobilize or remain dormant, but the option to advance their interests through trade unions would be uncontested.

This position is abhorrent to capitalists, as it invariably presents a risk of militancy and disruption. Oddly enough, Marxists and self-proclaimed supporters of worker rights also oppose a blanket union as undemocratic. This book will provide evidence that national unions which offer workers all-encompassing membership are in fact far more effective in advancing workers' interests against capital and the state and are invariably under the scrutiny of workers. The absorption of all workers into the ACFTU in the 2010s represents a far more significant weapon for workers against capital and the state than contracting unions in the West and throughout the world, especially with the imposition of neoliberal capitalism and global supply chains which require a weak labor movement to extract surplus labor from workers.

7 Uncovering Misrepresentation of Trade Unions in Socialist States

The dominant narrative in Labor Studies is that competitive trade unions within capitalist economies are the optimal form of organization and the system best suited to advancing the socioeconomic interests of the working class. Liberal capitalist democracy is, it is argued, the optimal mechanism for the formation of trade unions, which represent the interests and aspirations of workers. Liberal capitalist societies supposedly allow workers to freely decide the trade union most suitable to represent their class interests to employers in the private and public sectors of the economy. If workers in liberal democracies have free will to decide their representation, the decline in union membership in most of the world implies by extension that workers prefer not to join unions. Workers alone do not constitute an organizational form but have a collective relation to their employers and their work, whether or not they are members of unions. Taking this position for granted, workers prefer to directly engage with employers rather than hand over this responsibility to trade unions. This model does not consider the possibility that workers can form their own organizations to address workplace concerns: wages, working conditions and benefits. In the absence of trade unions, workers would be compelled to individually negotiate their terms of employment or, more likely, accept the terms which management offered in exchange for their physical exertion or services necessary to complete tasks.

Taken together, the majority of workers today, as ever, have not had the choice to decide to join or form a union. In most countries, the formation of unions is restricted and on occasion banned by government authorities. In this way, most workers do not have the capacity to act collectively unless they engage in forms of unauthorized collective action. In fact, a segment of the labor literature which is gaining traction asserts that unconventional organizing by workers through anarchism and syndicalism, and collective action without the intent to negotiate contracts with management, are the shape of things to come (Atzeni 2021; Brenner 2026; Clover 2016).

As this book will demonstrate, virtually all Western Labor Studies scholars wrongly claim that unions in single party socialist states are controlled by government authorities and are of no value in improving wages, working conditions and benefits. Workers in socialist states, the argument goes, are not permitted to choose between unions or to form independent ones. Therefore, workers have no choice about furthering their interests in socialist single party states and are even more deprived than workers who "choose" not to join unions in non-socialist states. In socialist states, trade unions are stripped of a meaningful voice and are no more than agents of single party states, which only serve to provide a façade of democracy.

This book challenges that dominant perspective as flawed. The free market democratic ideology was forged by the dominant system of capitalism in the post-Second World War era and consolidated as a doctrine after the emergence of the US as the dominant imperial power following the disintegration of the Soviet Union. This book challenges the Labor Studies view that unions in states with compulsory union membership are incapable of representing workers and that Western models are far more effective. The Labor Studies literature which rejects AES as adverse to the working class fails to recognize the notable achievements of socialist unions in advancing working-class interests.

I hold that it does so cynically as a way to debase the anti-imperialist state striving to maintain relevance to the working class. The socialist national liberation movements strived to give meaning to the state as an agency, not as an arena for party competition which is subordinated to their former colonial masters.

Labor Studies scholars tarnish the reputation of the AES in order to restrict its effective political and economic autonomy. Lacking any familiarity with global South, anti-imperialist socialist states, Caraway, Cook and Crowley posit that they are reflexively authoritarian:

> For much of the late twentieth century, unions in Eastern Europe, Latin America, and Asia labored under authoritarian regimes that set strict boundaries on their political and economic activities. Although the "workers' states" of Eastern Europe created unions with near-universal membership, those unions were subordinate to ruling Communist parties, had little to no independent voice, and sought primarily to ensure that workers were productive members of society. (Caraway et al. 2015, 1)

Western academic literature on China is an echo chamber of critics devoid of balance. It applies a narrative of the ACFTU and labor rights. To all intents and purposes, it has become a cottage industry echoing the US State Department, including its progeny the National Endowment for Democracy (NED) which was established in 1983 under Ronald Reagan and supported by the AFL-CIO Solidarity Center, the international body of the American Federation of Labor and Congress of Industrial Organizations. Likewise, NGOs are a leading force behind the condemnation of China, and students and scholars who advance the negative critique of China and the ACFTU are more likely to receive funding from private foundations.

8   Neoliberalism and the Decline of Trade Union Membership

Contrary to dominant claims by advocates of conventional Western unions and labor representation, liberal bourgeois states have cracked down on the capacity of unions to mobilize workers into unions and engage in concerted activities, including slowdowns and work stoppages. In the US, successive anti-union decisions by the Supreme' Court have impeded workers' capacity to join unions and banned the right to strike against private and public enterprises. In June 2023, the US Supreme Court ruled 8:1 that Kellogg's, the multinational cereal brand, had the right to file lawsuits against trade unions striking for improved conditions if the work stoppage resulted in property damage: for example, inability to pour concrete, or causing food to decay by not transporting it to consumer markets for the company. The judgment set a precedent for trade unions being technically banned from performing their primary function of withholding labor to improve wages and working conditions. The decision could lead the Supreme Court in future to further restrict strikes and expand the capacity of employers to file damages against trade unions, revealing the undemocratic nature of the US labor regime compared to AES countries' labor regimes, which US human rights organizations and NGOs accuse of being repressive (Kruzel 2023). By contrast, workers in China always have the right to strike and suffer no damages. Indeed, as the ACFTU is an arm of the CPC, striking against state enterprises and even private domestic or foreign firms is protected by the state. The denial of labor stoppages in the US confirms the pervasive charade which is the Western left's critique of China as deficient and inferior to the West in defending the democratic and economic rights of workers.

The dominant trade union research privileges the global North as the origin of working-class representation and resistance. In fact, the major trade unions in the global South are vestiges of the colonial legacy which established labor laws to restrict the power of the working class and privilege capital. As 85 percent of the world's population live in poor countries of the global South, this book provides a Southern perspective (uniquely well-substantiated in terms of its range and contemporary relevance) on the imperialist formation of labor unions and on challenges to the dominant legacy which endured even after decolonization and independence. Crucially, this demonstrates that, since independence, Western trade unions have endeavored to maintain their own dominance and that of the labor regimes privileging multinational corporations and free market policies for the benefit of capital formation.

Global Trade Union Decline, 1975–2025

That all efforts aiming at the great end hitherto failed from the want of solidarity between manifold divisions of labor in each country, and the absence of a fraternal bond of union between the working classes in different countries; that the emancipation of labor is neither a local nor a national, but a social problem, embracing all countries in which modern society exists, and depending for its solution on the concurrence, practical and theoretical, of the most advanced countries. (Karl Marx 1864)

1 Organizational Regression and Membership Loss

The worldwide decline of trade unions is underway even as the global working class expands in the global South and employment is expanding in the global North. This regression defies predictions by Labor Studies scholars that unions would expand as workers entered manufacturing and production industries which are predisposed to socialized workplaces and expanded exploitation as direct investments grow in countries which have low wage labor and are integrated into global production chains. However, contrary to expectations, labor organization is failing to keep pace with the expansion of industrial labor in the global South, and unions are incapable of mobilizing workers in the new employment forms of logistics and the digital economy. Labor historian Marcel van der Linden (2021) asserts the paradox that worker union membership is declining in both advanced and developing economies at a time of industrial transformation which demands strong organizations to protect and advance the economic and social exigencies of labor.

Global working class membership in trade unions has fallen over the past half-century in the wake of three substantial changes: first, the imposition of neoliberal capitalism from the 1970s to the 2020s; second, the fall of the Soviet Union in 1991 and the end of the requirement for post-socialist states to occupy (typically unionized) sectors considered essential to advancing the political economic interests of the state; and third, accelerating technological transformation and the tapering off of higher paid skilled jobs and the rise of digital labor.

Even as capital worldwide has gained hegemony over labor, the enigma is that the deterioration in trade union organization is not in response to declining working class demand for trade union representation. On the contrary, most workers entering new sectors of the capitalist economy continue to mobilize in both the expanding industries of the global South and in the digital economy which is growing worldwide. The problem is that trade unions are not forming despite it being in the interests of workers to have union representation. Implausibly, in the absence of strong unions, workers unmistakably continue to organize against employer exploitation worldwide; from delivery workers in the digital economy of the global North to industrial workers in rapidly expanding industrial sectors of the global South.

Hasty conclusions that workers seek to form independent organizations or no organizations at all but simply spontaneously oppose serial corporate efforts to extract excess surplus value are disproved by demands for stronger working class organizations. For Lenin, spontaneity reflected the failure of organization and in today's context the concept appeases the bourgeoisie as it fails to lead to class consciousness as well as the posturing by anarchist and other left scholars as they celebrate the "bottom-up" activism which already occurs through unstructured job actions. Most Western labor unions do not practice bottom-up organizing. On the contrary, an evaluation of the All-China Federation of Trade Unions (ACFTU) shows that Chinese labor comprises both bottom-up and top-down attributes of organizing. Bottom-up organizing is effectively the equivalent of Lenin's spontaneity: a form economism. In the absence of an effective organization, spontaneity does not advance the working class interests, or the difference between economism and socialism.

In *What is to be Done?* Lenin asserts:

> [T]he adherents of the "pure and simple" labour movement, the worshippers of the closest "organic" contacts with the proletarian struggle, the opponents of the non-labour intelligentsia are compelled, in order to defend their positions, to resort to the arguments of the bourgeois "pure and simple" trade unionists. ... [S]ubservience to the spontaneity of the labour movement, the belittling of ... "the conscious element" ... *whether one likes it or not, growth of influence of bourgeois ideology among the workers.* All those who talk about "exaggerating the importance of ideology," ... imagine that the pure and simple labour movement can work out an independent ideology for itself, if only the workers "take their fate out of the hands of the leaders." But in this they are profoundly mistaken. ... Since there can be no talk of an independent ideology being developed by the masses of the workers in the process of their movement *then the only choice is*: Either bourgeois, or Socialist ideology. There is no middle course. Hence, to

> belittle Socialist ideology in any way, to deviate from it in the slightest degree
> means strengthening bourgeois ideology. (Lenin 1929)

Lenin incontrovertibly rejects spontaneity as a means to build a working class movement. Today, worker spontaneity indulges scholars who embrace anarchism or fail to grasp the significance of organizations able to represent and maintain working class interests. For such rebel phrasemongers, meaning is found in words rather than sustained movements: an imaginary lexicon of "the left," "subversion," "anarchism," and "radicalism" adding up to a metaphysical idealism which inspires and uplifts foreign activists but fails to address worker interests. According to such proponents, rather than attaining any objective, it is better to fight and lose while appearing to form a social movement which is typically supported monetarily by NGOs created by imperialist opponents of socialism (Ruckus 2023; Wetzel 2022). But, in the absence of trade unionism, it is the devotion to spontaneity (accounting for the failure of trade unions to establish organizational capacity) that has given rise to right wing populism. In the past decade, as trade unions decline, workers are portrayed as helpless victims without agency who only seek the satisfaction of immediate demands through riot or uprising without consolidating labor organizations capable of continuously representing worker interests through the creation of strong and capable trade unions. While workers are continually engaged in struggle, trade unions today are at an unprecedented historical nadir (Clover 2016; Ness 2023a).

2 The Rise of Precarious Work in the Global Core and Periphery

In 1996, Jan Breman, a Dutch anthropologist of India and Pakistan, formulated the term "footloose labour" to define the typical worker in South Asia, one that could have been applied in most of the developing world. Steady employment was illusory for precarious workers habitually moving from one workplace to another (Breman 1996). Working class organizations were only available for privileged laborers employed in the public sector and critical sectors of the economy. Most laborers in the same factory performing identical jobs were paid a fraction of the wages and were devoid of job security. Trade unions were unable to help as efforts to integrate all workers into the same bargaining unit were almost always prohibited by management. Those workers seeking to form autonomous unions were harshly repressed, dismissed and even jailed (Hammer and Ness 2021; Ness 2015; Nielson & Rossiter 2017). For all but a few workers in the global North, the social contract established from the 1930s to 1960s in Western Europe and North America between private employer and worker that ensured labor's fair wages, decent working conditions and job security are gone as labor laws have been gutted and government monitoring of the workplace has all but disappeared.

Since the 1970s, a central feature of neoliberalism has been the transformation of the traditional work relationship between employer and worker to reduce employers' obligation to provide decent wages and benefits and working conditions. Neoliberalism represented the withdrawal of the state from all facets of the economy, including monitoring management respect for labor law and workers. For almost all workers in poor countries of the global South, precarity has always been ubiquitous. More often than not, workers in rural and urban regions have never had job stability and have always eked out a living with low pay, working under arduous and hazardous conditions without job security and with no hope of improving their conditions through training or education. In 2011, Guy Standing identified the formation of a precariat in the developed countries of the global North in the wake of industrial restructuring and outsourcing of production, and their replacement with low wage temporary jobs which most workers entering labor markets did not intend to stay in as careers (Standing 2011). In the global North and South, even professional work (including academia, accounting and health care) was typically not accompanied by gainful and permanent employment (Ayala-Hurtado 2022; O'Brady et al. 2025). However, labor precarity in the global South is far more endemic and widespread than in the global North. Research on the extensive decline in trade unions and the rise of precarious labor in developing economies has expanded precipitously as anti-union policies have been promulgated within restructured industries as a means to avoid unionization (Scully 2016).

Beverly Silver's seminal *Forces of Labor* (2003) examines the rise in collective action through the lens of World-Systems Theory and finds that class conflict historically forms in global regions due to the globalization of capital to circumvent higher wage labor in the global North and advanced economies using spatial, temporal and technological fixes. Still, a distinction must be drawn between unauthorized wildcat strikes in the absence of trade unions, which most certainly occur in new regions of capital investment, and the organization of durable trade unions. The organizational question is essential for understanding the propensity for sustained working class activism. In most cases, foreign capital investments in new industries contribute to greater productivity and improved wages. But for those workers who are employed in precarious employment, unions typically are uninterested in mobilizing low wage workers as they pose a challenge to trade union leadership and do not increase union dues which are indispensable in keeping them operating, as dues are not paid by private employers. Consequently, labor unions are unwilling and frequently lack the capability to organize precarious workers in opposition to firms which seek to dodge responsibility for essential laborers. And, even if workers are themselves motivated to organize and form militant unions in manufacturing, supportive and oppositional state policies will certainly influence the success of unions. The record of new trade unions emerging to represent new employment forms is negligible (Bieler & Nowak 2022; Ness 2023b; van der Linden 2021). India, Indonesia and other developing states frequently seek to attract capital investment through promoting the absence of trade unions (International Commission for Labor Rights 2013).

3　Chinese Global Labor Exceptionalism: All-China Federation of Trade Unions

As organized labor worldwide has precipitously declined over the past 50 years, the working class membership of the ACFTU has grown dramatically from 2000 to the present. In 2025, the federation represented 300 million members, about 75 percent of China's 402 million workers. The ACFTU is a Marxist-Leninist organization charged by the Communist Party of China (CPC) with organizing and advancing the material interests of the Chinese working class. In the People's Republic of China (PRC), trade union representation on all levels requires a diligent trade union to advance the interests of the working class. The ACFTU is a democratic centralist organization which educates its members and responds to the democratic aspirations of the working class. In a market socialist economy, the ACFTU must absorb and comprehend the material interests of workers. This does not take place instantaneously but as the exigencies of the working class are recognized and the Federation and all its affiliates respond to worker demands on a grassroots and national basis. The ACFTU is the clarion of socialism, devoted to maintaining and expanding the power of the working class through steady progress.

As trade unions have declined worldwide, the ACFTU and its provincial, municipal, district and street level workers organizations have unmistakably built the capacity to advance the material interests and democratic and consultative objectives of the Chinese working class. Undoubtedly, the institution of the market economy produced hardships, but the CPC and ACFTU have been proactive in responding to the expectations of workers. Working class demands remain and the ACFTU seeks to address these today and in the future. Taken together, organized labor in China is on the march and growing effective unions. Self-described leftist critics who expect change without delay fail to understand that the transition to socialism is a slow and bumpy course which is not devoid of obstacles. But, unlike trade unions in capitalist states, the ACFTU promotes the interests of workers to mobilize into organizations and hold democratic elections.

4 Global Trade Unions in Decline

This chapter assesses trade unions worldwide to understand how the Chinese labor movement compares and why a clear distinction must be drawn between global labor and the ACFTU.

Over the past 50 years, working class power has been in freefall and is now weaker than at any time since the beginning of capitalism. The decline in working class agency is a logical result of decades of opposition from the state and the capitalist class in liberal democracies and the collapse of socialism since the end of the Soviet Union. Capital formation, backed by a capitalist state, precedes dialectical counterhegemonic forces. In the quest for capital accumulation and profits, the working class is formed through the expropriation of surplus labor. Technological innovation has been the dynamic force transforming primitive accumulation and all subsequent forms of production into systemic crisis. As capital must remain profitable, it must destroy existing forms of accumulation to survive and expand its productivity through one of two means: (1) the exploitation of labor power; and (2) technological development which cheapens the cost of labor through machines producing new lower cost forms of work.

The zenith of labor's leverage is when technological advancement is at its nadir and cannot dislodge workers from a relatively advantageous position under capitalist accumulation. Yet, for Karl Marx, these moments of relative working class power set the stage for scientific and technological development which undermine the gains workers have achieved through development of the skill to master production, circulation and distribution and leverage control of labor's share of profit.

5 Actually Existing Capitalism and Actually Existing Socialism

The political economy literature is dominated by research which views capitalism as monolithic but with a range of forms that distinguish each state from another. For most scholars in the field, capitalism is ubiquitous and is only distinguished by the relationship between dichotomous states and economic systems which have emerged according to historical legacies. Ben Clift defines comparative political economy simply as the degree to which nation states regulate economic systems (Clift 2021). In every instance, states are capitalist, and variations of state intervention reflect a range of historical and socio-economic factors. For Clift, socialism does not exist and state ideology that has emerged from socialist revolutions only defines the type of capitalism. By defining states as types of capitalism which exist on a continuum between high and low levels of state intervention, the legacy of socialism in the 20th and 21st centuries are rendered as nothing more than a type of state participation in an economic system.

The historic legacy of the Soviet Union, PRC, Cuba and other states which began to end capitalism and establish socialist economies based on the dictatorship of the proletariat as advanced by Marx and Engels in their *Manifesto of the Communist Party* (1848/1898). While few advocates of and subscribers to the *Manifesto*'s tenets stop to think about the implications of putting it into practice, the philosophy and positions have been taken seriously and diligently applied by communist theorists and political leaders seeking to adopt the principles of overthrowing the bourgeoisie to liberate the working classes from capitalist exploitation and ensure that the bourgeoisie is defeated and does not reemerge after the socialist revolution. The popular pamphlet is beyond doubt a most radical document, one that even socialists may find too exacting.

But, from 1917 to 1990, socialism became a major economic system encompassing 30–40 percent of the world's population. The end of the Soviet Union and the Eastern Bloc diminished the world population living under socialism but certainly did not end socialism or variants of Marxism-Leninism defined as the dictatorship of the working class.

The unipolar moment which established US global hegemony certainly challenged extant socialist states but absolutely did not bring them to an end. Even as the PRC shifted to market socialism, rooted in the dictatorship of the working class, leading Western political scientists proclaimed that the end of the Soviet Union denoted that the Marxist ideological concept of historical materialism was entirely irrelevant to understanding the world. Rather, the rise of the US to global hegemon pointed to a permanent future of Western liberal democracy, a premise that the US pursued to remake the world in its own neoliberal bourgeois image (Fukuyama 1992). However, the era from 1990 to the present also gave rise to a deeper criticism of socialism and a return to anarchism as the desired form of resistance. To many, anarchists, autonomist Marxists and others who oppose organizational forms and the consolidation of government rule, social transformation could occur without taking state power (Graeber 2013; Holloway 2002; Öcalan 2023). In *A Brief History of Neoliberalism*, David Harvey declared the Chinese socialist system exhausted as a consequence of the development of the market socialist economy (2007). By doing so, Harvey applies a global capitalist absolutism and applies a purity complex that was not even advocated by Mao Zedong in the formative years of the foundation of the PRC. As early as 1953, Mao accentuated the necessity to develop and industrialize to improve the material well-being of China's population.

We must lay emphasis on the development of production, but consideration must be given to both the development of production and the improvement of the people's livelihood. Something must be done for their material well-being, but neither too much nor nothing at all. At present there are quite a few cadres who ignore the people's livelihood and couldn't care less about their sufferings (Mao Tse-Tung/Mao Zedong 1977/2021, 87).

Mao and his successors had strived without end for economic development from the origins of the PRC to the present (Wen 2021). But Western Marxists seek absolutes which are never possible in the real world and thus hold China up to a bar that is detached from material reality. Thus, in lockstep, Harvey denounces the PRC's socialist system which adheres to a one-party communist state directed by a proletarian democracy and dictatorship of the working class. For fastidious Western Marxists, a one party socialist state is indistinguishable from authoritarianism even as working class democracy flourished in towns, villages and workplaces throughout China. Moreover, Harvey and adherents of globalism advance notions about the capitalist world economy in the absence of a historic understanding of the pivotal role of the state and omitting China and its authentic and unremitting initiatives by the CPC to modernize and develop into an advanced economy through ending poverty (Robinson 2014; Slobodian 2023). Globalists consider actually existing socialism as a static political system incapable of adapting to global circumstances, notably the rise of neoliberal capitalism. Even Marxist political economists did not recognize the necessity for socialist states to develop the means of production to improve standards of living and develop and apply technology to serve the demands of the working classes (Ness 2024). The Western Marxist non-revisionist perspective only considers socialism in its purist form and does not consider the imperative of sustainable economic development to improve the material conditions of workers in urban and rural regions. Under these circumstances, any form of technological advancement has been viewed as an attack on the working classes; socialist states would have no input into international ecological crises and would remain at the mercy of capitalist market economies imposing conditions for the future. Among many socialists, the notion of development is anathema and those states that defined themselves as socialist would be forced to comply with the developed capitalist economies directing all technological and productive forces.

To understand the ACFTU it is necessary to clarify the practice of trade unions under capitalism and socialism with Chinese characteristics and a market economy and capitalism. From 1975 to 2025, actually existing socialist states (AES) have developed a market economy to attract new technology for modernizing and improving the social and material conditions of workers. However, new technology under both socialism and capitalism presents a similar conundrum: the erosion of workers' capacity to maintain and increase wages and benefits. In the capitalist economy, the application of new technology is exclusively applied to undermine the bargaining power of workers in the capitalist market. Technological investment is used to directly deskill labor through reducing their productivity. The subsumption of capital in new industries increases productivity and diminishes labor's collective power to maintain its share of wages and capital's capacity to lower costs and increase the extraction of surplus value.

New technology is a product of surplus value extraction in the previous stage of production and is developed through investing profits in new technology. Profits produced through labor exploitation are appropriated in the work process and are the foundation of the expanded expropriation of surplus value from labor in each successive stage of capitalist accumulation. In this way, labor is the foundation of its own demise. However, labor's role in the deterioration of its own wages is concealed through the capitalist market. Capital formation is dependent on the extraction of surplus value from a previous interval of production and will likely never work in the new industrial sectors.

6   The Western Model of Unionism

This chapter demonstrates that as the traditional Western model of mass production trade unions established in the early 20th century has regressed since the 1980s, so the imposition of neoliberalism and the domination of capitalist hegemony over labor has grown worldwide. From 1975 to 2025, the evidence overwhelmingly demonstrates that the Western model of labor relations which proliferated through most of the world has become obsolete. The primary elements of Western trade unionism (formed through the emergence of mass production industries and labor militancy, which motivated capitalist state reforms) is contingent on the development of labor-law supervision of the labor–management relation. In theory, this entails national labor institutions' creation of a complicated process for the formation of trade unions to become the official representatives of workers in bargaining collective agreements on their behalf with private firms. But in practice, it has become a means to deter worker mobilization and collective action against employers, who are then able to crush unions lacking a militant working class base.

The formation of trade unions began with the development of mass production industries in Western Europe and North America in the 1930s. But trade union militancy was quickly compelled to conform to capitalist imperatives to ensure labor discipline, corporate profits and state regulation over labor–management relations. This culminated in the passage of the National Labor Relations Act (NLRA) in the US in 1935 and formed the basis for unionization in other advanced capitalist countries. In the aftermath of the major strikes in the auto and electronic sectors, labor unrest continued to proliferate from the 1940s to the 1980s, but most disputes typically were short term disruptions which bought labor peace following the negotiation of new bargaining agreements. Labor conflict in the West was almost always overseen by nation states and quickly settled and did not impede the long term profitability of capital. Labor–management conflict in advanced capitalist countries under the supervision of state labor bodies have almost always been dominated by labor leaders promoting cooperation with corporations. Consequently, the labor–management accords have in effect excluded workers from determining their own conditions. Labor militancy only appeared when trade unions could not control workers from going on wildcat strikes. The most notable cases of labor unrest in the US typically occurred in the public sector among postal, mass transit workers and air traffic controllers as neoliberal policies and new technology began to undermine the rights and power of labor. In Britain and other states which had state-owned firms, privatization chipped away at the organizational power of trade unions and workers.

The labor–management accords which culminated in the US with the passage of the NLRA were typically conducted through imposing labor discipline on workers. However, the gains which were achieved by workers in capitalist states were gradually eroded as capital and rapacious labor-law firms circumvented the power of workers. Notably, the introduction of neoliberalism and the restructuring of capital have severely weakened the capacity of trade unions to effectively represent workers and negotiate adequate collective contracts. The unraveling of trade union membership began in earnest during the 1980s and reached its apogee in the 1990s, after the end of the Soviet Union, as capital flight to lower wage regions undercut bargaining agreements which had engendered labor peace from the 1930s to the 1960s. Up to this point, trade unions in capitalist countries had significantly raised wages through the formation of formal labor–management relations. The expansion of trade unions had a ripple effect across the labor market as non-union industries commonly raised wages to match rates in organized workplaces. It was not even uncommon for non-union firms to pay workers even higher rates than unionized workers to maintain management control through union avoidance. These earlier gains of workers in advanced capitalist countries of the West were eviscerated.

The restructuring of capital through financialization of production demonstrates how finance capital in the West inflects economic development from emerging new technology. Advanced capitalist states expand finance into affluent consumer markets in order to extract profits as economies deindustrialize and shift away from manufacturing. It is clear that, in developed economies, financial appropriation is extracted through consumers who always benefit from the unequal exchange in trade which allows workers in the global North to afford commodities which are produced in the global South (Emmanuel 1972/2025; Lapavitsas 2013, 62–70). Absent from Lapavitsas' analysis is the shift in production from the advanced capitalist countries to poor countries in the developing world. However, it is imperative to direct attention to the former colonial territories as sources of resource extraction and the global system of economic imperialism. Even with sustained and augmented capitalist investment, global South workers remained exploited through the unequal exchange of trade. The fact that most capital invested in the global South is later reappropriated by imperialist countries for investment in the rich global North further clarifies the dominance of imperialist finance capital and explains the decline of trade unions in rich countries. In addition, the export of capital to low wage regions has contributed to the decline of trade unions (see Table 1).

Plainly, the exporters of finance extract far higher returns through the system of unequal exchange of trade which enriches the North and diminishes the value of exports from the South (Emmanuel 1972/2025). Even China, the world's second largest economy, is a developing country subject to the extraction of surplus value by financial capitalists in the North. But, just as the socialist economies of the Soviet Union and the Eastern Bloc came to an end, Labor Studies scholars in the 1980s and 1990s took succor in the assertion that labor militancy was expanding in the newly industrialized regions, notably Brazil, South Africa and South Korea. However, in the intervening years, global capitalism has restructured, and trade unions seeking a share of surplus value through collective bargaining have declined.

TABLE 1 OECD Trade union density, 1975–2018, % of employees (selected region and countries) (Source: Derived from OECD. 2025. *Membership of Unions and Employers Organisations and Bargaining Coverage: Standing but Losing Ground* (Policy Brief) 30 September. https://www.oecd.org/en/publications/membership-of-unions-and -employers-organisations-and-bargaining-coverage_fe47107c-en/full-report.html and OECD. 2025. OECD/AIS ICTWSS Database on Institutional Characteristics of Trade Unions, Wage Setting, State Intervention and Social Pacts [Dataset] 28)

Country	1975	1985	1995	2005	2015	2018
Australia	50.1	46.1	32.9	22.5	13.7	13.7
Austria	52.6	51.3	41.1	33.8	27.4	26.3
Canada	34.8	35.3	27.7	26.5	25.9	–
Colombia	9.6	9.4	–	–	–	–
France	22.6	13.8	10.5	–	–	–
Germany	34.6	34.7	29.2	21.5	17.6	16.6
Italy	47.5	42.5	37.6	33.8	34.2	32.6
Japan	34.5	28.8	24.0	18.8	17.5	17.0
Korea (South)	15.8	12.4	12.5	9.9	10	11.6
Mexico	40.5	16.9	13.1	13.1	12	–
Netherlands	37.8	27.7	25.3	22.1	17.7	16.5
Poland	34.7	23.8	–	–	–	–
Spain	12.7	18.6	15.5	14.4	13	–
Sweden	74	81.3	84.8	75.7	67	65.5
Turkey	40.4	27.9	16.7	10.3	8	9.2
UK	43.8	45.3	33.9	28.6	24.7	23.4
US	25.3	17.4	14.3	12	10.6	10.1
OECD[a]	38.7	32.1	24.2	19	16.5	15.9

a Estimated union density for OECD region.
Note: Figures derived from OECD Data Explorer, Trade Union Density (2023).

7 Capitalism, the Decline of Labor in the West and the Rise of Unions under Socialism

Affluent countries which are members of the Organisation for Economic Co-operation and Development (OECD) and have adopted European and North American models of trade unionism have experienced a five decade decline, notwithstanding growth in traditional industries. The imposition of the Western model of trade union representation is no longer a viable means to organize workers into unions. The Western model has been adopted by newly independent countries following the end of colonial rule in the aftermath of the Second World War, but this replication has not increased union density in the global South at the periphery of the world economy. In contrast, democratic unionization in the PRC through the ACFTU has dramatically improved conditions for its members and expanded to represent 75 percent of all workers in the state through effective responses to worker demands for improved wages, working conditions and benefits. The success of the socialist model with Chinese characteristics is not dependent exclusively on strikes but on establishing a structure of responsibility among both state-owned enterprises (SOEs) and the private sector (non-public employees). The private sector now employs about 80 percent of all workers, who, under the holistic ACFTU model, have improved their material and working conditions dramatically in the first quarter of the 21st century. This has been achieved by effectively challenging employers through the most comprehensive labor dispute adjudication system in the world. Workers typically win over 95 percent of cases brought by the ACFTU against management (Social Sciences Academic Press 2024).

In contrast, trade unions in the West have experienced an unprecedented decline, which has led some observers to view organized labor as a spent force. Labor unions, the historic preserve and political expression of working class power under free-market capitalism, have experienced a five-decade organizational decline in influence in the private sector. In the US, the heart of neoliberal capitalism, opposition to labor unions is omnipresent and the lack of an authentic party based federation has undermined any attempt to build a strong union movement against the all-encompassing power of capital and the support of the capitalist state. Consequently, from the 1970s to 2025, labor unions have become far less relevant to the US working class and have limited efficacy among precarious workers working in home care, delivery and logistics industries (namely: women, racial minorities and immigrant laborers) essential for private sector profits. Since the 2010s, the capacity of unions to represent public sector workers has been significantly eroded by Supreme Court decisions and under Donald Trump in 2025, as federal government bargaining rights have been revoked in key government agencies (Beitsch 2025; McCartin 2025; Sainato 2025a).

Most Labor Studies analysts in the US and Western Europe attribute the decline to the expanding power of international finance capital and the US neoliberal state, which has inexorably challenged organized labor thorough a range of union-busting tactics and restrictive policies which disempower workers. In the 1980s, labor management policies fostered the redistribution of wealth from the working class to the upper classes. Concomitantly, the labor literature has since been dominated by discussions of how to energize a working class apathetic to trade unions or stymied by the power of capital. The most popular works are either historical accounts of past successes, present failures, or handbooks prescribing newfangled approaches to organizing workers better and more successfully (Burns 2022; Greenhouse 2020; McAlevey 2020; Moody 2017; Womack 2023). The most evident manifestation of the decline of the US working class is the export of finance and capital investment from manufacturing at home to low wage regions of the world to produce commodities at higher profits for major consumer markets such as North America, Western Europe and increasingly China, Southeast Asia and South Asia.

Even if the vast majority of Labor research converges on the economies of the wealthy countries at the Western core, where union organization has deteriorated to a historic low in 2025, with few exceptions, most Labor Studies scholars continue to applaud existing and proposed models of organizing as the inspirational basis for expanding trade union density. While workers in states with higher density have a propensity to go on strike, the decline in union membership has curtailed political strikes (Lindvall 2013).[1] Still, despite several exceptions, labor strikes are broadly inconsequential and have yet to contribute to a meaningful growth in trade union membership in Western Europe, North America and worldwide (McAlevey 2020). As capital restructures labor markets into new forms of work on dispersed terrains, organized labor can scarcely keep up with technological innovation and globalization of information (Huws 2014). Incredibly, notwithstanding the hemorrhaging of trade union membership, Labor scholars focus on the rare cases where workers mobilize, go on strike and even win election campaigns (Blanc 2025). Notably, the Starbucks Workers United have won elections to represent 11,000 baristas but have struggled with management for a union contract (Kaye & O'Brien 2025; Sainato 2025b). In the event that Starbucks workers do win a union contract, it is unlikely to palpably improve their wages and working conditions. Campaigns at Amazon warehouses have garnered worker support and even several union election victories but no collective bargaining agreements. Eric Loomis is more honest in his appraisal of union success in the US, which

---

1 Paradoxically, the People's Republic of China, with the highest union density rate in the world, tends to have fewer strikes due to the extensive expansion of administrative courts to settle labor disputes.

reveals a history of working class activism and strikes, sometimes succeeding but often going down to defeat (Loomis 2018).

Significantly, as workers worldwide increasingly enter a digital economy, oppressed laborers employed by technology firms are almost always considered independent contractors and do not have the capacity to gain employer recognition let alone collective bargaining agreements (Cini 2025; Huws 2014; Ness 2023a; Rothstein 2025; Scholz 2017; Tassinari & Maccarrone 2020; van Doorne et al. 2022) As we shall see in Chapter 5, bottom-up and top-down holistic trade union organizing among platform workers in China has reduced the share of workers who are not directly employed by service providers. Service and retail workers are also prevented from gaining union recognition as employers are averse to unions, even if workers legitimately vote for union recognition. The fledgling election victories at Amazon warehouses and among Starbucks baristas have restored a modicum of hope to Western union enthusiasts, but none has led to a substantive bargaining agreement similar to those at the Wal-Mart and big-box retail chains a decade ago. As government legislation and lack of enforcement and legal regulations have become increasingly opposed to the formation and presence of organized labor, the prospect of rebuilding trade unions in the US and developed countries has become ever more daunting and hostile to workers, even if they have wanted to join unions. In the manufacturing sector, the bastion of trade union growth from the 1930s to 1950s, trade union organizing has failed, even with significant resources. Trade unions are necessary to lessen economic inequality but require a reconstituted labor regime as well as resources and international solidarity to counter the effective union avoidance industry which thwarts organizing campaigns in the US (McClelland 2022; Silvia 2023). Technological change and industrial restructuring have further complicated the capacity of existing trade unions to organize workers. As trade unions weaken, the attention of Labor Studies scholars has shifted towards the prospect of social movements rather than union formations (Clover 2016; della Porta et al. 2023).

8   Western and Non-Western Models of Trade Unionism

The global labor movement is composed of trade unions in two international federations: the World Federation of Trade Unions (WFTU), formed in Paris in 1945, and the International Confederation of Trade Unions (ITUC), founded in Brussels in 2006 through a merger of trade unions which embrace capitalism. The ACFTU is not an international federation but has more workers who are members than both organizations combined.

8.1   World Federation of Trade Unions (WFTU)

The WFTU was formed in 1948 by the Soviet Union as an international bloc of communist trade unions with shared principles of anti-imperialism, anti-colonialism and socialism. In the immediate aftermath of the Second World War, the WFTU also hoped an international union federation would advance a common political perspective to compete with that of liberal unions intent on maintaining colonial structures after independence. The ITUC and the WFTU competed for trade union affiliates as part of competition between capitalism and socialism.

The WFTU proclaims itself to be a class oriented trade union movement fighting against capitalist/imperialist barbarity and fighting for a society free of humans exploiting humans. In 2022, the WFTU had 105 million members in 133 countries. Throughout its history, the WFTU has played a central role in the struggles against apartheid, racism, colonialism, as well as against the policies of the US, Israel and NATO and its allies. It has been at the forefront of the struggles for labor and union rights. Its history is rich, with action and struggles on central, regional and sectoral levels aimed at: uniting the forces of the working class in class struggles; uniting the workers regardless of their ideology, religion, language, gender and ethnicity; uniting the people in the struggle against capitalist exploitation and imperialism.

While the ACFTU was formed in 1922, the WFTU is the oldest existing *international* trade union federation. It was founded in Paris, France on October 3, 1945, moving to Vienna, Austria from 1953 to 1956, Prague, Czechoslovakia from 1956 to 2004, and Athens, Greece in 2005, where it remains today. The WFTU maintains divisions on all six continents with sectoral International Trade Unions (TUIs) in every industry. It has permanent representation at the United Nations and holds consultative status in the International Labour Organization (ILO). In 1948, the WFTU advanced the international right of workers to organize. Its trade unions are primarily situated in developing economies and have advanced an anti-imperialist policy.

8.2   International Confederation of Trade Unions (ITUC)

The ITUC, claiming 190 million members in 2018, is composed exclusively of national unions in capitalist countries. The unions are found in the European ecumene, North America, former colonies of European imperialist states that inherited the institutional regimes of their former colonial rulers and states in the US sphere of influence in the Western Hemisphere. ITUC trade unions seek continuity with the past and do not seek to transform liberal democracies dominated by private business, even as the ITUC represents unions which are dependent on public funding derived from state taxation for education, health care and social services. ITUC-affiliated unions do not seek to gain political power and dominance but to expand wages and social benefits for members and also to increase the share of workers who are members of trade unions. Indeed, ITUC unions are primarily motivated by simple unionism, avoid participation in politics and increasingly do not even advocate for political parties which have supported unions in the past. Most unions are transactional and seek a greater share of public funding and policies which favor their discrete industries and jurisdictions. In the private sector, ICTU trade unions seek government policies which restrict free trade, if they are in countries which have large consumer markets and promote exports. Trade unions support government labor policies which facilitate organizing new members, often contrary to attracting finance capital. In short, ITUC unions support protectionism, promotion of exports and governments which facilitate recruitment of union members.

Paradoxically, even as it criticizes the ACFTU for not interfering with socialist China, the ITUC does not engage in political activity and generally does not maintain an ideological perspective other than advancing the material interests of its unions. Even if members may maintain political perspectives, they rarely influence union policy.

9 Decline of Unions in Core Capitalist States, 1975–2025

Following the emergence of neoliberal policies and the dismantling of social welfare programs, trade unions in Europe, North America experienced corresponding decline from 1975 to the present (see Table 1). In Europe, where trade union membership has plummeted in the past 40 years of neoliberal capitalism, Labor scholars recognize the decline but point to a bygone era when unions were stronger as inspiration for the future (Holgate 2021). Even the Nordic region, where unionization had been highest, is experiencing a decline. In post-Eastern bloc Europe, emergent states have adopted neoliberal policies and compete for foreign investments through promising lower labor costs and union-free workplaces, significantly undermining trade unions. In the OECD region, successful labor union organizing campaigns leading to collective bargaining agreements are a rarity. Labor scholar Jelle Visser attributes the decline in trade union membership to the restructuring of labor markets and the inability of trade unions to attract young workers entering labor markets even when the historic conditions for unionization are favorable: for example, inflation and rising consumer prices, the revival of labor militancy and higher levels of government intervention to stabilize markets. In the OECD zone, Visser asserts:

> If ever there was a time for the trade union, it is now. Unemployment is lower and labour markets are tighter than has been the case in many years. Inflation has sharply risen after a long period of price stability. In many countries there is a recent upward trend in work stoppages, and more workers are involved in strikes. (Visser 2024, 629)

Visser considers the conditions to be propitious for a restoration of government as a solution to social and economic crises and support for labor market policies which are more advantageous to workers. This sentiment is rising among labor policymakers in the OECD zone in the aftermath of economic crises, rising inequality, climate change and the COVID-19 pandemic.

Organizing is in decline throughout the world, a point raised by Marcel van der Linden (2023), who argues that whilst European workers benefited from an apogee of union organization, most workers in the global South never had the opportunity to join trade unions to improve their conditions. Thus, a clear distinction must be made between US and European workers and those in poor countries of the global South (whose numbers have grown dramatically under neoliberalism) as equivalent victims of capital's neoliberal turn and the attendant decline of labor unions, but between whom there is a massive difference in wealth and income adjusting for purchasing power parity. Moody (2017) and his acolytes assert that the decline of labor is a result of multinational capital. He dismisses the disjuncture of labor interests between rich and poor countries even as GDP per capita in the OECD countries of the global North is significantly higher than in the global South (see Table 2). Instead, the "new terrain" provides the capacity for the development of working class movements in the US which will challenge the state. Accordingly, the new labor force of logistics workers worldwide poses a militant risk to capital through mass action, and the election of candidates supportive of corporations to mitigate this risk manifests the power of capital to influence the political sphere. More recent treatments by labor sociologists (Vivek Chibber 2022) posit that labor can regain its vitality through building social movements and working class political parties. But, if labor unions are on the back foot and failing their members, allegedly it is not because of an apathetic working class but a failure of tactical and strategic organizing (McAlevey 2020).

TABLE 2 GDP per capita, 2018–24 (constant 2021 international $) (Source: World Bank (Database) derived from World Bank Group. 2025. DataBank world development indicators (Database) https://databank.worldbank.org/source/world-development-indicators/Series/NY.GDP.PCAP.PP.KD)

Region	2018	2020	2022	2024
OECD members	49,543.0	47,938.0	52,125.4	53,311.4
Low income	2,395.3	2,322.4	2,291.7	2,228.1
European Union	50,726.6	48,792.1	53,686.6	54,291.0
United Kingdom	52,071.3	47,144.7	52,982.2	52,518.0
United States	67,719.8	67,342.1	72,679.3	75,491.6
East Asia & Pacific[a]	15,925.0	16,816.9	18,599.5	20,452.2
Europe & Central Asia[a]	41,007.4	39,619.5	43,268.7	44,689.5
Middle East, North Africa Afghanistan & Pakistan[a]	9,498.7	9,162.5	9,636.7	9,792.6
Latin America & Caribbean[a]	18,120.2	16,754.7	18,419.7	18,935.3
North America	66,672.0	65,982.8	71,185.0	73,461.8
South Asia	7,622.3	7,399.2	8,522.0	9,653.4
Sub-Saharan Africa[a]	4,595.9	4,374.7	4,502.9	4,535.1
World	19,063.0	18,698.1	20,281.5	21,267.7

a   Excluding high income.

10 Perspectives on the Decline and Possible Resurgence of Union Membership

Do the US and the American Federation of Labor and Congress of Industrial Organizations (AFL-CIO) represent a model for trade union resurgence? In 2023, US trade unions declared that they were undergoing an unprecedented turnaround in the wake of labor-union strikes and collective bargaining successes in major industrial and logistics sectors, in particular the United Auto Workers (UAW) contract campaigns in the big three leading auto companies: General Motors, Ford and Stellantis. Notably, the UAW won wage increases ranging from 25 percent to 33 percent, expedited wage increases in the future and secured unionization in new battery factories without employer resistance, an objective which labor unions had demanded but typically failed to achieve since the late 1980s. Remarkably, through a targeted strike campaign, the UAW, under its new national president Sean Fein, forced management to abolish the tiered wage system it had instituted in 2004 which had severely eroded union membership and wage standards in the industry and set higher wage workers against lower wage ones. However, although workers covered by union collective bargaining agreements registered a marginal increase in numbers, union density, not including membership, remained at 6.8 percent in the private sector, the same rate as in 2022. Due to the Janus decision by the Supreme Court, permitting workers in unions to opt out of paying dues, ever more workers covered by collective bargaining agreements are not union members (Janus v. AFSCME 2017). Right-to-work laws in the US are a leading factor in the decline of membership and have been replicated in other Western countries. Thus, workers may benefit from collective bargaining agreements but reject membership and the requirement to pay dues to employers. Most union analysts believe that the true unionization rate in the private sector is below 5 percent.

Since the merger of the AFL and CIO in 1955, it has been the sole labor federation in the US during a historical low point in union membership numbers. It is significant to note that the US is dominated by a single labor federation as Labor scholars often claim that socialist countries like China and Cuba have a single federation, linked to a political party without competition. The difference for the US is that the AFL-CIO is loosely allied with the Democratic Party as an interest group lacking in substantial influence over political decisions. At least, unions directly affiliated to political parties maintain the power to

TABLE 3　Union membership, coverage, density and employment: Private sector workers (Source: Derived from Hirsch et al. (2025) *Unionstats: Union membership and coverage database from the current population survey* (Database) Unionstats.com https://unionstats.com/)

Year	Sample Size	Employment (thousands)	Union Members (thousands)	Membership (%)
1973	40,245	61,886.5	14,954.1	24.2%
1980	55,246	71,440.7	14,331.6	20.1%
1990	152,197	87,066.4	10,299.4	11.8%
2000	134,554	101,809.9	9,147.7	9.0%
2010	137,980	103,040.4	7,091.9	6.9%
2020	111,050	111,587.0	7,082.3	6.3%
2023	105,475	122,994.1	7,408.1	6.0%

Note: Data is based on the US Government Current Population Survey.

influence decisions in favor of labor. As union power in the US is measured by density in the working population, trade unions in the private sector declined to an all-time low which has remained relatively constant despite efforts to mobilize workers into unions and take militant strike action. Union membership in the private sector declined between 2020 and 2023 from 6.3 percent to 6.0 percent, and Supreme Court decisions further eroded union membership and power through undermining labor's capacity to collect union dues, both in the private and public sectors (see Table 3).

11 Factors in the International Decline of Trade Union Membership

Union membership has declined throughout the world in the neoliberal period since 1975. Scholars have historically attributed this in the US to government and Supreme Court policies and legal decisions hostile to unions. Others assert that unions lack internal democracy, thus repelling workers from social organization at the workplace (Moody 1988). However, the evidence shows that as trade unions are ineffective in defending labor, a growing share of workers prefers to remain independent from unions and are largely uninterested in joining new union campaigns. The rise of neoliberalism and the precipitous decline in union density poses a significant dynamic in the economies of wealthy states in the affluent West as wages decline and fewer can afford housing, transportation and other necessities. This helps explain why trade union strategists believe that organizing new forms of worker organizations that include youth, women and immigrants entering the labor market will boost the size of collective trade unions (Kochan et al 2023; Visser 2024). But trade unions, workers' organizations and NGOs have shifted from direct organizing towards advocacy campaigns to increase membership, hoping that workers will achieve wage increases as a result of lobbying rather than direct action. Consequently, wage gains are applicable to NGOs and government minimum wage laws rather than union organizing activity. Concomitantly, the wage gap between union and non-unions jobs is becoming less significant. Often, in unskilled jobs, government minimum wage laws set by elected officials are the basis for setting wages rather than being an advantage which unions gain from mobilizing members. In skilled jobs, workers are apt to bargain directly with employers rather than depend on a union to do so on their behalf.

Scholars have attributed the decline in unions to legal and political restrictions on labor organizing and membership (Gould 2022; Lichtenstein 2013).

Certainly, the US labor courts (biased against trade unions), and corporate lawyers have significantly constrained the capacity of workers to strike and engage in concerted action to improve conditions and have limited their rights to represent workers. But legal restrictions alone do not explain the anemic state of the labor movement in the US. In addition, union wages are not appreciably higher than non-union wages, and workers have been beneficiaries of the privileged position they hold compared to workers overseas. While Black and Latino workers have a propensity to join unions, the record shows that employer anti-union campaigns pose formidable legal obstacles to organizing. Moreover, in comparison to other countries in the West and OECD region, white US workers are less interested in labor representation due to employer opposition (Bronfenbrenner 2009; Wang and Young 2023). Race also is a factor in unionization, but if white workers are already members and realize that interracial solidarity is beneficial to all workers they are more likely to unify on class rather than identity (Frymer and Grumbach 2020). William Gould, chairman of the National Labor Relations Board in the US from 1994 to1998, contends that labor laws have been a barrier to union organization, but such impediments do not explain the wide gap between US and overseas workers in this respect. Instead, in his most recent work, Gould asserts that unions in the US lack internal democracy in the workplace (Gould 2022; Levitt 2021). During this time, most labor unions throughout the world have had restricted rank-and-file participation and have often been complicit with employers in negotiating and enforcing contracts. This view has long been maintained by union democracy reformers in the Teamsters, UAW and other major unions (Brenner et al. 2010; Burns 2022; Crowe 1993; Moody 1988; 2017). They believe that the spectacle of rank-and-file militancy in those cases takes precedence over establishing genuinely strong and viable unions capable of overcoming the power of capitalist exploitation. Rising capitalist exploitation in the West and the decline of existing trade unions have eroded the living standards of workers, characterized by Guy Standing as "the precariat," who, lacking in representation, constitute a dangerous class which has the potential to politically destabilize society, an outcome which has come to fruition with the rise of populism (Standing 2011).

The growing number of workers eschewing unions does not negate the fact that workers are seeking to mobilize to obtain wage increases. But, due to occupational mobility, it is unlikely that workers will view unionization and wage gains as a significant change in their working conditions. Workers seeking unionization are the most vulnerable and view unions as a means to secure wage growth, protection from employer abuse and, for undocumented migrant workers, deportation.

12   Unequal Exchange and Inexpensive Commodities

The decline in trade unions is in part a function of the deindustrialization of the economies of wealthy states, where the industrial working class comprised the most militant workers. Service and technology workers are far more concerned with low cost services and inexpensive commodities, which are obtained from the unequal exchange of trade between wealthy and poor countries (Emmanuel 1972/2025). In the West, even workers benefit from the extensive availability of low cost commodities. Admittedly, they are subjected to higher costs of living, and the US has the highest level of inequality of income and inequality among rich countries, but the evidence reveals that per capita GDP in the West is far higher than in the rest of the world and growing (Chancel et al. 2022). In the post-industrial economies of North America and Western Europe, the workforce has shifted away from industrial manufacturing and towards services and new technology. Wage inequality stems from the growth of the digital economy and the expansion of new labor markets, including ride hailing, delivery, logistics and workers who have become dependent on digital platforms where technology companies typically have no responsibility for them.

Trade unions primarily increase wages among low wage workers. Most other workers do not require labor unions to defend and improve wages, but, as they are independent contractors, trade union organizing is highly challenging or impossible for them as they do not have an official employment relationship with technology firms. A large segment of the digital workforce is composed of migrant laborers who are considered essential workers employed in jobs which are in high demand but where there is a shortage of labor. Thus, the correlation between trade union representation and wage growth applies only to low wage workers and not those who form the "labor aristocracy." This view was advanced by Marxist economists as early as the late 19th century as they sought to understand why organized labor in rich countries was not interested in defending the interests of destitute workers in poor countries.

To begin to overcome this failure of international class solidarity, we must recognize that, from the transformation of primitive accumulation to the origins of capitalism, proletarianization has not been uniform but has reflected multiple class contradictions. The origin and development of capitalism is not monolithic and mirrors the manifold developments of capital formation and the essential introduction and application of new technology (Emmanuel 1982). The asymmetrical churning of capital formation is decisive in economic development and the formation of interclass and intraclass privilege. On a world scale, the poorest in developed societies have been better-off than the wealthiest in poor countries of the global South, patterning class conflict within societies and reflecting imperialist economic privilege among countries. The dual shift takes place through internal conflict within states and patent conflict expressed through imperialist privilege between the core and periphery, with non-uniform distinctions among social formations. It is the progression of interstate divisions which gives rise to a labor aristocracy and has been identified by major philosophers from Karl Marx and Friedrich Engels to eminent Third World political economists of the 20th and 21st centuries; namely, Arghiri Emmanuel, Ruy Mauro Marini, Samir Amin, Immanuel Wallerstein and the World-Systems school.

The concept of unequal exchange advanced by Emmanuel in the 1960s has been revitalized in the 2020s and has shifted a growing share of the Marxist literature away from its dominant proclivity for structural theory towards studies focusing on the dialectical relationship between humans and the material reality, fostering research on the non-equivalence of wages between rich and poor countries (Brolin 2007; Cross 2021; Dunaway & Macabuac 2022; Frame 2023; Hickel 2021; Hornborg 2011; King 2023; Lauesen 2024; Malm 2020; Marini 2022; Ness 2023b; Osorio & Reyes 2023; Raffer 2023; Ricci 2022; 2023).

13   Workers in the Capitalist Core and the Aristocracy of Labor

As the dominant imperialist power from 1945 to the present, the US has reaped economic advantages from its hegemonic economic, military, cultural and political status. The abundant literature in political economy has demonstrated that the formation and consolidation of the financial order in the postwar era has benefited the capitalist class and supported attendant economic benefits for its working classes. The dominant capitalist fractions in the US required a strong working class as consumers of its products and services. Workers also obtained economic advantages from their privileged status at the center of the global empire.

As US dominance extended from the 1970s to the early 21st century, the relocation of production from the US to new low cost sites in the global South transformed the labor market as well paid jobs in manufacturing were replaced by ones in services, retail and finance sectors. Taken together, the reconstitution of the US labor market away from production has solved the overproduction problem of the 1970s and removed a major source of economic and political instability. The unemployed reserve army was shifted from the US and other countries of the global North to the global South. In the postwar era, lower unemployment was always an indicator of an overheated economy, as capitalist markets worried that wages would creep up and reduce profitability. When unemployment rates decline today, markets stay stable, as they indicate that the consumer market remains vibrant.

Though wages have moderated as a consequence of the decline in trade unions, the US relies on a strong consumer class to purchase goods primarily manufactured overseas. Consequently, the capitalist markets require a working class which can afford foreign goods. The purchasing power of the US consumer market is the largest in the world and, based on GDP per capita, is growing. In the modern era, this satiated working class in the US and imperialist core constitutes a labor aristocracy which benefits directly from the superexploitation of foreign labor. Thus, as Lenin noted, today's US and European workers do not share common political material interests with 85 percent of the world in the global South but are in alliance with their national bourgeoisie (see Amin 2017). A majority of the US and metropolitan working class are members of the labor aristocracy, disinclined towards forming a common class interest with workers in the global South, which is articulated through national chauvinism with an unambiguous objective of maintaining their economic advantage derived through imperialism.

To understand the nature of populism in the US and elsewhere we need to revive the concept of the labor aristocracy as a prime driver in class consciousness and political action. The presence of a privileged sector of labor is not an abstraction but allows us to understand the unsettling impact of working class fragmentation. As Labor scholars and socialists, it is far more comfortable to perceive the working class as a cohesive unified force. It is preferable to lay blame for the decline in working class unity on rapacious employers controlled by a compliant capitalist state than to gaze at the internal divisions within the working class. Of course, it is the upper strata of labor which join with the bourgeoisie and capitalist state to advance a mutual set of interests.

As a graduate student recently related, the idea that the world capitalist system is defined by a labor aristocracy is a bitter pill to swallow. Indeed, it is a challenging normative position to conceive of workers as divided and compels scholars of the working class to reconsider our enduring perspectives on the challenges which circumscribe and restrict class unity and collective action.

13.1   Labor Aristocracy in the Global Core Today

Working class populism is directly implanted in the turbulence of the global divide between rich and poor and intensification of the imperialist center's struggle to preserve its economic privilege, which has not declined but deepened through superexploitation of natural resources and labor in the global

South. Accordingly, we can begin to delineate the alarming growth of right wing populism in the US working class. While populism is also expressed on the left, the unmistakable erosion and disappearance of trade unions (which had advanced ideas of justice and social rights on a national basis, though certainly not on a global basis) have left workers abandoned with no form of organizational representation. Though trade unions in the US have had a tenuous relationship with their members, once jobs disappear, that connection completely disappears and workers are left to fend for themselves. (On the decline of US trade unions and other social organizations, see Putnam (2001).) Workers are more likely to join religious institutions that advance social chauvinism. However, as unions decline, most do not join any competing social organizations whatsoever.

While the wealthy countries in the global North have experienced wider income inequality, reflected in the catchphrases "1 percent," "precarious labor," "anti-fascism," and growing interest in "socialism," a close examination of the movements of the left exposes a reformism that does not seek to address questions of global poverty and exploitation but a redistribution of wealth within the wealthy countries of the global North. The social movements and political currents of the 2010s in the US, notably "Occupy Wall Street" and the dramatic growth of the Democratic Socialists of America after the election of Donald Trump in 2016, are devoted to addressing national rather than global inequality.

14 The Growth and Expansion of Trade Union Representation in China

The premise of this book is that China's ACFTU is a model for trade unionism worldwide. Detractors on the right and left may reject this view, asserting that the ACFTU is controlled by the CPC. However, upon the foundation of China in 1949, the ACFTU had adopted a Leninist model of trade unionism, advocating the mobilization of workers into unions but rejecting the participation of unions in independent political activity which could potentially undermine the mainsprings of a socialist society. Opponents either do not recognize the importance of the CPC's political leadership rooted in the working class and the ACFTU's consistent shapeshifting and metamorphosing of its organizing strategies in response to the application of new technology that also have a bearing on workers' job stability. But to be sure, Chinese trade unions affiliated with the ACFTU elected their leaders democratically and reflect the demands of the Chinese working class for improved wages, conditions of work and benefits. The trade union federation has been recognized by the ILO as exemplary in responding to technological changes that affect workers and has assigned the ACFTU to strengthen trade union capacities to advance South–South cooperation.[2] The ACFTU's antagonists do not consider cause and effect of technological change and focus on the temporal interval before the implementation of new organizing strategies.

The ACFTU has successfully adapted to the rapid modernization of China's economy and has reflected the subjective needs of an urban proletariat. It had significant challenges to overcome in the development of China's economy which required understanding of the objective requirements of the working class. No social organization can respond immediately to the organization of markets, especially the insertion of foreign capitalist markets in the formative stages of China's opening up. The advances of the ACFTU reflect the unremitting progression of a socialist trade union organization to address worker demands.

15   Conclusion

Opponents of the ACFTU, almost exclusively leftists outside of China, expect it to instantaneously change its organizing practices without absorbing the multifarious features of the economy. To absorb the changes, the ACFTU, like all organizations, must ascertain how to respond in the interests of the working class. In this sense, it reflects both the Leninist transmission belt of a Marxist organization and a bottom-up federation which responds to the demands of workers. Surely, we do not live in a utopian world and grasping demands is often imperfect and laden with barriers which reflect internal and external forces. In a natural world, change does not occur immediately but swells up from the rank and file and the working class forces which represent the Chinese ACFTU. Juxtaposing Chinese labor-union representation (which mobilizes workers, increases wages, benefits and rights) with the inept Western capitalist form highlights the distinctiveness of a society which is dedicated to advancing the rights of the working class. Chapter 6 examines the ACFTU's leadership

---

2   In 2024, the ILO renewed an agreement to "enhance trade union capacities in Asia and the Pacific." The ILO has charged the ACFTU to expand its initiatives to assist unions to "advocate for policy reforms and improve working conditions" for workers through trade unions. The ACFTU will impart its effective organizing strategies in the digital sector to trade unions in Asian and Pacific countries. In addition, the ACFTU was charged with working with unions in the global South to meet Sustainable Development Goals (SDGS) for decent work, "including gender equality, social dialogue, occupational safety and health, transitions and forced and child labour" (ILO 2024).

in organizing workers in the platform economy. The Chinese success in organizing workers in logistics and the digital economy stands in stark contrast to unions' failure to organize this rapidly expanding sector of workers elsewhere in the world. No other state encourages the democratic organization of workers in the public and private sectors. Trade union organization in China has tangible benefits: significantly higher wages, benefits and social security, as well as improved standards of occupational safety.

Unlike most countries across the world, China does not pride itself on low unionization rates to promote foreign investment. As a socialist state, it encourages workers to join local unions where there is a high level of democratic representation through elections for union leaders on the firm level. However, China's high union density rate and attendant high wages do not inhibit foreign investment in the country due to the country's high productivity, technological development and subsumption of capital into production.

While the ACFTU has mobilized workers into unions, raised wages, benefits, social insurance and improved working conditions, the federation is charged by the CPC to continually work to improve the lives of Chhina's working class. As a socialist society which is dedicated to the working class, the ACFTU must never consider its efforts complete as the material conditions constantly change. Consequently, the ACFTU must consistently improve wages and working conditions in new labor market sectors, such as services and logistics, while organizing new workers into the federation. A key challenge today is ensuring that all workers have contracts with their firms. Those workers who do not work directly for employers do not have equivalent benefits. However, the ACFTU has successfully transformed the status of workers on the provincial, municipal, district and street levels. In contrast to unions globally, it is on the march and exhibiting to the world that it surpasses trade unions based on Western metrics and is moving towards an equitable socialist society.

Migration, Floating Labor and Urbanization

> Marxist philosophy holds that the law of the unity of opposites is the fundamental law of the universe. This law operates universally, whether in the natural world, in human society, or in man's thinking. Between the opposites in a contradiction there is at once unity and struggle, and it is this that impels things to move and change. Contradictions exist everywhere, but they differ in accordance with the different nature of different things. In any given phenomenon or thing, the unity of opposites is conditional, temporary and transitory, and hence relative, whereas the struggle of opposites is absolute. (Mao Zedong, 1957)

One must understand the condition and revolutionary nature of the Chinese working class to properly understand the major demographic transformation from 1978 to the present. During the post-Mao era, China has transformed from a fundamentally agrarian society to an urban one and, concomitantly, the primarily rural working class economy has become an urban industrial and service society. Under Deng Xiaoping and his successors, the rural economy has transformed into an urban "market socialist" economy which has set the stage for the application of a developed form of socialism. The contradiction of socialism without development was solved by releasing the forces of production. Under any dialectical process, contradictions are not resolved without adversity and struggle. If Mao's era was characterized by the application of socialism in 1949, Deng's rise in 1978 was directed at the institution of market reforms under a socialist state, preparing the foundation for the emergence of a more effective socialist state dedicated to the expropriation of capital under Xi Jinping from 2012 to the present (Bu 2022).

1 Introduction: Anti-Imperialist Revolution and the Struggle for a Socialist Path to Development

When the People's Republic of China (PRC) was established in October 1949, just under 90 percent of its 541.2 million residents lived in the countryside and just over 10.6 percent resided in urban areas. Under the leadership of Mao Zedong, from 1949 to 1976, the capacity to survive on the countryside was considered a vital form of economic security, and the Chinese state consistently emphasized improving the lives of rural workers through collectivization and state social programs. The "iron rice bowl" provided China's rural population with the capacity to survive, no small achievement in view of more than 100 years of imperial occupation and pillage from the early 19th century to the rise of the PRC. From the mid-1950s, China established a *hukou* residential system, which ensured all citizens had the right to a domicile and household, a development which contributed to the vast rise in basic living standards: for example, life expectancy, infant mortality, food and nutrition which eradicated stunting, and so on. The hukou was viewed as a social benefit ensuring the right to maintain households. Notwithstanding efforts to thwart Chinese development by the US and the West, the PRC provided basic protections which preserved the capacity of people to live in rural regions. This is why Marxist sociologist Robert Weil (1996) regarded rural state security under the socialist system of the PRC to be a significant achievement which safeguarded the Chinese rural proletariat from economic calamity and devastation.

Chinese government statistics and academic research have shown a direct nexus between the extraordinary expansion of migration from rural agrarian regions to urban agglomerations as essential to stimulating the rise of the manufacturing industries for export and a burgeoning urban economy. Within only two decades, from 1980 to 2000, China became the world's foremost industrial producer and exporter of commodities for consumers chiefly in North America and Western Europe. In the next 25 years, from 2000 to 2025, the Chinese economy rose to be the second largest in the world, measured by the value of goods and services, without taking into consideration unequal exchange and the inequality of the value of goods and services produced in China and the US. If the true value of goods and services were factored in and unequal exchange of trade were removed, China would have the largest economy in the world (Ricci 2021a; 2021b).

Marxist political economist John Bellamy Foster (2024) lays bare the magnitude of unequal exchange from developing to developed countries:

> It should be emphasized that the Global North's contemporary drain of economic surplus from the Global South, via the unequal exchange of labor embodied in exports from the latter, is *in addition* to the normal net flow of capital from developing to developed countries recorded in national accounts. This includes the balance on merchandise trade (import and exports), net payments to foreign investors and banks, payments for freight and insurance, and a wide array of other payments made to foreign capital such as for royalties and patents. (Bellamy Foster 2024)

Jason Hickel et al. observe, on a global scale, unequal exchange of trade between North and South is extensive and durable:

> Our analysis confirms a substantial and persistent pattern of unequal exchange between the global north and South. In 2021, the global North imported 906 billion hours of embodied labour from the South while exporting only 80 billion hours in return (a ratio of 11:1). On average across the period, the North imported 15x more labour from the South than it exported in return. ... This net appropriation occurs across skill categories, including high-skilled labour. On average the North imports 4x more high-skilled labour from the South than it exports, together with 17x more medium-skilled labour and 29x more low-skilled labour. ... Net flows from China to the North account for roughly one-sixth of total net South–North flows. It is worth noting here that the net South–North flow of embodied labour is not "paid for" by an opposite net flow of embodied land, energy or materials (on the contrary, large South–North flows occur across all input categories. (Hickel et al. 2024, 3–5)

The disproportionate shift in human labor and resources from the South to rich countries of the North, and particularly from China to the North, discredits the assessment of most academic critics of labor exploitation who live in the North and are beneficiaries of the uneven exchange of trade. Moreover, the Chinese government and trade unions have had to respond to social dislocation and inequality triggered by Western trade policies. That Chinese workers and trade unions are successfully improving conditions through organizing trade unions exposes the actuality of the internationalization of class struggle (Hammer and Ness 2021; Mihci 2022; Moussaly 2022). Further underpinning the achievements of the PRC is the fact that, despite its major strides, the country remains a developing country which is exploited economically by the West and recognizes the difficult task for other countries.

From 1949 to 1976, the Communist Party of China (CPC) encouraged and advanced proactive policies to reclaim the land and capital from foreign imperialists and large landowners. Rural collectivization provided the Chinese people with dignity but, in part due to the Sino-Soviet split in 1956, US sabotage of the Great Leap Forward, and Mao Zedong's meeting with US president Richard Nixon, the economy was dependent on foreign alliances for development and required the technological means to advance. In effect, China could not develop because foreign countries, and especially the West, stymied efforts to provide capital and technology. It is highly mistaken to contrast the introduction of socialism under Mao from 1949 to 1976 and Deng Xiaoping's opening of "market socialism" in 1978. As Wen (2021) describes, China has endured a series of crises under the planned socialist economy and the introduction and expansion of the market economy. However, the socialist market economy has had the most significant impact on the Chinese working class through the migration of rural workers to urban regions.

This chapter examines the most significant demographic transformation in world history over the last half century: the migration of the majority of China's population to urban areas and the attendant consequences of urban mobility on the Chinese working class. The urbanization of China's population is the basis for substantial analysis and critique as it was accompanied by the withdrawal of social protections by the state which had been the mainstay of the socialist economy under Mao Zedong from 1949 to 1978. Political economists and sociologists examining China in the ensuing years have delineated the rising societal tensions during the formative era of the application of "market socialism" by Mao's successors. For many in the West, political identification and support for the CPC under Mao was replaced by disheartening appraisals that the PRC had turned away from socialism. Countless Maoists in the West abandoned support for the PRC, resigned to the adverse consequences of market socialism. Western Marxists, anarchists, and social democrats who reject Marxism Leninism, Maoism and socialism with Chinese characteristics have reveled in disingenuously caricaturing the project as a turn to capitalism. Duplicitously, most liberal and Marxist scholars have been even more rancorously opposed to the Mao era than they are to the Chinese state today.

2   Internal Migration, the ACFTU and the Chinese Labor Movement

The "opening up" of the Chinese economy to market forces in the 1980s was the foremost factor shaping the nature of labor in the last half century and will continue being so in future. In 1978, less than 16.7 percent of China's nearly 963 million citizens resided in urban areas. For millennia, Chinese people had been reliant on the land and agriculture for sustenance. In the 40 years after 1978, urban residents came to compose nearly 65 percent of China's more than 1.41 billion population. Whereas China's urban migration is the most significant demographic factor in China's economic transformation, the presence of nearly 500 million residents in rural areas cannot be discounted, as that population represents a formidable social and economic force. However, migration to urban agglomerations is the primary driver in the development of the Chinese working class. Rapid urbanization is the primary dynamic which defines the Chinese economy over nearly half a century. Moreover, urban migration has grown so quickly that the task of integrating the urban working class into cities of all sizes has been the most formidable charge for the PRC and its institutions.

The All-China Federation of Trade Unions (ACFTU) has had a formidable task to absorb the Chinese working class within urban areas into constituent unions across labor markets, 23 provinces and 11 additional administrative regions. As the Chinese state does not restrict union representation and all workers who want to form unions have a legal right to do so, the ACFTU has had to adapt to conform to the transition from a rural agrarian to an urban industrial economy. In the initial period, from 1980 to 2000, the ACFTU had to keep pace with multinational corporations, foreign investors, offshore contractors, and internal subcontractors to make sure that labor rights ensconced in China's labor law were observed by frequently rapacious capitalists unconcerned with municipal wage rates and occupational safety. Notably, ensuring that labor-union membership rights were adhered to also presented a challenge to the ACFTU. Frequently, private capitalists practiced union avoidance, circumventing labor laws by designating workers in their firms as independent contractors and not permanent employees. This tactic is ubiquitous throughout the world as a means to prevent workers from joining labor unions and collecting equivalent wages and benefits. In the US, where unions are far sparser than in most other capitalist countries, their absence has significant consequences for workers.

In China, a country with a legacy of collectivization, the right to form a union at the workplace is considered de rigueur. To be sure, union membership is acutely significant for migrant laborers who have relocated from rural areas and have yet to gain local residential registration. It is necessary to reinforce the fact that almost all Western literature on Chinese labor distorts the effectiveness and accomplishments of the ACFTU and fails to account for the federation's leading role in the unfolding dialectical relationship between private employers and the working class. Beyond a doubt, the federation serves as the facilitator in the protection of labor through improving job security, wages, social insurance, working conditions and more. Even though the ACFTU has consistently endeavored to protect labor rights, formative research in the West during the early 2000s to the present has sought to disparage it for facilitating resolution of labor–management disputes even as the rights of labor have improved substantially. Instead, such commentators search for the spectacle rather than the application of labor rights. For example, Zhu (2004) admonishes the ACFTU for facilitating bottom-up organization by migrant workers in foreign enterprises in the formative years of China's industrialization in the 1990s and early 2000s and chastises the ACFTU's efforts to broker agreements to avert strikes in state enterprises as a means of bureaucratic control, implying that migrant workers would be better off without unionization. This paradox recurs among almost all Western Labor scholars, analysts and journalists, frequently but not always writing from abroad and focusing on rare events which may have been orchestrated by powerful Western NGOs. Typically, they do not consider the progression of government practices and policy evolution in response to identification of rapacious business practices by foreign multinationals. To reiterate, they see historical materialism as rooted in Xi Jinping's seminal anti-corruption campaigns and poor business practices (Bieler and Chun-Yi Lee 2017; Chan et al. 2020; Friedman 2014; Gallagher 2005; Harney 2008; Lee 2007). Once again, this critique does not impute that most opponents of China's labor regime are engaging in ideological conformity in the West. For most left opponents, since 1978, China has become state capitalist, a stance that typically requires ideological conformity. This Western purity complex applied to actually existing socialist states, non-assessment of change over time, and an absence of painstakingly examined factual information. However, after advancing disparaging perspectives on any academic subject, changing material evidence should spur scholars to change their assessment based on empirical facts. To do so requires, reappraising one's previous research and admitting error. Unfortunately, a complex of well-funded organizations collaborates to advance the anti-China narrative, and many China academics are directly linked to them. Others are committed to applying anti-China jargon and profit from US NGOs established in the West (Friedman 2014).

The evolving labor-studies literature in the West condemns the PRC and the ACFTU for extending labor protections to all workers and opposing discrimination against women and migrant workers, as enacted in the 2007 Labor Contract Law, which took effect in January 2008 (Labor Contract Law 2007). In the aftermath of the passage of the new labor law, some Labor scholars honestly assessed the strategic transformation of the ACFTU rather than applying a uniform position to union organizing in China, as most other Labor Studies scholars did. Notably, Mingwei Liu, writing in 2010, identified distinct patterns of organizing and representation in a nuanced approach. Liu showed that the form of union organization framed the type of union organizing. Notwithstanding the perfunctory critique of the nature of the ACFTU as an arm of the

CPC, Liu found that union mobilization strategies take on three patterns of organizing: traditional ACFTU pattern, the union association pattern, and the regional, industry based bargaining pattern" (Liu 2010). Writing 15 years later, Ying applies a careful empirical approach to analyzing the developing Chinese labor market and its challenges, without recourse to mockery or ridicule, examining the growth of urban migration, demographic shifts and the labor employment change as service and digital employment expands (Ying 2025).

The Chinese working class is overwhelmingly composed of recent migrants who have relocated to urban agglomerations from c.1990 to 2025. Initially, workers migrating to urban areas have been paid low wages, primarily by contractors for multinational corporations and within Special Economic Zones (SEZs) established along the eastern littoral. Each municipality has competed with others for foreign direct investment (FDI) through lax taxation, availability of low-wage workers, and infrastructural developments such as road, rail, ports, warehouses and other logistics. Taken together, the migrant working class can compete, even if earning higher wages, as high technology and efficient supply-chains have further reduced costs (surplus labor).

China's hukou registration classification for residency in a locality initially restrained wage growth as every citizen was tied to a specific place. For example, at the outset of China's industrialization, there was no established plan to modify the residential status of workers from rural to urban and semi-urban workers (Chan 2021). In the absence of residential status, Chinese laborers did not have the legal right to reside in their new locations and lacked access to the attendant housing, health care, and education since social benefits were determined on the basis of one's legal habitation. Accordingly, as in the case of most urbanizing societies, workers frequently spent long periods away from family members in rural areas or other provinces. As will become apparent (see "Market Socialism, Urban Migration, and the Rise of a Floating Population" below), this problem was later addressed. Even though China's population is nearly three times greater than that of Europe, migrant laborers have typically had authorization to work in the country's growing urban centers and metropolitan areas. It is pointless and unreasonable to compare the conditions and rights of China's internal migrants to those of migrants in Europe or North America, where workers are rendered "illegal" and forcibly restricted from legally participating in the labor market even as they are essential workers. In China, rural migrants' conditions are continually improving as they receive legal status to stay and reside in destinations with their families. In the US, no legal path to citizenship is available to undocumented migrant workers who typically migrate alone, without their families, and are employed at low wages, lack occupational safety protection and are subject to perpetual abuse as they face arrest, imprisonment and deportation. Paradoxically, migrant workers are essential workers and employed in the most dangerous jobs, a factor which became especially evident during the COVID-19 pandemic (Hernández 2024; Ness 2023b; Reid et al. 2021).

3   The ACFTU, Floating Migrants and Worker Representation

The key contention of this book, as adumbrated in the Introduction, is that the Chinese labor movement is the most inclusive and democratic in the world. We aim to dispel the prevailing critique of China among Labor scholars, which is based on impossible standards.

not even approached by labor movements in the West. China is unique among nations as a worker's state which is striving to improve conditions for the working class. Even if the market economy here introduced reforms which pushed the rural working class into low wage jobs, the state has sought to soften the effects through advancing their socioeconomic status, an objective which has been achieved but which the CPC and ACFTU continually seek to improve upon. The Chinese working class has the highest union membership rates in the world. This does not imply that the ACFTU has achieved all its goals or that workers are not exploited; but fundamentally, the Chinese state is responsive to their demands. Moreover, workers who are members of unions typically are motivated to advance their collective interests and improve the wages and conditions of all workers in a firm, as all workers are represented by the union and entitled to the same conditions. Nevertheless, hostile Labor scholars have raised the bar for China and ceaselessly condemn the ACFTU for not achieving socioeconomic goals which are not even on the agenda in the West, where labor unions are on the back foot and vanishing. Most significantly, the People's Republic of China, CPC, and the ACFTU are accomplishing the goal of incorporating migrant workers into unions. Where worker conditions are substandard, the ACFTU will intercede, resolve disputes and improve wages, benefits and safety. This is not to say that strikes do not occur in China, but disputes between labor and management are adjudicated and mediated within the interstices of the ACFTU. Undoubtedly, the ACFTU could not have been expected to anticipate the extent of the mass wave of internal urban migration. Consequently, it and the CPC responded to worker discontent with national labor laws protecting labor in 1992 and 2008, at the height of neoliberal reform and the redoubling of enforcement from 2015 to the present under the leadership of Xi Jinping.

On October 22, 2024, the People's Republic of China Ministry of Ecology and Environment published an official position on the significance of migrant workers to urban centers and the requirement to incorporate them as vital workers with full rights. According to the CPC organization, a central plank of building a modern workforce is to:

> Cultivate migrant workers into high-quality modern industrial workers. Focusing on industrial transformation and upgrading, strengthen skills training for migrant workers and widely implement the "Study and Dream" program. Promote the integration of migrant workers into cities, further relax and expand urban settlement policies, and ensure equal access to basic urban public services for migrant workers. Increase public legal services to benefit migrant workers, protect their legitimate rights and interests, and promote stable employment. (Ministry of Ecology and Environment of the PRC 2024)

In spite of the CPC's policy initiatives to promote worker rights, most of the research by Western Labor scholars ends in 2015 and primarily advances a critical and judgmental perspective on the treatment of new urban migrant workers. A considerable share of the Western hostility arises from Western NGOs. The PRC considers NGOs' research to be directed by antagonistic foreign researchers resolved to invent inadequacies rather than initiatives to improve the conditions of the Chinese migrant workers as indispensable to its working class. Indeed, this is precisely what Labor research does in the West. The narratives are almost never favorable towards the Government in power. Regrettably, the penchant for criticizing and condemning draws attention away from constructive research which identifies complications in need of improvement. Westerners apply their own models of labor–management relations when they have no relevance to China. In closing, it must be stressed that the ACFTU unions have no monetary incentives to favor members over non-members of unions as they are not subsidized by dues but by the government and sometimes employer levies. Union members do not fund union bureaucracies.

Notwithstanding this, Booth et al. (2022, 997) have found that "[t]he membership premium is particularly remarkable for wages, for which the advantage for the members is twice as large as for the non-members." It is clear that wages, "happiness and mental health" are a function of union membership, which corresponds with improved pay, benefits and access to social insurance, participation and self-management. Thus, it stands to reason that migrant workers will require workplace and residential rights to improve their conditions as lack of hukou rights provokes anxiety and social discomfort.

The International Labour Organization (ILO), the foremost and most esteemed labor institution affiliated with the United Nations, works closely with the ACFTU and conducts studies on logistics, platform labor and cutting edge labor questions in China. The research demonstrates that the Federation is far advanced in representing migrant workers in urban workplaces, even if it faces significant challenges from businesses which do not grant labor status to workers (Wei & Wang 2024). We must question if the termination of Western research is related to the inherent bias against the ACFTU and China as a whole (Friedman et al. 2024). The negative findings by Westerners who have conducted research in China do not account for extenuating factors, notably the necessity for the Federation and its constituent unions to identify those firms which do not comply and dissuade migrant workers from unionization. To expect any union to respond in advance of gaining knowledge, gathering evidence and mobilizing workers is an unreasonable bias. It is irrational to expect any organization to respond before it has drawn together information and developed a response. This does not negate the need to improve and encourage the ACFTU to increase response rates and closely monitor worker complaints. However, in comparison to any other national trade union federation, China's ACFTU is far and away the most responsive to workers on all spatial levels of government. Remarkably, unlike most Western unions, the Federation encourages workers to file objections to employer actions and has a comprehensive mediation and arbitration system in place which increasingly extends to internal migrants as more floating workers gain residency permits. Westerners view work stoppages and strike as creating spectacles of mass unrest and conflict. Effectively, to Western leftists, the mass strike takes on the form of a commodity to be observed, exhibited and fetishized as a tradable good (Dubord 1967/1994). In a socialist state, dialectical materialism and class conflict exist and a workers' state intercedes to address the legitimate demands of workers. This is in contrast to capitalist bourgeois democracies, where workers frequently have no recourse but to quit or go on strike and if they do, risk losing their jobs and livelihoods.

4   Primitive Accumulation to Socialist Construction: Labor and Urban Migration

In *The Transition from Feudalism to Capitalism*, British political economist Maurice Dobb wrote that the primary element in establishing a capitalist society is the application of Newtonian physics to the natural world (Dobb et al. 1985). The building blocks for developing a modern society require not just conceptual knowledge but its application to the productive forces in society. This crucial insight was advanced by Karl Marx in *Capital* (1867/1990) and remains the genetic code for the formation of capitalism. Thus, it is only after one applies the theory to the material world that we can begin theorizing about the transition from capital to socialism.

The foregoing necessitates considering how primitive accumulation evolves into more advanced productive practices. We can begin to understand appropriate and necessary technology that is required for the next step in a higher form of agricultural production. In the absence of technology, it is impossible to even begin to consider the organization of production. It is in this way that political questions about mobilizing the rural masses around socialism must begin. In the case of China, the rural population had already been extricated from primitive accumulation through the formation of a socialist state economy and the development of rural cooperatives. Unlike capitalist economies, China already had a working class in the rural areas and had developed a proletarian subjectivity. Accordingly, the Chinese working class remained dedicated to the CPC and maintained a working class consciousness. However, for many workers employed in urban areas of the PRC, the state ceded to an organized "market economy" to generate capital. In that transformation, even the Chinese state recognizes the attendant class contradictions for its working class when multinational corporations and capitalist contractors became dependent on FDI, chiefly for export production. In a state deemed to be directed by a proletariat, the opening of the economy to "market reforms" posed challenges for its workers. Deng Xiaoping, who presided over the opening of the socialist economy to global market forces and cut social benefits in the countryside, remained steadfast in his position that China had adhered to socialism. On August 20, 1991, Deng wrote:

> The future of China hinges on adhering to [socialist] policies. ... We must continue to stress the need to combat bourgeois liberalization. In carrying out the reform and the open policy and in shifting the focus of our work to economic development we are not abandoning Marx, Lenin and Mao Zedong. ... The problem is to get a clear understanding of what socialism is and how we can build and expand it. (Deng 1992, 240)

Deng takes a longer view of the transformation of China from imperialism, ending feudalism and then bureaucracy as a revolutionary process necessitating the fundamental change of impediments to "the development of the productive forces and to establish a vigorous socialist economic structure that will promote their development," viewing reform to be a component of liberation

(Deng 1992, 241). The migration of rural workers to urban centers, including SEZs, was an essential for opening up and, through class struggle, the emancipation of the Chinese working class from poverty.

5   Evolution of the Chinese "Floating Population"

Applying a Hegelian dialectical perspective to actually existing socialist (AES) government involves learning to advance policy in response to the principal contradictions extant in a society. In socialist China, from 1990 to the present, internal migration and the question of a "floating population" of workers represents China's key challenge. The socialist party must adapt and apply transformational policies to attend to the subjective needs of the working class. The dictatorship of the working class is not pursuing utopian policies which have no relevance to the natural world, which continuously presents itself with internal conflict. We must distinguish between the Chinese socialist state endeavor to reflect the interests of the working class and the reality that must be confronted by the PRC. Market socialism under Deng was an interval of reform and economic difficulty for the rural working class from 1978 to 2012, as the absence of economic and technological development had been the principal contradiction of the PRC. The rise of a capitalist class in China does not negate the genuine nature of a state which is commanded by a communist party and strives for socialism. Deng asserted on December 24, 1990, that a dictatorship of the proletariat would become necessary to seize control of the economy. The market economy was only necessary to gain access to technology from developed countries. In its absence, Deng asserts,

> … we would have … to reconcile ourselves to lagging behind. But maintaining a Socialist path was just as essential. … For a fairly long period of time the proletariat, as a new, rising class is necessarily weaker than the bourgeoisie. If it is to seize political power and build socialism, it must therefore impose a dictatorship to resist capitalist attack. To keep to the socialist road, we must uphold the dictatorship of the proletariat, which we call the people's democratic dictatorship. (Deng 1990, 236–237)

China's Seventh National Population Census (2020) demonstrates the proactive nature of a state striving to improve the conditions of its internal migrant working class. However, the data shows that even as a responsible socialist government is energetically adopting policy to respond to the unprecedented rise of rural–urban and urban–urban migration, socialist policy is not static but persistently adapts to the new contradictions inherent in a rapid demographic transformation. The 2020 Census reveals the unevenness and "mismatch between people's place of residence and place of household registration" (Cheng & Duan 2021, 1). The Census reveals "cognition" (Mao) within the interstices of the CPC and the Chinese state of a need to continue efforts to regularize the "floating population" through crafting and implementing urban policies to reflect the transformation of the demographic composition of the Chinese working class. While the state's recent accomplishments are remarkable in shifting from a planned rural economy to absorbing and serving an urban working class constituting most of the population, the pace of internal migration has exceeded expectations. In turn, the government comprehends the scale of population change and the requirement for both residence permits and services (Cheng & Duan 2021, 275–284). A not insignificant fraction of the floating population remains, not because its people are unable to establish residence permits in urban areas but because of their desire to maintain a bond to the land through rural hukous. Of course, as most migrant workers move to urban areas, rural towns are often underserved, a challenge which the Chinese state recognizes and is addressing.

In contrast to the critics, Chinese scholars of internal migration to urban areas maintain that obtaining an urban hukou is relatively smooth and seamless for most. Cheng and Duan assert:

> Chinese people can now freely choose the city where they work and live. Generally speaking, the change of the locale of a person's household registration is usually accompanied with the change of his or her dwelling places. (2021, 277)

The authors maintain that, despite a shortfall in housing due to the unexpectedly large growth in urban migration, the Chinese government is effectively addressing most who relocate from rural–urban and urban–urban locations and now must tackle unforeseen rural–rural and urban–rural migrant populations. The 2020 Census shows that the rural–urban migrant population grew nearly 75 percent between 2010 and 2020 and the urban–urban population expanded by 90.7 percent. Still, the state continues to promote education, medical services and public housing for newly arriving migrant workers in search of higher wages in China's megacities.

The ACFTU must continuously adapt to the often-unexpected swings in populations requiring new forms of representation. For example, the dramatic growth of migration from mid-size to major urban agglomerations has expanded the share of contract laborers who do not work directly for employers (Zhang et al. 2023; Interviews, food delivery workers, Beijing, November

16–18, 2024). Unquestionably, a precarious migrant labor population is growing in China's megacities. The ACFTU reports that 43 percent of couriers, food delivery and e-hailing drivers in three major cities had been successfully mobilized into trade unions in 2018 as recognized workers for employees, compared to a 90 percent national rate of unionization in China. By comparison, in most other countries, digital and platform workers have practically no representation through established trade unions and if they join unions, they do not have lawful contracts with employers but are typically considered independent contractors. Most digital delivery couriers in Amsterdam, Berlin, New York and other major cities in the West are petrified to even discuss unionization due to fear of deportation (Ness 2024b; van Doorne 2023). In the US, the Taxi Workers Alliance, an NGO which formed in NYC and is now a constituent national union of the AFL-CIO, has no contracts with employers and workers voluntarily pay dues for assistance with unfair local government regulations and fines against drivers. In the platform ride hailing and delivery sector of New York City, migrant workers must pay for all costs, including mobile phones, motorized bicycles and repairs. In addition, digital delivery workers face legal charges for minor traffic violations and are forced go to court for adjudication. No other country apart from China has even 1 percent of platform workers organized with legally enforceable employment contracts (Ness 2023c). A clear distinction must be made between workers who are employed under contract and those who have joined grassroots unions with no collective bargaining agreements with technology companies. However, even if existing unions eschew platform workers or workers are disallowed from joining trade unions, in Europe, according to Vandaele et al., about 13.4 percent of non-traditional unions represent workers, using a metric of density within the entire working age population, typically about half of laborers who are in the working population. Moreover, the definition of union is extended to "grassroots unions" who are not engaged in collective bargaining, as is the case in China (Vandaele et al. 2024). The same figure of 13.4 percent was used in a similar report issued in 2018 (see Chapter 5).

6   Market Socialism, Urban Migration and the Rise of a Floating Population

In the late 1990s, Chinese internal migrant workers had been designated a "floating population" by scholars as they did not have residency status in urban areas. The term "floating population" does not refer to a defined type of urban dweller but to a range of migrants who move to cities for diverse purposes and live under dissimilar conditions (Goodkind and West 2002). However, the Chinese government steadily implemented national plans to reform restrictions on hukou, which were lifted as it became evident that urban workers required permanent residency in a locality. Due to worker efforts to gain rights from 1978 to the present, the hukou system is in continuous reform to serve the burgeoning Chinese working class. The most notable reforms in 2012 were advanced by President and CPC General Secretary Xi Jinping and the Chinese government with the establishment of a formal migration system permitting workers to establish residence with their families in urban centers.

Since 2008, China has enacted and implemented successful plans to regularize urban migrant workers who have constituted almost all those seeking to transfer their official residency classification from rural to urban locations and with interprovincial migration. All but four first tier cities incorporate and are standardizing residency for floating migrants and the largest cities are recognizing migrants, especially high skilled migrant workers relocating from outside their home provinces to major cities and foreign countries (Koslowski and Ding 2024). Empirical research contradicts critical reflexive dogma advanced in the West, that significant wage differentials endure in the largest urban agglomerations in China, producing perpetually higher wages among local urban workers and floating migrants from rural areas, small cities and remote regions beyond the Eastern littoral coast. Recent data shows that labor market reforms contribute to an equalization of wages between long term residents as migrant worker wages steadily increase over time and the wage premium disappears. Certainly, as with anywhere in the world, migrant workers initially receive lower wages than local or migrant workers who maintain or acquire higher skills. However, without a doubt, wage differentials are higher in capitalist economies than in China. Notwithstanding this, the ACFTU trains workers to learn new skills and the degree of union activism contributes to a propensity to acquire skills and consequently earn higher wages (Wu et al. 2024).

The majority of China's working class are workers who have migrated to urban regions. Thus, an examination of the Chinese working class is roughly synonymous with migrant laborers. The extensive research on China's labor movement inescapably focuses on internal migrant laborers. However, the extensive research deriving from North America and Western Europe ignores crucial evidence, as it discounts the significance of the ACFTU's systematic efforts to absorb internal floating migrant workers and integrate them into the social and economic life of major cities. More and more, as the pace of household registration accelerates, Chinese migrant workers gain access to housing, education and health services. Critics living in capitalist societies who have not visited China in a decade or more set up a straw man which can never be achieved in the natural world as a measure for what constitutes a socialist and capitalist society. Seemingly, most Western Marxists' benchmark for socialism is a utopian society where people lived in rural areas and did not engage in work in rural China before the market reforms took hold in the 1980s. Consequently, it is difficult to take opponents seriously without distinct information about why they disparage the evolving socialism with Chinese characteristics. Such Western scholars' lists of supposed defects appear endless. Through applying partial anecdotes and shunning government statistics, academics and activists establish a basis to deride and insult the socialist project in China. Apart from a few prominent serious scholars (e.g. Roland Boer (2023), Enfu Cheng (2021) and Michael Dunford and Weidong Liu (2015) among others), until 2017, due to an inherent bias, few Westerners had conducted research in China. Joel Andreas, who has conducted research in China, still rejects the notion of a state and institutional capacity to learn and adapt to changing demands and circumstances and the possibility that migrant workers in state owned enterprises (SOEs) have the capacity to engage in democratic unionism. Most other critics, whether scholars, NGO operatives or activists, lack credibility when discussing migrant laborer incorporation (Andreas 2019; Yu; Franceschini & Sorace 2022; Friedman et al. 2024; Ruckus 2021). Unfortunately, in the pursuit of opposing China and its long struggle towards socialism, anti-imperialism and improving living standards, a close examination of the works shows a bias and absence of an analysis rooted in historical materialism. Those scholars who have conducted serious unbiased research often default to the same conclusions, as division and rupture from the anti-China intellectual cottage industry is a taboo among Western critics.

Drawing on my research of Western Marxism and anti-communism, I share Viren Murthy's reflection upon Japanese philosopher Takeuchi Yoshimi: that Asia and in this case China and its market reform and effort to improve the lives of migrants, are "more an idea than a geographic space" (Murthy 2023, 152). Given this Sinophobia, the evolving form of Chinese socialism is dismissed by Western scholars. Thus, while anti-communism is associated with imperialism, opposition to China today is a universal project which emerges among Western scholars and activists.

Instead of focusing on the prodigious achievement of absorbing an ever increasing population of urban migrant workers, scholars who study Chinese migration emphasize the obstacles for those who have yet to apply or complete local household registration. Internal migration in China is growing, and most Western research focuses on those who are left behind. What is absent is a practical grasp of the fact that policy implementation is not a magical development which is promptly resolved upon the initiation of new plans. In 2021,

Kam Wing Chan, undeniably a highly reputable scholar of China's internal migration, writing for a publication of the World Bank, directed attention to the gap in achieving policy goals. Acknowledging that China's internal migration had more than doubled between 2010 and 2020, Chan asserted:

> China achieved the 100 million urban hukou conversion target by 2020. However, this progress was offset by faster growth in migration, resulting in a much larger migrant population without local rights (between 261 million and 376 million, or 18.5 percent and 26.6 percent of the country's population) and thus making the 15 percent target set by the 2014 Plan impossible to meet. Thus, instead of narrowing, the social benefits gap in cities and towns has widened, edging to a worrying level of 26.6 percent of China's population. (Chan 2021, 3)

Chan is an established scholar of Chinese migration and demographics working in the West who does not resort to innuendo or speculation. As is to be expected and as is clearly evident in China's census data, an unanticipated upsurge in internal migration contributes to a household registration gap in urban areas (NBSC 2021a). But the literature generally disparages China for the rise of a "floating population" and faults the government for not anticipating the higher migration rate and need to convert a larger share of workers and their families to being urban residents (Østbø & Speelman 2022).

Similarly, Zhou and Chi-Man Hui (2022), real-estate scholars at Hong Kong Polytechnic University, assert that internal migration favors the educated, skilled and wealthy, resulting in wage discrimination rather than demonstrating the higher standards of living for China's migrant working class. Once again, we are presented with the deductive and illogical double bind. Western research focuses cynically on families omitted from health care and education, rather than on the unprecedented achievements of the Communist government between 1949 and 1978. Western capitalists and Western Marxist academics and activists benefited from the opening up. Capitalists and investors earned vast profits through seizing upon hundreds of millions of Chinese workers who had been exploited through unequal exchange of trade between poor countries and the imperialist West.

Western Marxists and activists designated China as a "state capitalist" economy without contemplating the preservation of the CPC as the primary political, economic and social force in the country. Even as China adopted market reforms, the emergence of a socialist market economy was under the guidance and control of a socialist state; what Torkil Lauesen deems to be the principal contradiction pertaining to the expansion of markets. Certainly, market reforms had deleterious consequences for Chinese rural workers living in relative security, as noted by Robert Weil. But Lauesen adopts the Maoist concept of the "principal contradiction," that had shifted in the course of the transformation of China from a colony of extraction to a socialist state. However, academics identifying as Marxists reject a dialectical approach grounded in historical materialism and class conflict, a concept embraced by Xi Jinping and the CPC leadership. China's absorption of migrant families is remarkably successful in view of the massive scale of urbanization. Even the Chinese government did not anticipate the magnitude of migration from rural to urban areas (Lauesen 2024; Losurdo 2024; Ness 2024).

Figure 3 shows a dramatic shift in China from a predominantly rural to urban country. China's population of 541 million people in 1949 increased to more than 1.4 billion in 2025. In nearly half a century, from 1978 to 2025, its urban population increased from approximately 10 percent to nearly 65 percent. This

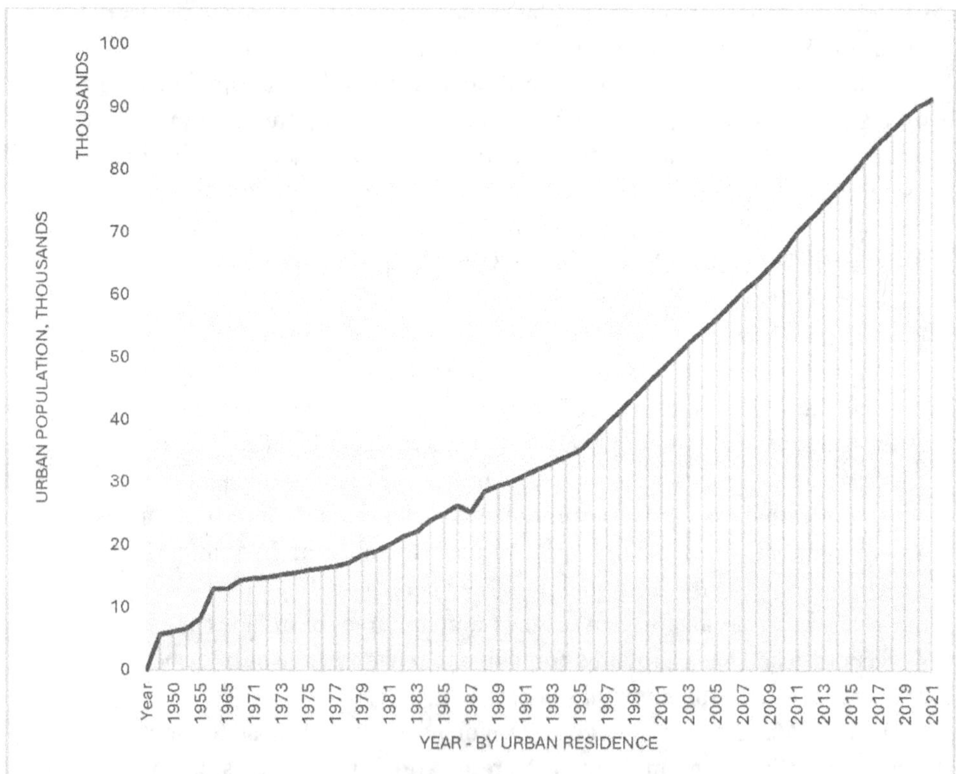

FIGURE 3   Urban population share of total Chinese population, 1949–2021 (Source: China National Population Survey (2021a)) (Notes: (a) Figures before end of 1981 are from household registrations. Figures for years 1982, 1990, 2000, 2010 and 2020 are the census year estimates. Figures for the remaining years are estimated on the basis of the annual national sample survey of population. (b) Total population includes the servicemen of the Chinese People's Liberation Army, who were reclassified as part of the urban population in population by residence.)

shift is perhaps the most important demographic change in both the Chinese and world populations. The urbanization rate far eclipses the capacity of any nation to absorb. That the growth in the urbanization of nearly 376 million people from 2010 to 2020 occurred peacefully is a testament to the public's support of the PRC (a population larger than that of the US) and an unprecedented achievement. According to the National Bureau of Statistics of China, "the population who lived in places other than their household registration but still in the same city totaled 116.94 million and the migrants numbered 375.82 million, a 69.73 percent increase in migration" (NBSC 2021b). In fact, urbanization occurred systematically and without social conflict, on a scale unprecedented in human history and with relatively little exploitation of the working class. Certainly, Western opponents will focus on several incidents of conflict, strikes and social dislocation, but the record reveals that the urban areas have successfully, though not fully, absorbed the floating population; a goal which the Chinese government is consistently seeking to address, especially under the CPC and the leadership of General Secretary Xi Jinping and the ACFTU.

7 Urbanization: Planning, Workers and Sustainability (2013–Present)

Academics consistently conduct research on the challenges encountered by China through urbanization, overlooking the historical political economy of the rural–urban nexus. From the origins of industrialization in the mid-19th century, in capitalist or socialist economies, development scholars view agricultural productivity as the basis for the creation of an urban population which advances economic growth and improves the standard of living. The remarkable transformation in China, an economy which has been tied to the land for millennia and continues to have over 500 million people in rural regions, is a challenge which is likely to entail socioeconomic ordeals for masses of people. The pursuit of modernization could never be unproblematic under a socialist system with "Chinese characteristics" ingrained in the historic legacy of a society which has viewed agriculture as sacrosanct. Consequently, the spectacular population shift from rural to urban areas is arguably the most significant socioeconomic policy of the 50 years from 1975 to 2025.

The socialist "market economy" which emerged in the early 1980s, a form of economic planning rather than chaotic capitalism, has had significant implications for China's 1.4 billion citizens. It has principally occasioned urbanization and population mobility from second, third and fourth tier urban areas to megacities and regions; as well as, for a not insignificant share of the population, a return back to rural regions. Surely, the immense scale of the population movement has been accompanied by socioeconomic requirements for rebalancing., but to implicate the hukou as solely an obstacle to economic transformation fails to consider that a significant share of migrants have acquired new household registration in specific cities only to seek relocation several years later. As Wang et al. conclude, "China's urban transformation has gone well beyond the dual sector model and has resulted in new types of migration flows and new migrants such as the tens of millions of residents resettled to make space for urban development and major infrastructure projects." It is imperative to understand China's development and government policies to "recalibrate our understanding of Chinese migration" (2023, 317).

Instead of focusing on the determinantal effects of migration, the Chinese government considers the "organic combination" of a balanced economy (which privileges both urban and rural regions and is committed to the uplift of newcomers to China's burgeoning cities) to be a practice based not just on hope but on planning, policy and implementation (Zou 2024).

8 Systemic Western Aversion to the CPC and the ACFTU

Critical perspectives on the state of Chinese labor conditions fail to account for fundamental aspects of government policy in a workers' state and are based on idealistic notions of a society dominated by representatives of the working class, a society dominated by representatives of the working class, the CPC and the ACFTU in transition to a socialist society. Opponents are one of three sorts: (1) those who maintain idealistic perspectives of a workers' state which is not grounded in reality; (2) Labor scholars seeking to transform the workers' state into a liberal-bourgeois democracy, with competitive labor unions akin to those in the West, where nation states are controlled by the dictatorship of the bourgeoisie; (3) geostrategic opponents of the Chinese state who seek to reprimand a society which is advancing the conditions of the nation's burgeoning working class.

This chapter continues the assertion that China and the global working class must be viewed through the principal contradiction which exists at a given historical conjuncture. The principal contradiction, as advanced by Mao Zedong and more recently Torkil Lauesen, asserts that each epoch has principal and secondary contradictions which are rooted in dialectical materialism reflecting the human and societal relationship to the natural world as it evolves over time. Thus, even if the working class is not seemingly ascendant in a precise era, that does not negate the actuality that China under the CPC is a workers' state controlled by democratic centralism. Every so often, the principal contradiction may shift, for example, from an impoverished agrarian socialist society to a state that has applied modern technology to the political economy. If, for a time, secondary contradictions appear which may produce distortions of socialism, the socialist state remains under the control of the proletariat. The negation of the contradiction is inevitable and restores the essential features of a socialist society. Yet, this requires unity in a communist party which is motivated by advancing the conditions of the working class. Even when open class conflict may appear between multinational capital and the working class, the state will defend the interests of the latter. This analysis accounts for setbacks and regression during eras of modernization and during the introduction of market socialism. The long term interests will always remain controlling even when deviations in economic policy may lead the idealist or utopian to believe that the socialist state has lost its way and trans-formed into a capitalist society dominated by the bourgeoisie and globaliza-tion untethered from a state. In fact, the socialist state recognizes the principal contradiction to carry forward the interests of the working class. Nonetheless, the socialist (communist) party apparatus (the central committee and the leadership) must unify to defeat degenerate actors and policies. We find this to be the central position of Antonio Gramsci in his letter to the Central Commit-tee of the Soviet Communist Party. He was firmly committed to a unified party but also maintained that retrograde forces must be purged from its leadership (Gramsci 1926).

> There is yet another motive for the international bourgeoisie to take account of the possible split, or the aggravation of the internal crisis within the Communist Party of the USSR. The workers' state in Russia has existed already for nine years. It is true that only a small minority of the labouring classes, and even of the communist parties themselves in other countries, are able to reconstruct in its whole the full development of the revolution and to find, even in the details that make up the daily life of the State of the Soviets, the continuity of the red thread lead-ing to the general perspective of the building of socialism. ... In these countries, the large masses cannot understand the discussions that take place in the Communist Party of the USSR, particularly when they lead to the current violence and affect not one aspect of the detail, but the whole political line of the Party. Not only the working masses in general, but the very mass of our parties see and want to see in the Republic of Soviets, and in the party that is in government, a united combat unit acting in the general perspective of socialism. And it is

> only because the masses in Western European see Russia and the Russian party
> from this point of view, they accept voluntarily, and as a necessary historical
> fact, that the Communist Party of the USSR should be the leading party of the
> International, so today only the Republic of Soviets and the Communist Party
> of the USSR constitute a formidable element of organization and revolutionary
> impulse.

The necessity for unity has been decisive in building socialism, and all deviations from the fundamental interest of establishing a strong workers' party may initiate dissent managed by bourgeois elements when competition surfaces outside the internal activities of the party and the trade union.

9   International Labour Organization and Chinese Internal Migration

The ILO has a more balanced perspective than Western trade union critics on China and its labor institutions and their relationship to the "floating population" of migrant workers to urban prefectures and cities within and between provinces. The ILO has adjusted its assessment of the ACFTU's reaction to changing circumstances. It has done so without resorting to the kind of ideological biases advanced by opponents who: appeal to ethereal objectives which no other country is subjected to; or, in the absence of utopian objectives, completely distort unfolding events and the historical record; or report on notorious cases which were then addressed by the ACFTU; or omit to include facts which reveal the achievements of the ACFTU; or, in some cases, knowingly report fabrications of places and events to create a sense of opprobrium and illicit condemnation from readers seeking to learn about internal migration and the Chinese labor movement (Chan et al. 2020; Friedman et al. 2024). If one challenges these false narratives and seeks to correct the record on the basis of factual information drawn from accurate government reports and site visits, one is exposed to censure and exclusion. No doubt, there are disputes that require the ACFTU to become more active; for example, the ACFTU's goal should not be 90 percent of workers in unions but 100 percent, and this requires organizing private employers.

Notwithstanding the cottage industry of the PRC's opponents, who are mostly anarchists and others who prefer spectacle to effective resolution of disputes, the ILO tends to produce unbiased reports. The ILO, the leading tripartite organization representing labor, management and the state, strives to advance the interests of workers through best practices and resolution of disputes rather than escalation. However, the West seeks to stoke the embers of minor disputes while their own labor practices and those of their low cost producers overseas are almost always ignored.

However, in a report on the conditions of migrant workers in China during the most challenging historical period, the ILO recognizes the constitutional status of the ACFTU as the legal national union in the PRC but also recognizes the presence of other associations which protect migrant workers in China. In 2006, the ILO found that the ACFTU "is providing more protection to the newest members of the working class" and projected that the growth of migrant laborers in each year compelled a continuous policy of absorbing more and more migrant workers into the Federation (Tuñón 2006, 26).

Policies of the ACFTU have responded directly to systemic labor abuses, chiefly by multinational corporations and private contractors. The ILO study commended the ACFTU for organizing migrant workers into unions and reported that the Federation projected to organize and represent 70 percent of all migrant workers in 2008. In addition to organizing workers, the ACFTU engaged in "promoting decent wages and working conditions" as well as "training opportunities and campaigns on behalf of migrants" with an emphasis on ending the "practice of delayed wages" by foreign multinationals and unscrupulous private contractors. Comprehending the notion of cause and effect, the ILO acknowledged the challenge of eradicating poor working conditions, organizing new members, workplace safety and even migrant workers' need to meet living costs. It must be noted that the ACFTU had advanced these policies ahead of its policy to absorb all Chinese workers into the national labor federation to improve the bargaining power of internal migrant workers through direct representation before the Chinese state required all workers to join unions (2006, 26). The shortcomings of the ACFTU must also be placed in historical perspective. The ILO report was issued two years before the revised Labor Contract Law came into effect. Additionally, labor conditions have vastly improved for migrant workers as most who wanted residency status in localities have subsequently relocated to urban areas, as is evident from the increased size of China's urban population as a proportion of the whole. As early as 2003, the ACFTU acknowledged the challenges of mobilizing the migrant labor force. According to Su Liqing, the Federation's vice president:

> "they are still a weak group in society and there remains much to do to protect their rights. The most common problem for migrant workers is that they often cannot get paid in time and are fired very easily as the employers usually do not sign contracts with them," Su said. Besides, workplace safety is also a very serious problem for migrant workers. (People's Daily Online 2003)

The mass urban migration in China from 1985 to the present has posed severe challenges for the ACFTU which can only be addressed after they occur under a socialist state developing an advanced economy. The creation of a "floating population" has been among the most formidable tasks over the past 40 years, and the inflow of foreign capital also contributes to the uncertainty and the inescapable creation of informal labor in provincial urban areas seeking foreign capital investment. Changing the urban working class's status from floating informal workers to formal laborers with residence permits requires mobilization efforts which the ACFTU has striven to advance. Soaring membership in the ACFTU and its affiliates demonstrates that a significant share of the population have become formal workers with residence permits. Concomitantly, rural provinces will also inevitably confront dwindling populations and changing demographics which destabilize communities. Regularizing a "floating population" of internal migrant workers has drawbacks for rural workers who are left behind, and the Chinese government has responded with specific policies to upgrade the socioeconomic conditions where populations decline.

Starting In 2015, under Xi Jinping, China has significantly relaxed the hukou system through granting residence permits to migrant workers and their families who have been employed and lived in urban households for six months, as well as students who have attended school regularly. Additionally, the expediting of hukou reforms has greatly expanded the population of urban workers. However, the process of granting workers and their families residential permits cannot be expected to be implemented instantaneously as urbanization has occurred at a far more rapid pace than expected by the government. According to Sun Wenkai, since 2015, the Chinese government has unremittingly advanced efforts to stabilize the urban population. In the 13th five-year plan (2016–20), legal obstacles to granting residency hukou status for rural migrant workers in urban areas were to be consistently removed by the PRC and CPC. A recent study has found that an average annual rate of 13 million residents has been granted urban residency permits each year. The rate of urban hukou registration has expanded to 45 percent, leading to an increase of the permanent urban population of more than 2 percent from 2013 to the end of 2020. Those workers seeking to return to rural areas also maintain rural residency rights (Wenkai 2022, 7–9).

The capacity to absorb urban migrant workers and equalize pay scales is a formidable task for local, municipal, regional, provincial and national governments as urban migration has far exceeded predictions. Less educated rural migrants are paid lower wages than more highly educated workers, but recent studies have found that the wage gap has narrowed significantly in the last decade:

> This is also a refutation of the view that the public sector has advanced at the expense of the private sector in China. Of course, working in the public sector

establishment still provides pay advantages for some groups. Through regression analysis, it is found that the wage differentials between inside and outside the establishment mainly exist among low-income labourers, which chiefly consist of labourers with a low level of education and labourers with a rural hukou. At the same time, the proportion of these labourers working in the establishment is relatively low, and it is more difficult for them to enter the establishment than other groups. Only a small number of people can enjoy the dividend of working in the establishment. (Wenkai 2022, 190)

For per capita income differentials (US$), Engels Co-efficient, and wage by ownership see Figures 4, 5, and 6.

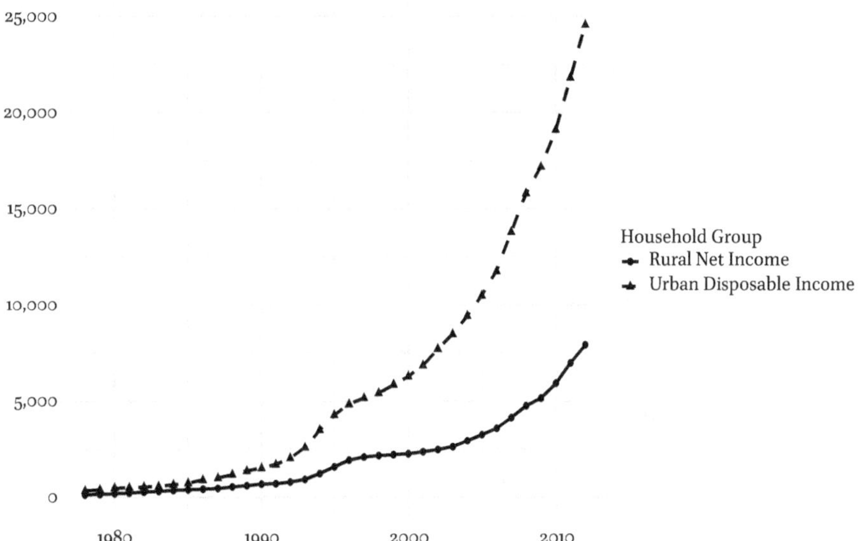

FIGURE 4   Per capita annual income of urban and rural households, 1978–2012
(Source: Derived from National Bureau of Statistics (2024) China statistics yearbook (2024) 4–9 average wage of employed persons in urban non-private units by registered statistical category. Beijing: National Bureau of Statistics. https://www.stats.gov.cn/sj/ndsj/2024/indexeh.htm)

While the ILO honestly raises shortcomings and weaknesses, most of these result from the rapid increase in private sector enterprises. However, significantly, the election of Xi Jinping in 2013 as General Secretary and President have contributed to ameliorating workplace violations in the private sector and an emphasis on expanding SOEs, disquieting international finance capital, which seeks to extract profits and expand the private sector. Consequently, rural–urban migrant workers have mobilized more effectively into unions in SOEs.

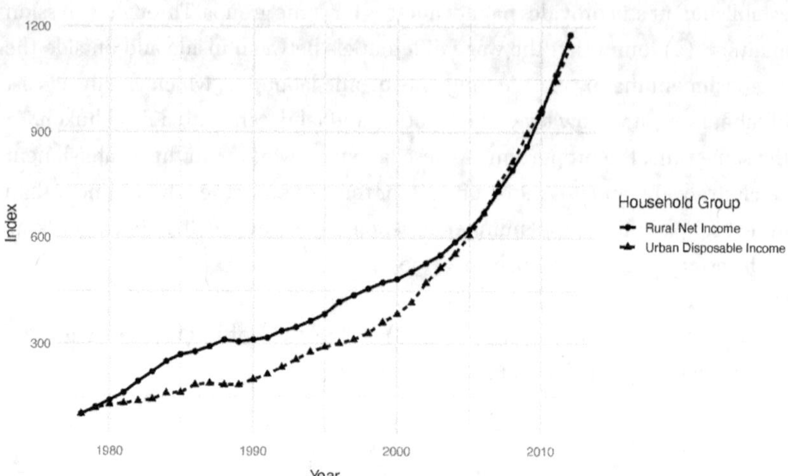

FIGURE 5   Per capita income ($US) and Engel's coefficient of urban and rural
households, 1978–2012 (Source: China statistical yearbook (2024) 11–2
per capita income and Engel's coefficient of urban and rural households,
1978=100 (Beijing: National Bureau of Statistics of China) https://www
.stats.gov.cn/sj/ndsj/2024/indexeh.htm)

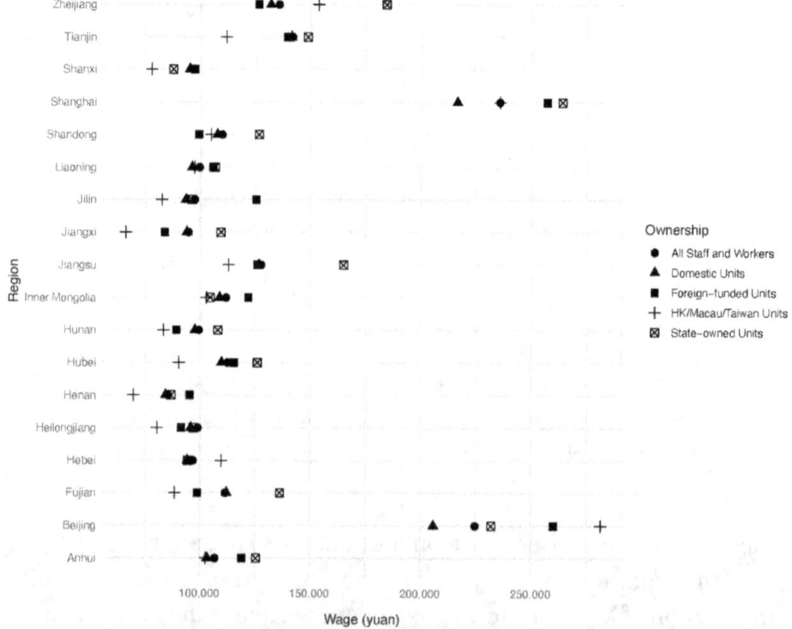

FIGURE 6   Average wages in China by ownership type, 1995–2023 (Source: China
statistical yearbook (2024) 11–2 per capita income and Engel's coefficient of
urban and rural households, 1978=100. (Beijing: National Bureau of Statistics
of China) https://www.stats.gov.cn/sj/ndsj/2024/indexeh.htm)

Though organizing is more challenging in private sector firms, all workers have the right to form unions without opposition from employers and tend to advance their authorized power if they intend to remain on the job for an extended period of time. As we shall see in Chapter 6, workers who are working temporarily while they train for new jobs may not have the equivalent investment in improving conditions through joining a union. In still other scarce instances, workers had been manipulated by NGOs with foreign financial support to generate the illusion of discord through intentionally disregarding ACFTU organizing policies. A notable example of foreign-funded NGO interference was the 2018 Jasic Technologies case in Shenzhen, orchestrated to generate international opprobrium rather than to improve wages and conditions of work. Private employers are ever more instructed of worker rights to form unions. From 1990 to 2015, China even permitted foreign NGOs to operate in China, a policy that would be forbidden if Chinese NGOs or labor institutions operated in the US or European Union. These NGOs primarily engaged in undermining the ACFTU through mobilizing a small number of workers to engage in anarchic actions which sought to "educate, agitate, and organize" workers into Western-styled labor organizations directly opposed to the workers' state. Both foreign capital and Western NGOs share a common perspective that the period from 1990 to 2015 was the apogee of their ability to extract profit and to organize workers in opposition to the ACFTU and the PRC. The shared position of finance capital and Western labor NGOs is consistent with constructing an unregulated market, which benefits capital and NGOs capable of using the chaotic conditions to organize workers to oppose the Chinese state. Xi Jinping put an end to the neoliberal era of unregulated foreign influence.

In addition to promoting decent wages and working conditions, the ACFTU and its industrial, provincial, and local affiliates are continuously improving conditions and responses to expand opportunities for migrant workers and the Chinese labor movement as a whole. Furthermore, the ILO reported that the All-China Women's Federation (ACWF) serves the interests of women migrant workers who were subject to abuse by foreign capital and corrupt private employers. The same report published by the ILO in 2006 commended the ACWF for its energetic role in defending the rights of women (Tuñón 2006, 26–27).

10   Conclusion

Worldwide, the latest data provided by the International Organization for Migration estimates there were 740 million migrants in 2009, the vast majority being within countries of the global South. The figure for international migration based on 2020 data is 281 million (IOM 2024). Among the more than

1 billion migrants in 2020, an estimated 72 percent are internal migrants, while 28 percent are international migrants. The challenge of incorporating internal migrants is more formidable than the significant challenges of fostering the rights of international migrant laborers.

The prevailing literature asserts that urban migration contributes to economic development and growth as well as upgrading migrants' standard of living. However, in almost all Western academic accounts, the focus is on the deleterious consequences of migration: higher levels of exploitation, lack of social services, splitting of families and households, men and women, children and parents, and leaving the aged behind (Pun & Chan 2012; Solinger 1999; Xiang 2007). This double standard reveals a bias in the literature which dismisses the net economic and social gains of internal migrants and their families. China is the exception to the rule as the destructive consequences of migration are emphasized by Western observers rather than the contribution of migration to social and economic well-being for migrants and all urban residents. Moreover, a plethora of research was conducted over a 25 year period from about 1990 to 2015, when the Chinese state and institutions were responding to the most adverse and unforeseeable consequences of migration resulting from market socialism. The national demand for FDI promoted competition among municipalities through a proliferation of SEZs and often unregulated free trade zones hosting multinational corporations (Hussinger and Palladini 2025; Jiang and Waley 2023; Renaldi 2025; Wang et al. 2022; Zeng et al. 2024).

Instead of assessing China's mass migration from a historical perspective, most interpretations employ a static and reductionist approach which fails to absorb the CPC's struggle to keep up with a tumultuous transformation. The whole of the ubiquitous critical literature on China's development fails to account for the temporal and political responses to improve the negative effects of policies chiefly imposed by foreign capital on a developing society. Accordingly, Western research on Chinese migration focuses on the time lapse between episodic changes in the countryside and the formation and implementation of policy to address negative consequences (including family disruption caused by migration) rather than policies advanced to address undesirable socioeconomic consequences of market socialism. In so doing, it tends to neglect the significance of stages in migration and economic development. Rather, time seems to be fixed and stands still. As a result, research is prone to focus on the same old notorious cases, notably the Foxconn worker suicides in 2010, the escalation of strikes from 2010 to 2015 and the Jasic Technology case in Shenzhen in 2018. In the latter case, the local ACFTU affiliate sought to address the workers' complaints only to be outflanked by a foreign-funded Hong Kong NGO, Workers Empowerment, which sought to counter efforts to resolve the dispute.

Migration is the major feature of the Chinese workforce. However, Western critics and NGOs practice a form of cultural imperialism by applying often erroneous and offensive norms to Chinese internal labor migration. Moreover, Westerners fail to recognize the nature of the Chinese socialist state. For them, China is not unique but one state among many others. The leftists refer to China as "state capitalist" or, more recently, simply "capitalist." As such, Western critics lack understanding of the time and space of labor migration and the fact that the ACFTU can only respond after recognizing systemic problems, as it did with the Labor Contract Laws of 1994 and 2008 and subsequent amendments. The ACFTU has become more responsible and active in representing workers in the wake of the strikes and disputes from 2010 to 2015. Rather than understanding migration as a process which includes the establishment and implementation of state policies, multiple institutions and global forces, Western migration theorists who criticize China do not take into consideration that state policies to address social concerns must follow migration and a recognition of the outcomes and difficulties which migrants encounter. Policy follows a process of learning and adapting to the social obstacles and challenges which are recognized by the state. This logic, for Hegel, the imperfect government, acquires information based on experience to develop policies for advancing citizens.

Moreover, the critique is often misplaced as the hukou laws enacted in the 1950s were in response to the challenges of the time, as were labor law and policy on migration. The hukou registration system was originally established in the 1950s to regulate migration and protect the economic and survival needs of an agrarian population, not as an obstacle to rural–urban migration. Yet Western academics, activists and NGOs repeatedly apply a reactive response which does not account for the specific nature of the state and the notable achievement of integrating the largest ever wave of migrant workers into cities. While China faces tremendous obstacles (Chan and Zhang 1999; Li 2019), the demographic transformation and the government response to hundreds of millions of internal migrants are nothing short of extraordinary. Taken together, the migration literature about China exclusively applies Western concepts to the exclusion of dynamics in the Third World and socialist states.

Digital and New Economy Workers in China: from Precarity to Job Stability

The varied, apparently unconnected, and petrified forms of individual processes now resolved themselves into so many conscious and systematic applications of natural science to the attainment of given useful effects. Technology also discovered the few main fundamental forms of motion, which, despite the diversity of the instruments used, are necessarily taken by every productive action of the human body. (Karl Marx, 1867)

1 Primitive Accumulation and the Transition to Capitalism

The emergence of industrial capitalism and labor exploitation as the dominant mode of production and trade in the 18th and 19th centuries was a direct consequence of unequal exchange of trade between poor and rich regions and nations. This engendered the international division of labor. In *Capital, Volume I*, Marx examines the manifold systems of expropriation of labor power under primitive accumulation, which had reached its highest point through European private colonial control over trade in East, Southeast and South Asia. In the 19th century, the expansion of European colonialism was driven by private capitalists seeking to profit over low-cost production in what Marx termed "so called primitive accumulation." This relied on the imperially authorized seizure of wealth, natural resources and labor. Marx recognized that the imprimatur of the state was integral to the development of capitalism through the authorization of totalitarian force for colonial expropriation:

> These methods depend in part on brute force, for instance the colonial system. But they all employ the power of the state, the concentrated and organized force of society, to hasten, as in a hothouse, the process of transformation of the feudal mode of production into the capitalist mode and to shorten the transition. Force is the midwife of every old society which is pregnant with a new one. It is itself an economic power. (Marx 1867/1976, 915–916)

The colonial state alone conferred the legitimacy for state-chartered private capitalists to plunder feudal and semi-feudal societies and the "right" to extract minerals, commodities and low-wage Indigenous labor. Marx underscores the significance of the British government granting the British East India Company an exclusive monopoly to expropriate wealth from China and India in the mid-19th century as an apogee of rapacious capitalism. Hence, capitalism and the expropriation of surplus value from labor could only exist with a strong state.

Significantly, the plunder of natural resources, agriculture, commodities and then labor hinged on the capacity of a dominant capitalist class to control state power through colonial rule from the 17th century to the early 20th century. Political economist Amiya Kumar Bagchi asserts that European colonial powers compelled most colonized natives in Asia and Latin America to abide by their edicts through the imposition of free trade, which benefited only the British, Dutch, French, Japanese and American imperialists. European, North American and Japanese imperial rule in China was especially destructive.

The situation of China over the period 1850–1949 must have been much worse because it witnessed two Opium Wars, the hugely destructive Taiping Revolt, a Japanese assault which led to the loss of Formosa, foreign aggression to quell the Boxer Rebellion and a period of warring landlords and full-scale Japanese aggression from 1931 culminating in civil war from 1945 to 1949 (Bagchi 2021, 10).

Once local authorities had been weakened or overthrown, imperialist corporations could gain concessions to extract profit from the global South through annexation, impoverishment of local and regional populations and displacement of rural labor. In most of the developing world, displaced, landless rural labor has transformed into a permanent precarious labor force living at the margins of cities in South Asia, Southeast Asia and Latin America (Breman 1996; Davis 2004/2017). By conferring the right of the colonial state to extract value from poor regions of Africa, the Americas and then Asia, European capital emerged and expanded through intervention and undermining and eradication of Indigenous political and economic systems, only permitting local leadership once European dominated trade had been asserted and spread within colonial trading zones.

Capital investment flows from developed countries with higher labor costs are transmitted to developing countries where the ability to extract surplus value from workers is far higher due to lower labor costs. Likewise, at the global periphery, internal inequality between rural and urban areas is an inescapable consequence of capital formation and urbanization. While urban regions become more affluent, rural areas often lag behind through the internal division of labor. In market economies, urban–rural inequality is far more prominent and challenging to balance. Over 40 years of neoliberal globalization, the unequal exchange of trade has become a dominant, global economic dynamic which is essential to imperialist profitability and accumulation in the core and poverty and extraction at the periphery.

By 1950 it had become clear that the development of industry at the periphery depended on the relocation of rural subsistence labor into urban agglomerations. Capitalist modernization in Western Europe and North America was viewed as the prototype for developing countries seeking to establish modern economies. In most advanced economies, migration of labor from rural areas to urban agglomerations was essential to developing a low wage working class. This development model did not consider holistic development of society in both rural and urban areas but focused on the mechanization of agriculture and the displacement of peasants from rural regions to the urban centers. By the 1960s, Western countries had become almost entirely urban as rural agriculture was commercialized and dominated by multinational companies which had centralized control over food production among several major multinational corporations. Mechanization of agriculture was facilitated through the development of profitable urban markets where consumers benefited from the creation of advanced economies. Multinational agribusiness had become so strong that, by the 1970s and 1980s, it even penetrated into economies of poor countries of the global South with their predominantly rural populations. In developing countries, surplus value from low-wage workers and technological advancements has sharply expanded productivity and profits, enriching multinational corporations in rich countries. Even technological innovation applied to manufacturing benefited capital formation and accumulation in the North. Concomitantly, the most impoverished countries in Africa, south of the Sahara, have rarely obtained advanced technology to increase worker productivity. Western foreign investment is intentionally designed to purchase the less advanced technology to maintain dominance over the most impoverished and least developed countries of Africa and elsewhere, ensuring that most profits are realized in rich countries at the top of global production chains (Emmanuel 1982).

Extraction of surplus value in the South and realization of profits in the North through the sale of commodities allows global production chains to benefit rich countries at the expense of developing ones. Marx's concept of primitive accumulation is thus apropos to understand the dichotomy between workers at the periphery and in the core from the 18th century to the present. Under primitive accumulation, labor works under conditions of obsolete capital accumulation. In many industries, the lack of technological innovation is used to extract profit without commensurate investment, yielding high profits for capitalists. Maurice Dobb has demonstrated that primitive accumulation is used as a means to both increase profits and to threaten workers employed in industries where minimal investment and the subsumption of new technology result in redundancy and mass unemployment.

A firm market for the assets with which the bourgeoisie were trading and an elastic and cheap supply of the commodities they were now investing in were required to create surplus value in pre-capitalist societies that exist simultaneously with capitalism. The latter condition may even be considered the more important of the two, since the existence of the positive inducement of extracting surplus to invest in industry was more decisive at that time than the mere absence of deterrents to the sale of other types of assets. To bring about the ideal conditions to extract surplus value, the primary requirements were plentiful reserves of labor and easy access to supplies of raw material, together with facilities for the production of tools and machinery. Without these conditions, industrial investment would inevitably have been discouraged and further progress arrested, however splendid the wealth and status to which the bourgeoisie had previously grown accustomed (Dobb 1946, 183).

In the post-colonial era, foreign investment in advanced industrial technology has been relatively scarce in the developing world as exploitation of human labor removed the necessity to increase productivity. Production devoid of modern industrial technology has given rise to higher levels of labor exploitation in poor countries and the expansion of low-cost consumer goods in the imperial center. Rather than investing in new technology, capital extracts profit from superexploitation of workers. The introduction of neoliberal capitalism in the 1970s repositioned a share of foreign investments to the South, intensifying the extraction of surplus value of workers and the production of commodities at even lower cost. However, the emergence of the digital economy has further extracted profits, shifting the burden of payment for new technology from new industries to workers, who must bear responsibility for smartphones, e-navigation systems and even—as the drivers for e-navigation technology firms—renting, buying and maintaining auto bikes and motor vehicles.

2 Technological Change and Responsive Representation of Workers' Interests

The introduction and institutionalization of market socialism over nearly 50 years have posed significant challenges for stabilizing China's rural and urban working class during development of a national economy matching advanced industrial countries' standards while applying technology to build the economic conditions for a modern socialist economy. The All-China Federation of Trade Unions (ACFTU) has been instrumental in defending, steadying and improving the conditions of the Chinese working class during this dramatic transformation, which has brought about the concrete foundation for a prosperous socialist economy. Since the opening of the market socialist economy in 1978, the ACFTU has been consistently stretched in adapting to the inevitable vicissitudes of China's technological development and economic modernization. It has been compelled to develop the capacity to serve a far more diverse working class in manufacturing, construction, social services and, since the 2010s, the digital economy.

With high confidence (based on the author's research in China labor archives, randomized sample interviews, ethnographic conversations and participant observation), one can say that the ACFTU has successfully mobilized the Chinese working class in all sectors of the economy from industrial enterprises to the platform economy: a formidable accomplishment for any trade union federation and a colossal endeavor for the world's largest trade union. In 2024, an estimated 400 million workers were ACFTU members; more than all trade union members combined in the rest of the world. To accommodate unionization, Chinese labor law grants workers a legal right to join and form their own unions. Public and private employers must recognize and bargain with ACFTU-affiliated unions to negotiate higher wages and ensure safe working conditions.

3 ACFTU Organizing New Employment Forms and the Digital Economy

Unambiguously, trade unions worldwide outside China have failed to organize workers in new employment forms even as labor continues to challenge capitalist exploitation and improve working conditions. Today's trade unions are weakening, and new forms of worker organization (NFWO), unduly praised by innumerable Labor Studies scholars, are incapable of challenging capital alone. They stand out as popular models among scholars who view nebulous organizations with ties to labor as preferable to strong organizations that have the capacity to represent workers' democratic interests. NFWOs—including workers' centers—may have had minor public relations victories but do not challenge capital because they depend on funding from private foundations (Frantz & Fernandes 2018). From 2000 to the present, workers' centers and advice offices may have received plaudits from the neoliberal press in the West, but almost all have transformed into advocacy organizations bereft of ability to meaningfully mobilize workers, a condition which is replicated throughout most of the global South by labor-based NGOs dependent upon Western funding or donors (Kerswell & Pratap 2019). In the course of 25 years' research, this author's honest assessment of new employment forms and NFWOs exposes the deficiencies of Western organizational models and those imposed by Western NGOs in the global South. The best NGO labor organizations may raise worker consciousness and rank-and-file activism but reveal themselves to be no replacement for existing unions formed in the early 20th century. Consequently, precarious and contract labor are on the rise worldwide with almost no representative agency reflecting working class subjectivities (Ness 2023a).

In sharp contrast, the monumental achievements of the ACFTU have been praised as exemplary by the International Labour Organization (ILO). In the last decade, the organization of workers in the rapidly expanding digital economy and new forms of employment has been unmatched by any trade union elsewhere in the world. Notably, the ACFTU is organizing digital workers employed in the burgeoning logistics industries (including trucking, ride hailing and delivery) comprising approximately 200 million workers. Digital platform workers have unique challenges, including regulating the hours of work and meeting wage standards. In China, most digital workers are employed for identifiable technology firms in the ride hailing and delivery sectors and beyond. The ACFTU is advocating for platform workers to be directly hired by platform technology firms, ensuring minimum wage standards and organizing new workers into the union.

As the Chinese labor market transforms through the introduction of new technology, the ACFTU is directing efforts to mobilize in the new forms of employment sectors that conventionally have not had equivalent rights to those enjoyed by industrial workers. By 2021, the ACFTU had achieved notable success integrating workers in new employment forms into its unions. According to an ILO report:

> By the end of 2021, the number of trade union members newly developed by the All-China Federation of Trade Unions for platform workers exceeded 3.5 million, of which all 12 head enterprises in four typical industries, namely truck drivers, online taxi drivers, couriers and take-away delivery workers, have established their trade unions. (Wei & Wang 2024, 42)

In addition, local unions have organized workers and signed collective bargaining agreements with the largest employers in the logistics and delivery industries, which include increased compensation, safety equipment, education and skills training and other benefits. Workers and the ACFTU have significantly increased wages, working conditions and benefits. Trade union organizing of logistics and delivery workers is not limited to China's largest first tier cities but is occurring throughout China among the largest platform technology firms (Meituan, Ele.me and J&D.com) as the reserve army of labor decreases, fostering greater competition for workers (Wei & Wang 2024). As of January 2024, the ACFTU and its affiliates have mobilized 26.5 percent of platform workers into trade unions, even if a minority are full-time workers (2024, 34).

As the ACFTU is committed to unionizing all new forms of employment in logistics, the digital economy and beyond, it has focused on developing campaigns on the provincial, municipal and district levels. In 2025, it succeeded in organizing workers in China's leading platform delivery firms as the industry is seeking reliable full-time workers. Unlike Western trade unions, the ACFTU and its affiliates directly bargain with platform technology firms and file grievances on behalf of workers, a model for trade unions worldwide. The ride hailing industry is notorious worldwide for opposing drivers as employees and fighting all forms of responsibility for their welfare. In 2020, a public ballot measure in California, Proposition 22, passed, disqualifying ride haling drivers from being considered employees of Uber and Lyft among other digital riding platforms. Instead, the drivers were classified as independent contractors in business for themselves and disqualified from wages and benefits. The ride hailing behemoths were not even responsible for the health and safety of the drivers. The public law was the bellwether that disqualified all ride hailing workers from becoming employees in the US and worldwide.

By way of contrast, under the directive of General Secretary Xi Jinping, the ACFTU is mandated to mobilize workers in new forms of employment. At a press conference on July 17, 2023, Zhang Xiaohui of the ACFTU stated unequivocally that the federation was holding fast to the directive, stating that "workers in newly employed sectors, including truck drivers, ride hailing drivers, couriers and food delivery workers, have reached 84 million nationwide, becoming an important part of the workforce." The ACFTU inaugurated a "Three-Year Action Plan for Deepening the Work of Trade Unions for Workers in New Employment (2023–2025)," requiring the trade unions to deploy resources to deepen the mobilization of workers in the new sectors into trade unions (Bo & Jin 2023).

In China, the ACFTU has been successful in unionizing the ride hailing giant Didi Chuxing since 2021. Ever since, ACFTU has been converting ride hailing drivers into employees of Didi and organizing new workers into the union.

On July 30, 2025, the Hunan Provincial Federation of Trade Unions successfully mobilized thousands of drivers in search of membership into the union. In 2025, the union expects 20,000 provincial drivers to join the union (Li, W. 2025). The digital technology company has recognized drivers throughout China's major cities. Didi's recognition of drivers as both workers and union members of ACFTU affiliates with the right to bargain exemplifies the dramatic growth of unionization in the digital economy which is climbing rapidly throughout China.

This achievement sets the ACFTU apart from other established unions in the world. No other union worldwide has organized even 1 percent of workers in the platform economy, due to fierce employer resistance to recognizing digital laborers as employees; a response which serves as a disincentive for trade unions to organize workers in the industry. At best, workers in the UK and the US have formed independent associations with scant support from established unions. Although Labor researchers in Europe claim that 13.4 percent of workers are organized into unions, almost all are grassroots organizations which do not have collective bargaining agreements with digital technology companies, as noted in Chapter 4 (Vandaele 2018; Vandaele et al. 2024).

Labor analyst Lu Zhang asserts the crucial significance of the transformation of the organization of the labor process in the Chinese workplace through the application of Labor Process Theory (LPT), which examines the whole enterprise including management, supervision and division of labor (Zhang 2024). Factory regimes are not static but a dynamic process as new forces come into effect in response to the application of new technological investments or the absence of advanced technology. As China's industrial production process develops and modernizes, those industries which innovate contribute to a decline of labor due to productivity growth. Those industries that fail to modernize may also lead to unemployment as workers are rendered redundant. Thus, in China, the state actively supports the development and application of new technology into industrial production to catalyze and stimulate productivity. At a machine tools firm in Guangzhou in April 2025, the enterprise was devoted to investing in new technology and modernizing its machine tools. The enterprise's plant with markedly more workers had fewer new machines than its plant with cutting-edge equipment. Notably, the firm received financial support and encouragement from the state to increase worker productivity. Suggestively, to the observer, the Chinese-operated enterprise had also invested in skills training to integrate all workers into the technologically advanced production process. Additionally, the firm's managers reported that its workforce would grow if demand remained strong and younger workers were hired.

However, the introduction of new employment forms outside of industry also expands the number of jobs in the platform economy, which tends to have lower job security. Chinese scholars have documented the ACFTU's unprecedented achievements in organizing workers in the digital economy and its organizing of assistance to unions outside China in protecting the rights of platform workers. Irene Zhou's ILO working paper states without reservation, "China stands at the forefront of technological innovation" and is well placed to educate unions on setting standards for platform workers. She concludes that, in response to the demands of precarious workers worldwide, "China is well placed in contributing to better seeing the dynamic of these new forms of worker and to supporting mutual learning between countries" (Zhou 2020, 5).

4   Representing Workers in the Digital Economy

China has been making efforts to develop the platform economy and protect platform workers' rights and interests. With the world's largest population and a quarter of the global workforce, it stands at the forefront of technological innovation and globalization. Understanding the regulation of digital labor platforms in China will contribute to better understanding the nature of and constraints on workers within these new forms of work and to supporting mutual learning between countries. In an expression of support in June 2024, the ILO recognized China's leadership in organizing workers employed in the platform economy and its future role in guiding European Union labor representatives to develop social protection for vulnerable workers in the sector.

The rapid introduction of the digital economy is unparalleled worldwide and has captured a large share of new workers in national labor markets. New generations enter these jobs due to demand for their work and will continue to do so. The initial stages of labor relations are typically fraught with controversy in all societies. Low pay and poor working conditions are often abysmal, and workers respond to ameliorate these. Most but not all Western scholars and NGOs deliberately neglect the ACFTU's achievements, instead seeking to disparage it. Notwithstanding this, the ACFTU continues its efforts, which have expanded under President Xi Jinping to recognize, address and change policy for workers in the new economy. Whilst the ACFTU's achievements in organizing and protecting new economy workers have not been acknowledged by Labor scholars in the West, they are recognized and highly regarded elsewhere in the world as an exemplar of successful organization. Western NGOs and Labor researchers, however, disregard or criticize the ACFTU's sustained success in organizing new economy workers and consider improvement of wages and conditions an anomaly.

5   Distortion of the ACFTU Achievements

Western NGOs and academic critics distort or completely ignore the ACFTU's achievements in organizing workers in China's digital and logistic sectors, and those who counter such unsupported and inaccurate narratives are ostracized. In the digital sector, the ACFTU's detractors have repeatedly enforced a collective gestalt even when organizational success has been achieved. For example, critics will enforce compliance to their narrative through a focus on shortcomings; for instance, the ubiquitous notion of top-down unionism, which is applied within otherwise correct labor accounts, even when workers are actively involved in advancing the cause. If the ACFTU participates and imposes employer compliance, cynics will focus on bureaucracy rather than the advantages of powerful unions affiliated with the Federation. Paradoxically, a dominant framework for analyzing trade unions in the West is through labor power resources vis-à-vis capital (Bieler 2018; Refslund & Arnholtz 2021; Schmalz et al. 2019; Tattersol 2010), or the capacity to marshal a coalition of forces to confront management and succeed in mobilizing workers. However, under neoliberal capitalism, the weakening of unions and the launching of new digital technology in the platform economy, labor's power is even further marginalized, and workers and their allies must formulate innovative organizing strategies to confront capital.

A French scholar's recent study of labor organizing in the digital sector (*Organizing Without Mobilizing: The Platformization of the Workplace and Its Impact on Chinese Trade Unionism* (Huang 2023)) convincingly details the success of a unionization campaign among food delivery couriers. After platform workers protested independently, the national federation "sought to unionize delivery workers by developing new modes of organization. At the same time, it developed a range of services for these workers. It is only recently that the ACFTU has become involved in the negotiation of collective agreements covering employment conditions and working of delivery drivers." It is perfectly understandable that the ACFTU would become engaged in organizing *after* a new labor market like this had come into being. However, Huang's puzzling conclusion states: "Even if the lack of hindsight makes it impossible to grasp the real scope of these negotiations, it nevertheless raises questions about the reality of trade unionism in China" (Huang 2023, 1). At the same time, the study reveals that the ACFTU example contrasts sharply with the situation in

Britain, France and elsewhere in Europe, where delivery workers are shunned by established unions. The Federation has uniquely managed to mobilize and represent workers in the industry despite the ambiguous legal relationship between platforms and workers, the multiple outsourcing and the geographical dispersion of contracting to third party companies which have challenged its traditional union organization patterns. In response, the ACFTU has created special unions at different levels for couriers by "innovating beyond the established system, abandoning the tradition of employer-controlled 'paper unions' and potentially gaining substantive bargaining power" (Huang 2023, 2).

In an era of trade union decline and virtually no union representation of drivers and delivery workers, worker militancy and union responsiveness culminating in unionization and improved conditions would be considered an example of success anywhere else. However, the conclusion drawn from Huang's otherwise excellent case study is that the food delivery workers should not have a strong and effective union with the capacity of subduing the excesses of the private sector.

Western NGOs and academics have devoted significant funding and research in casting organizational success as failure, using code words and inaccurate quotidian positions which denigrate the People's Republic of China (PRC) and the ACFTU. But despite such misrepresentation, motivated by an aversion to socialism, recent surveys of workers reveal the ACFTU has responded rapidly to labor market transformation after becoming aware of poor working conditions, wage abuse and non-payment of social security. Having understood the challenges faced by digital navigation workers and noting reports of worker discord and dissent against low incomes and poor working conditions, the ACFTU started negotiations between workers and firms to address and resolve persistent abuses through tripartite dialogue. The resultant negotiations resulted in direct employment relations between technology companies and workers and worker mobilization and affiliation with branch unions of the ACFTU. As direct employees of the technology firms, ACFTU members can speed resolution of worker grievances through mediation and arbitration for improvement of conditions within labor courts. If the drivers and delivery workers are unorganized, the ACFTU mobilizes them into unions to ensure employers comply with wage rates, safety standards and pensions. In contrast to advanced Western capitalist countries, where the capitalist class rules the economy, the working class is the leading mass social force in China.

As a result of the deepening of socialism with Chinese characteristics, tangible improvements have been achieved in workplaces throughout the country. The ACFTU undertakes to respond to changing material conditions which may alter labor wages and conditions and to challenges by private sector employers, inevitable in any state but far less prevalent in China. National labor law and local trade union practices have dramatically improved labor conditions in factories, the digital economy and beyond in response to technological innovation affecting the political economy. Consequently, the ACFTU encourages local democratic engagement in workplaces throughout industrial sectors, provinces and on the local level through street, neighborhood and district unions to increase wages and improve conditions, including providing social security to workers. In addition, digital and new economy employers must provide shelter for workers in hot weather.

6   Precarity and Disorganization

In the 2010s, digitization and development of geographic mapping systems have set the stage for the application of new technology as a highly profitable force which has stimulated hundreds of billions of dollars of capital investment in new service economy startup enterprises in the US and later worldwide. Notably, foreign direct investment has expanded into the global South, above all into states with inadequate public transportation services. Without delay, these new forms have accumulated capital to deploy digital communication technology in ride hailing, food and consumer goods delivery, logistics and even home services. In the process they have disrupted existing forms of capital accumulation and displaced firms which previously had direct relations with workers in the taxi, delivery and cleaning and care industries. On the whole, these industries had been controlled by small businesses with vehicles to rent or sell to drivers and delivery workers. In home services, digitization characteristically involved a direct relationship between a contracted worker and a firm or recipient of services. The new startup firms sought to revolutionize the entire industry and dominate ride hailing, delivery and attendant home services through harnessing digital technology to these labor markets. Notably, the firms were designated technology businesses not service providers, as they did not own the vehicles and did not consider laborers to be their own staff but independent contractors in business for themselves.

Classical Political Economist Joseph Schumpeter proposed that uprooting existing industries through the appearance of new technology and application of new methods of production is vital for capitalist progress. Of necessity, new technology doomed peasants and the working class to economic displacement. Yet, Schumpeter also supported the imperialist system of extraction of profit from workers and resources at the global periphery; especially through the formation of monopoly capital, which is indispensable for capitalist expansion and profitability (Schumpeter 1911/1934). While Schumpeter regarded technological modernization as an essential and positive feature of capitalist development, he all but ignored its effect on rural and urban workers, which Marx examined in *Capital* more than 50 years previously. Conversely, Marx regarded capitalism as a destructive and exploitative force on rural laborers and the working class.

7 Advent of the Digital Logistics Economy

The inception in 2010 of smartphone navigation apps for ride hailing and delivery was facilitated by the investment of billions of dollars of finance capital into technology companies. These formed and expanded exponentially in creating a new consumer service which removed the capital–labor relationship and expanded a labor market of precarious workers. The presence of the new technology in consumer markets throughout the world would not have been possible without a vast reserve army of workers entering an industry dominated by technology firms. Industrial restructuring in the West and urbanization and migration within and from developing countries expanded this reserve army and set in motion the proliferation of digital applications on platforms for driving, delivery and consumer services (Xu 2023). Precarious drivers and delivery workers were now challenged by aggressive firms devoid of workers and financed by major private investors chiefly in North America, Europe and Southeast and East Asia.

In the West, highly capitalized firms (including Deliveroo, Lyft and primarily Uber) required a large and obedient workforce drawn from a reserve army of labor among workers. Most drivers entering the industry were compliant, migrant, young unemployed workers. Some supplemented their wages through driving on a part time basis. Concomitantly, navigation technology became a major source of employment for unemployed industrial workers and rural laborers entering urban labor markets throughout the world. In China, the rapid development and investment in ride hailing and delivery firms were widespread by 2015. This period saw the emergence of new companies including Didi Chuxing, the leading ride hailing firm, and Meituan and Ele.me, the two leading digital food delivery firms.

8 Proletarianization of Informal Labor

Proponents of ride hailing and e-commerce worldwide contend that the new technology greatly benefits economic development and reduces poverty by pushing idle workers displaced by industrial closure, and migrants displaced from the countryside, into gainful employment. As independent contractors, drivers supposedly go into business for themselves. This is not a new idea but a formula which has been invoked since the emergence of neoliberalism in the 1980s. Even if unemployed and informal laborers can earn a modest income through selling their services on the app, drivers for digital platforms are forced to work long hours with low remuneration, poor working conditions and no social security. In most cases, ride hailing is a stopgap to earn a living for unemployed workers and migrant laborers. The evidence shows that in the West and worldwide, due to persistent low income and dangerous conditions, all but the most impoverished workers are unwilling to sustain the high intensity of work in the personal services economy for more than a few years (Katta et al. 2024; Malhotra & Agrawal 2025; Pankaj & Jha 2024). Ride hailing and delivery drivers are considered self-employed entrepreneurs in business, but they must work long hours to provide for themselves and their families. Most drivers enter the industry due to the scarcity of decent wages in other more productive sectors, and they are not really in business for themselves as they are highly dependent on the technology firm, which can discipline them through withdrawing the navigation systems for any of numerous reasons. All expenses (including purchasing, renting and maintaining e-bikes or motorcycles) are shifted to drivers. While drivers can take out loans, many of them are forced into long-term debt. They must pay for batteries, helmets and other gear, are responsible for accidents, are often subject to theft and incur high levels of personal health risk from stress and fatigue (Cohen 2025; Ray 2024).

9 The Digital Economy under Neoliberal Capitalism and Chinese Market Socialism

Internet e-commerce spreads in the West with the support of state policies which deem drivers to be independent contractors and not employees of ride hailing technology firms. California Proposition 22 in 2020, passed with the support of the technology industry, denies drivers the right to employment with the ride hailing firms (Jacobs & Reich 2020). In effect, this bars them from organizing into unions to protect their rights. International capitalists have also expanded outside of the imperialist core to where profit margins are far higher. As sources of super-profitability in North America and Western Europe have been exhausted or stymied from further competing with entrenched private taxi drivers, capital investment has expanded into Asia,

Africa and Latin America. The Western behemoth Uber was thwarted in China, as national investment capital poured billions of dollars into its own national ride hailing app, Didi Chuxing, a technology firm formed in 2012 with more than 550 million users by 2023 and approximately 23 million drivers in China (Smith 2024). Chinese investors are the major investors in the navigation app, while most other developing economies rely on US, Japanese and Western European capitalists. However, while Western investors have actively campaigned to disallow ride hailing and delivery workers from becoming workers, China and the ACFTU have encouraged and facilitated the conversion of independent contractors into workers directly employed by ride hailing and delivery firms. Through increasing oversight of delivery and ride hailing firms Ele.me, Meituan and Didi Chuxing, the ACFTU has increased driver rights. It has facilitated direct employment and regulation of the expanding industry to increase wages, occupational safety and labor protections such as unionization and social security. Employers are obliged to acknowledge drivers as workers and to permit unionization and payment of dues to the ACFTU to administer adherence to collective bargaining agreements. This is a development which even Western scholars must acknowledge (Chau 2022).

With its national government and working class expecting the strong ACFTU to ensure precarious workers in the gig economy are unionized and have adequate wages and benefits, China has proved exceptional. Whereas the Uber driver is an independent contractor everywhere else in the world, the American technology firm has been prevented from imposing that model in China, leading to its withdrawal from the economy there. By contrast, the Didi Chuxing Technology Company, China's most prominent ride hailing company, is typically obliged to negotiate collective bargaining agreements with workers. Didi began operation in 2012 when most drivers, known as "riders," had not previously been employed by taxi-fleet owners. This differs from the situation in the West (notably, the US), where taxi fleet owners had already ground down any modicum of a work relationship even before the navigation app came into practice. Taxi drivers in the US had continually worked without labor protections since those apps' introduction in the early 20th century. Since the 1980s, taxi drivers had not been employed by fleet owners but rather leased their vehicles, lacking a direct employer–employee relationship and depending on earning more than they paid out. Taxi drivers had highly precarious earnings as they depended solely on the demand for services (Hodges 2020; Mathew 2005).

In the 2010s (as the navigation app was launched and applied, and as demand grew and ride hailing proliferated worldwide), the employment relationship became even more tenuous when "technology companies" disavowed any work connections. Drivers in such contractual arrangements now have no option but to purchase their own vehicles and are at the mercy of the app controlled by the technology company for customers. Additionally, drivers are assessed by customers, who are not obliged to tip them for rides. Instead, the transportation app companies like Uber and Lyft and so on ask customers to rate each driver on the quality of their ride, including the relative luxury of the automobile, the time from pickup to drop-off, courteousness and other intangibles. These in turn inform algorithms which are based on multiple factors unconnected to the driver's proximity to the customer.

10   Precarious Independent Contractors

Western investments in privately controlled ride hailing and e-commerce navigation apps were projected to enrich foreign venture capitalists, technology firms and an emergent comprador class through monopolizing investment to exploit domestic labor. The distinction between comprador and national capital is pivotal to grasping the contrast between imperialist exploitation and national economic investments intended to foster economic development. The former is motivated by international capitalist investment and extraction of profits from the periphery. The latter is driven by a motivation to advance economies at the periphery. Accordingly, Chinese support for technological advancement and implementation through delivery technology firms prohibits foreign competitors and is integral to the development and modernization of the economy. Unlike most developing countries, where ride hailing and delivery navigation apps are designed and operated as a replacement for mass transit systems, in China, driver and delivery transportation apps complement modern, state owned, urban metro systems.

Proponents of ride hailing and e-commerce worldwide contend that the new system greatly benefits economic development and reduces poverty by pushing idle workers in the informal economy into the capitalist marketplace by going into business for themselves. This is not a new idea but a formula which has been invoked since the emergence of neoliberalism in the 1980s. However, even if some peddlers, taxi drivers and for-hire service providers can indeed increase their income through selling their services, most are forced to work long hours for low remuneration. Most are unable to sustain work in the personal services economy for more than a few years or to improve their standards of living. Drivers may think they are self-employed entrepreneurs in business, but they are forced to work far harder and longer to provide for themselves and their families. Drivers also incur major costs for purchasing and maintaining motorcycles. While drivers can take out loans, the informal sector forces more drivers into debt. The ride hailing industry bears a resemblance to micro-lending by the World Bank. Presented as a means to lift the poor out of poverty, micro-loans are in reality a way of extending capitalist control over highly dependent populations. Cyclists and workers for the ride hailing firms are responsible for purchasing motorcycles on credit which may be provided by banks associated with the ride hailing firms. They are thus more completely dependent on the firms (Go-Jek or Grab) than they were as private drivers. They must pay for fuel, helmets and uniforms, are responsible for accidents and incur high levels of personal health risk from stress and fatigue, driving four times as much as before the introduction of the apps. Go-Jek is not yet profitable but once it has pushed other taxi driving and transportation options out of the system, it will have no competition; drivers will then have no alternative but to register with them (Damanik et al. 2025).

This unique relationship between the rise of technology companies which do not employ workers and labor is documented by abundant research around the world on the detachment of capital from the means of production and the shifting of the burden to laborers in the expansive platform economy. Even as some trade unions and drivers have sought to organize their own fledgling labor organizations, government legislation in most countries has deemed the workers to be service providers in business for themselves. This transformation has been made possible by the development of apps and geographic tracking programs connecting drivers to customers. However, Chinese laws applicable to digital workers have advanced farther and are continuously updated to reflect the changes in the platform industry.

China has advanced legislation which protects platform workers through properly categorizing them as workers, providing the fundamental rights which accompany worker status. The impetus for improving the condition of workers has been advanced by General Secretary Xi Jinping, emphasizing the necessity for digital workers employed as couriers, online workers, truck drivers and others to be granted labor protection directly through the platform enterprise.

Since 2020, the ILO has issued numerous reports praising China for developing labor protections for digital workers (Zhou 2020). The country is advancing legislation which protects platform workers through properly categorizing them as workers and providing the fundamental rights which accompany worker status. The impetus for improving the condition of workers has been advanced by General Secretary Xi Jinping, emphasizing the necessity for digital workers employed as couriers, online workers, truck drivers and others to be granted labor protection through the platform enterprise. The Communist Party of China (CPC) and the ACFTU are at all times adapting to the changes in the industry to ensure the formation of a legal employee relationship with platform technology companies (Xie 2022).

11   Organizing Digital and Platform Workers into Trade Unions

Scholars of the digital economy focus on the significant transformation of the work relationship under the platform economy and the challenges faced by laborers in the new economy contributing to higher levels of informality and precarious labor (Rani & Gobel 2023; Woodcock & Graham 2019). Unlike industrial or public sector employers, the rapacious platform economy has successfully insulated itself from trade unions and government regulations in both the West and most developing countries. In Western Europe and North America, existing trade unions do little more than publicly support the rights of digital workers. Consequently, some digital workers may engage in periodic stoppages and even fewer form autonomous associations and organizations.

Almost all established unions are severely lacking in the capacity to tangibly defend worker rights. Instead, they self-represent their interests through collectives, online forums and other nebulous organizations (Cini et al. 2021). At best, established unions are cooperative towards digital workers but most do not have the organizational power and resources to represent them. In the absence of union recognition among most workers in Europe, digital laborers protest only infrequently unless blatant abuses are perpetrated by technology firms. Certainly, if digital technology firms were to support organizing, unions would likely represent them (Vandaele 2018; Vandaele et al. 2024). However, historically it has been more common for unions to shun workers who could potentially be organized and mobilized since they are reluctant to recruit members who might unsettle their jurisdictional membership bases.

In *Global Labour Unrest on Platforms*, Trappmann et al. (2020) contend that, in sharp contrast to the belief that workers have a capacity to challenge highly capitalized firms, they are in fact intimidated and consigned to their powerlessness. Labor scholars Schmaltz, Ludwig and Webster (2019) consider the capacity to gain and wield power resources indispensable to effectively challenging global capitalism.

12   Case Study: Organizing New Economy Workers in Shanghai

To demonstrate the ACFTU's strong support for workers in the new economy, we look at Shanghai as representative of the country as a whole. The city has been selected as it reflects the progression of a distinct organizing model for digital workers in the ride hailing and food dealing industries by unions on street, district and municipal levels. The city has been among the first in China where ride hailing and delivery technology have expanded rapidly for new economy workers, a labor market which was previously unfamiliar to conventional forms of trade union labor mobilization and organization. The examples below will focus on the rollout of new digital companies, including: Snouqi, Shenzhou, Yidao and Meituan.

Shanghai, with nearly 25 million residents, is the second largest city in the world. It is dedicated to the improvement of an efficient and environmentally sustainable transportation system which corresponds to the economic, civic and ecological conditions of the city and region. As a directly administered municipality, Shanghai develops policies which are relevant to the quality of life in the city. A central element is advancing a transportation development scheme for Shanghai, an ongoing process which corresponds to evolving changes in the municipality.

In October 2022, the Shanghai Metropolitan Transportation Commission issued a *White Paper on Transportation Development in Shanghai* to develop an integrated system conforming with the national goal of advancing the economy and serving the people. The White Paper accentuated a "people-oriented" integrated transportation network to provide a range of convenient travel options benefiting all citizens, from youths to seniors and focusing on a "high-quality healthy life." To meet this goal, the document emphasized reliable travel options extending into the suburbs of the city. Central to the plan was unceasing improvement and integration of a unified taxi and ride hailing platform to supplement Shanghai's mass transportation system.

Digital platforms and logistical networks are central to plans to modernize booking and waiting stations, encouraging carpooling and emphasizing public transit to reduce dependence on automobile use. Shanghai's transportation plan is directed to "strengthen the integration of transportation space with the ecological environment," improving energy consumption, ecological protection and low-carbon emission. Logistics and driving are essential features in improving the working and living conditions of truck drivers and ride hailing and delivery workers (Shanghai Municipal Transportation Commission 2022).

To accomplish the task of developing a transportation system which focuses on human needs and ecological sustainability, the municipal government and the ACFTU recognized the imperative to improve and standardize the e-navigation platforms' wages and working conditions for their rapidly increasing labor force. As the digital platform economy has emerged and expanded rapidly, the ACFTU has had to respond quickly to the unique and distinctive needs of workers in an often-unregulated technology industry with few rules governing the status and conditions of drivers in the private sector. For antagonistic Labor Studies scholars in the West, the platform economy was a target for opprobrium as critics do not acknowledge the specific material conditions in the new industry that require the ACFTU to evaluate and respond effectively. Western Labor scholars ignore or do not recognize that the application of new technology to the natural world requires responding to the material needs of workers. These can of course only be diagnosed after workers have expressed concerns and grievances. Likewise, labor laws regulating an industry can only take place after they are perceptible by workers and the union.

In Shanghai, once the platform economy was introduced, the ACFTU responded quickly to address the economic and occupational concerns of workers. Most importantly, the ACFTU intervened to ensure that the industry (which had eschewed drivers as employees worldwide) recognized workers as employees and would allow it alone to negotiate agreements on their behalf once the employee relationship had been standardized. Undeniably, regularizing digital ride hailing drivers and delivery workers as employees is a painstaking process not without complications and instances of failure due to unforeseen circumstances. Independent contractors in this industry remain a challenge for the union, which must respond as and when workers agitate and appeal to it for help.

Shanghai's multiple unions at street and district levels have effectively and promptly responded to the demands of the city's mushrooming ride hailing workers, and in 2018 the city became the first in China to develop such representation, just over five years after the private platform economy was established. As workers in the private economy, or non-public enterprises, represent most of the labor force in China, the ACFTU has established policies to address worker concerns. First and foremost, a scientifically grounded Marxist perspective must diagnose technological innovation and then recognize the conditions of workers in the new economy. Some Western Labor Studies scholars do not consider that the organization of labor follows the application of technological change. Instead, they expect workers to oppose outcomes before they are applied to the workplace; a position which defies any grasp of political economy.

12.1 Essential Role of Shanghai's Digital Ride Hailing and Delivery Workers

In 2018, the ACFTU's 17th Congress highlighted the significance of "deepening trade union organizational work" in response to the challenges of applying new technology. Dongming Wang, ACFTU Chairman, emphasized that the five years between 2013 and 2018 had been marked by significant change.

These five years have seen the further enhancement of the political, progressive and mass character of trade union organizations and trade union work, the continuous advancement of rights protection and service work, the deepening of trade union reforms and the continuous strengthening of party building in the trade union system and the powerful demonstration of the role of trade unions in the overall work of the party and the country (Liang 2018).

A focal point of the Congress was to fulfill PRC General Secretary Xi Jinping's "Thought on Socialism with Chinese Characteristics for a New Era," focusing on the reform of trade unions in non-public enterprises, the establishment and membership of trade unions for employees and protecting their rights and interests and the construction of trade union teams to respond to the economic transformations in private firms, which employ most workers in the economy.

12.2   ACFTU Mobilization and Membership in Shanghai

In July 2016, two years before the ACFTU Trade Union Congress, the Shanghai Federation of Trade Unions (SFTU) had commenced pilot projects through the Baoshan District Trade Union to mobilize digital ride hailing workers and establish trade unions to safeguard rights and manage trade unions in non-public enterprises. Subsequently, 18 pilot unions were formed in enterprises, within communities, termed "street level unions," government development zones (Special Economic Zones) and in 16 districts under the governance of the Shanghai Municipal Federation of Trade Unions. In this way, the federation is dedicated to strengthening grassroots trade unions within non-public enterprises through devoting staff, funds and resources to organizing and enforcement (Liang 2018).

In contrast to the common practice among Western unions of organizing dues paying members into their unions only to disappear until the next round of collective bargaining negotiations with management, SFTU branches are actively involved in increasing services for what it calls "New Employment Forms of Workers." In April 2024, the Shanghai Qingpu Trade Union affiliate of the ACFTU established a specific legal-services center specifically for "New Employment Forms of Workers" within designated companies. For example, a legal supervision committee was formally established in the headquarters of Shanghai Yunda Express, a logistics services firm providing delivery services and road freight transportation. The committee offered couriers legal services and care packages, lawyers, legal education and rights-protection policies in the industry (Longxiang 2024).

12.3 China's First Digital Food Delivery Worker Trade Union

On January 1, 2016, the Putuo District Online Food Delivery Union Federation was established as China's first union of its kind at the headquarters of a food ordering platform for workers in third party delivery companies. It subsequently began at each food delivery station. The union formed in response to the decentralization and flexibilization of new forms of employment and the demand for representation to address critical work issues in the new sector. Before the formation of the food delivery union, the Shanghai Putuo District Trade Union had researched the essential conditions of online food delivery workers and strived to provide caring and targeted services to them, earning the trust of both platform enterprises and employees and rapidly expanding membership in this essential yet demanding, sector of the digital economy (Qian 2018). Consequently, before formation of the online food delivery workers union, SFTU conducted in-depth research by deploying a trade union organizer to "experience the life of an online food-delivery worker first-hand" through working as a driver for a platform. In advance of even working on the platform, in spite of working at breakneck speed, the union staff member could not meet the specified delivery times and learned that drivers were required to upload a personal photo, health certificate and pay a deposit of ¥100 RMB through the crowd sourcing platform. Once on the job, he experienced significant impediments to delivering to customers over 72 hours of work. In advance of the unionization, the SFTU researched employer practices, administered questionnaires and directly visited delivery stations to learn about the primary occupational concerns and dilemmas workers experienced on the job.

The SFTU conducted a comprehensive study of the nascent food delivery platform industry to discern the organizational structure, labor management, compensation and demographics of delivery riders in advance of commencing an organizational campaign. Unlike unions in the advanced capitalist countries, where a main objective is to recruit dues paying members, here the union conducted in-depth research to gain understanding of the material conditions in the industry and to appropriately represent and advance the concerns and interests of workers through unionization. The SFTU found the primary challenges for workers were "excessive flexibility, insufficient safety, and imperfect protection mechanisms." It then formulated a "protective umbrella" which would extend legal rights and protect the interests of workers. The advantage of the SFTU's affiliation with the Communist Party of China was that not only could it bargain over wages and working conditions but also enforce rights through promulgation of laws protecting workers' interests. Finally, SFTU Chairman Mo Fuchun hosted a seminar to research and study the employment conditions of online food delivery workers at Ele.me, the second largest online food delivery platform, headquartered in Shanghai. Ele.me was initially ambivalent about or opposed to the benefits of forming a trade union, apprehensive that it would increase labor costs and reduce profits (Hong 2014). But the SFTU and Putuo District Committee encouraged Ele.me to recognize the establishment of a delivery worker trade union, the Federation of Trade Unions of the Online Food Delivery Industry, representing 16,000 workers at third party companies operating in partnership with Ele.me in Shanghai (China News Service 2018; Qian 2018). The Shanghai Putuo Trade Union, a district branch, played a decisive role in the unionization of food delivery workers through exploring distinctive new models which are unique to the platform economy. Subsequently, districts, municipalities and provinces throughout China organized food delivery workers (Daily Worker 2022). As part of its effort to register food delivery workers, the ACFTU has formed a representative negotiation system with members employed at Ele.me, according to Li Ke, dean of the School of Labor Unions at China University of Labor Relations. The mobilization and enforcement plan encompasses labor law enforcement and dispute mediation (Ke 2025). The food delivery union is not a paper union, but standardizes compensation, provides labor rights protection, legal services, skill promotion, welfare and other member services. The task of organizing dispersed gig workers employed as subcontractors for Ele.me or Meituan is not equivalent to mobilizing and organizing typically enthusiastic and informed workers in state owned enterprises or even large-scale private manufacturers which had emerged and expanded in the 1990s.

12.4   Wuhu City Federation of Trade Unions Officials' Experiential Research

In compliance with the General Secretary Xi Jinping's directive to mobilize workers in new employment forms in logistics and the digital economy, ACFTU district trade union federations across China are conducting research to learn about the constraints which workers regularly encounter on the job. In August 2025, ten union officials of the Yijiang District Trade Union Federation (YDTUF) of Wuhu City in Anhui Province engaged in participant observation to directly experience the multiple challenges of food delivery workers. Through direct experience on the job, union officials became immersed in the daily work of food delivery workers. Zhang Chunliu trailed a food delivery worker to understand the day-to-day demands, which included completing 20 deliveries within two hours. She gained familiarity with the primary tasks of taking orders and fetching meals to transport to customers and learned that the job entailed multiple tasks that were complicated by significant logistical complications and physical work, including carrying food up several floors in apartment buildings without elevators in the hot summer and restrictions on riding bicycles in some residential complexes. The rules limit the number of orders which can be delivered and lower driver earnings. Other obstacles include bottlenecks during peak delivery times, as riders have to wait to pick up orders.

The comprehensive on-the-job research of union representatives of the YDTUF prompted the Anhui Provincial Federation of Trade Unions to expand its "grassroots immersion work" among workers in new forms of employment. The Wuhu City Federation of Trade Unions required all trade union officials to engage in mandatory "experiential research" among platform companies and industrial parks. This prompted the federations to establish pre-employment training schemes for new delivery riders, upgrading the amenities and services of union service stations and developing policies to allocate deliveries on platforms during peak delivery hours to limit order delays for union members. Engaging trade union officials in new forms of employment provided acute awareness of workers employed outside of office buildings and factories, with new policies to respond to their most vital concerns. Holistic trade unions reinforced their mission to protect the rights and expand the skills of workers (Hua 2025).

12.5   Trade Union Density Generates Worker Mobilization

The prodigious achievements of organizing "new employment forms" since 2018 have inspired the ACFTU and its constituent unions to consolidate and amplify mobilization in the digital economy throughout China. In December 2022, the ACFTU issued the "Guiding Opinions on Deepening the Work of 'Bottom-line Construction'" to codify standards in the sectors and to stimulate democratic management among workers to advance their demands, notably welfare benefits, subsidies, extra breaks during inclement weather conditions and other measures to protect workers. In 2021, the ACFTU launched a three-year union drive to build worker power among digital logistic workers, including truck drivers, ride hailing and food delivery workers. The campaign directed ACFTU representatives to directly respond to worker demands for union representation as well as to engage in a rigorous campaign to conduct research and organizing among workers in new employment forms. Three years later, in 2024, the campaign succeeded in organizing 18.3 million new union members among logistics, digital and new economy workers (SCIO 2025).

In practice, trade unions responded to expand democratic management among drivers. In August 2022, SFTU and YDFTU and their members prevailed on food delivery giant Meituan to increase democratic management among workers in "new employment forms." Similar initiatives have sprouted among unionized delivery workers at Ele.me, especially to create mechanisms to mediate disputes between workers and management and to raise compensation and improve conditions, physical examinations and preventative care. These were concerns particularly prevalent during the COVID-19 pandemic and extremely high temperatures, which exposed new-economy workers to high levels of risk while protecting vulnerable populations in need of services and delivery of food and essential supplies (Wang and Liang 2022).

In addition, the governments on the provincial and city level have bolstered labor mediation and negotiation to resolve labor disputes, notably for workers' claims against dispatch agencies. According to Chinese Workers (2024, 21), on the municipal level, nationwide, the Chinese dispute resolution program has given workers far more power, "breaking through the 'last mile' in resolving grassroots labor disputes" through addressing distinctive worker concerns rather than applying a uniform approach throughout the country (Chinese Workers, 22).

In Shanghai, trade union organizing in the digital sector is pervasive and ongoing and new unions are formed to directly represent workers in diverse sectors of the economy. In December 2024, the Pudong Express Industry Trade Union Federation held its first congress. The Pudong District Union actively encourages workers in "new employment forms" to join to improve and standardize their earnings and working conditions (Jing'an News 2024a).

For Labor Studies scholars submerged in Western labor organizing models which are often platitudinous, lackluster and mostly theoretical in nature, the Shanghai online food delivery organizing campaigns, which significantly improved wages, benefits and working conditions, provide tangible evidence of improving the lives of workers which are almost never organized in Western Europe and North America. The examples of successful organizing in Shanghai and other municipalities throughout China demonstrate that, almost always, the workers, trade unions and the CPC have popular support and can marshal collective resources to compel private companies to adhere to decent labor standards. If the power resources are insufficient to resist rapacious managers in the private sector, the ACFTU and its constituent unions are persistently adapting their mobilization strategies to increase the power of workers. Capacity is a significant feature of successful organizing campaigns, and the widespread success of bottom-up and top-down organizing demonstrates that power resources are derived from the rank and file, as well as local community demands to upgrade services through improving the wages and working conditions of digital workers. Undoubtedly, the success of organizing digital platform workers is also engrained in the nature of a socialist workers' state, the CPC and ACFTU trade unions, all of which are dedicated to empowering and improving the lives of workers.

The ACFTU has flourished through high trade union density in Shanghai. In many respects, Shanghai is an unparalleled international union city as high density encourages an acceleration of trade union organizing and membership among non-union workers in the non-public enterprises which proliferate across the city. Workers in Shanghai and throughout China are not required to join unions but are highly motivated to do so by their grassroots nature, which regards digital workers respectfully and responds to the personal and economic needs of workers and their families in the digital economy. As advanced by Jane McAlevey (2018), "whole union organizing" through building meaningful relations with workers and communities has not been adopted by trade unions in the US but is a pervasive practice in the Baoshan District of Shanghai and throughout China. When grassroots unions encourage non-unionized employees to join unions, even among "micro-enterprises" with only 10–20 employees, it stimulates growth and enhances the power of workers who have subsequently been able to augment their technological skills.

As ride hailing drivers have proliferated in Shanghai and other Chinese cities, trade unions have formed in buildings, streets, parks, communities and villages. For those drivers in the digital economy in Shanghai too busy to sign up, trade unions facilitate organization and membership through the convenience of the Shengongshe app and WeChat. These simplify organization into nine district-level trade unions, facilitating services for workers in domestic services, logistics, delivery, medical care and online meal delivery, freight delivery and so on across the districts of the Shanghai Municipal Federation of Trade Unions (Liang 2018).

In April 2024, the Shanghai Putuo District ACFTU formed the first online car hailing industry trade union federation in the Shanghai region, representing more than 2,000 online car hailing drivers. This is poles apart from the experiences of established union organizing worldwide. The enthusiasm for having a delivery union which includes benefits and common activities is palpable. According to Mr. Feng, a driver from nearby Anhui Province:

> I have been driving online car-hailing cars in Shanghai for 8 years and I have been driving for Jugao for 5 years. After arriving here, I feel very different, especially the Xinyang Park has been provided us with warmth during the Mid-Autumn

> Festival and Lantern Festival and organizing cultural and sports activities. When I learned that I could join the union, I signed up early. … Joining the union will help us coordinate and resolve driving disputes, rights protection, personal medical insurance, social security and other aspects in the future. It is much better than being in the dark! (Shanghai City Spirit 2024)

The Shanghai logistics firm values the presence of a union which creates an experienced, professional and stable workforce with modern facilities in which to take breaks and eat hot meals and which has plans to expand to offer professional skills training, haircuts and other trade union benefits, as drivers maintain the security of a stable income. When drivers' vehicles are damaged or under repair, management provides replacement vehicles to prevent loss of wages. Unequivocal trade union support for ride hailing drivers in Shanghai is expanding. For example, in September 2024, during the Mid-Autumn Festival, Didi Shanghai signed a "Model Workers and Craftsman Assisting Enterprises" agreement with the Shanghai Jing'an District Federation of Trade Unions. This expanded services and benefits in collaboration with Didi Shanghai to assist with personal matters, career development, health protections and "multi-dimensional trade union services for drivers" (Jing'an News 2024b).

The ACFTU district unions in Shanghai effectively negotiated improved labor conditions for digital workers, especially ride hailing and food delivery workers who suffer from extreme heat and humidity in the summer. During the summer, due to the extreme levels of heat, drivers typically have more customers and are typically working longer hours. To ameliorate the effects of the high temperature and cope with the humidity, in July 2024, the Jing'an District Federation of Trade Unions and the Pengpu Town Federation of Trade Unions, local union affiliates of the ACFTU in Shanghai, requested that Didi, China's leading ride hailing technology company, build 20 cooling stations so drivers could take breaks and receive refreshments in a pleasant atmosphere with cool cushions. The trade union also requested that automobiles have air conditioning for both drivers and passengers and requested that Didi subsidize the cost of using air conditioners in vehicles through sharing in the energy costs of operating the vehicles (Chen 2024).

In sharp contrast to the symbiotic relationship between trade unions and platform workers in China, Western ride hailing and delivery workers unreservedly strive for trade union representation but are shunned due to legal and organizational barriers as well as a proclivity among trade unions for organizing only among employers (with substantial numbers of potential members) who will not oppose unionization, thus adding to the union coffers through union dues. The outcome is the creation of well-meaning yet ineffectual associations termed "indie unions." These primarily serve to boost the spirits of defenseless workers who have little option but to quit rather than remain gainfully employed in the new industries.

13 Trade Union Organization of Logistics and Trucking Workers

As the Chinese labor market shifts from manufacturing towards logistics and delivery as a consequence of robotization and investment in highly productive means of production, the rapidly rising labor market of trucking workers is considered by the ACFTU of significant importance. The ACFTU is relentlessly adjusting to the transformation of the Chinese labor market on national, provincial and municipal levels to foster organizing strategies to facilitate mobilization and unionization. In logistics and trucking, an industry which is also dominated by the platform economy is growing rapidly throughout China. Consequently, the ACFTU is devoting resources and staff to research the demands of workers. Through multifaceted dialogue with truckers in the industry and studying the unique nature of their everyday jobs, it aims to shape strategies which best suit the subjective interests of workers throughout the country. The rapid growth of the National Truck Drivers Union (NTDU) in China is emblematic of the prodigious endeavors of the ACFTU to ascertain and grasp the most significant concerns in the burgeoning industry and to mobilize workers into the union. On July 28, 2025, Ma Zhengqiu of the ACFTU reported that the NTDU had grown to 5.9 million voluntary members. The massive scale of organizing is reflected in the statement of Vice Chairman Zhengqiu at the Ministry of Transport in the most recent ACFTU report:

> Currently 12,000 new business trade union federations have been established at the municipal and county levels across China and leading platform companies in the road freight industry have achieved near-complete unionization at their headquarters and provincial branches. (Wu 2025)

To fathom the significant consolidation of the NTDU, it is essential to underscore that workers in China are *not* required to join trade unions but sign up voluntarily. To simplify organizing truckers and logistical workers, the NTDU has established a "Workers' Home" app and have set up unionization bases where truck drivers frequently park and rest, as well as other locations where they congregate. The union also draws on existing networks of truckers to establish and enforce wage, benefit and working condition procedures which assist them, including accident insurance, medical examinations at no charge and legal assistance. These campaigns have succeeded in mobilizing new members. The NTDU and ACFTU expect to mobilize over 600,000 truck drivers into unions in 2025 alone, the vast majority working for platform enterprises. Consequently, Zhengqiu emphasizes the magnitude of "building in key areas, building in industries and building as a safety net to promote platform enterprise unions to directly absorb workers in new employment forms into platform enterprise unions." Accordingly, the NTDU has developed the proficiency of organizing logistics and trucking workers directly through platform enterprises. She adds, "We will build on the previous work of 'building in key areas, building in industries and building as a safety net' to promote platform enterprise unions to directly absorb workers in new employment forms into platform enterprise unions" (Wu 2025).

14 Conclusion: Anti-China Propaganda and ACFTU Exceptionalism

Around the world, the formation of new technology firms using digitized communication has made the employer–labor relationship redundant. National governments have supported such companies and trade union responses have been lackluster at best. Almost everywhere in the capitalist West, digital workers have had no representation. The development of telecommunication through the mobile phone has in large measure established a new relationship between capital and labor and transformed the study of labor relations. In the 2000s, the emergence of the platform economy made it possible to use labor without establishing a direct relationship between the firm and worker. The platform economy expanded across the globe and shifted the obligation of directly paying labor for its services. According to the capitalist, such workers were in business for themselves but in reality, they were tethered to their apps, and technology companies could operate through algorithms which allowed them to provide services without the firm or company as the intermediary. Almost immediately, the labor–management relationship was broken, and technology companies became intermediaries between drivers and customers, extracting surplus value from workers.

In clear contrast to capitalist economies, in China, the ACFTU-affiliated trade unions have rapidly responded to driver needs through engaging in comprehensive labor market research, learning from workers about abuses and engaging with drivers to represent their concerns. Notwithstanding, most Western Labor scholars have disregarded this significant trade union participation in improving the conditions of workers through mobilization and unionization.

Undoubtedly, the emergence of technology companies has formed a new political economy which undermines the organizational power of workers through unions in capitalist and socialist countries. Yet, the literature on China, frequently advanced by self-proclaimed socialists and social-democrats, only recognizes capital and workers without recognizing that the Chinese state, CPC and the ACFTU advance holistic trade unionism through bottom-up and top-down practices. Both have the legal authority and capacity to determine the relationship between them. Such scholars do not consider the unique capability of socialist party trade unions (Chen 2018; Franceschini & Sorace 2022; Yuan & Zhang 2025). Numerous academic journals have proliferated in the last 20 years for the express purpose of disparaging the prodigious accomplishments of China under market socialism. Often embedded in leftist terminology, they are oblivious to the continuity of the PRC as a socialist workers' state and its undeniable expansion of labor rights and conditions from 2012 to the present. Scholarly articles from each of the aforementioned scholars engage in inconceivable disparaging rhetoric and are transparently advanced to oppose the ACFTU. They are alluded to for the purpose of demonstration, collectively contending that the trade union federation is non-responsive and even not a union at all.

In the context of labor relations, Western Marxist opponents of the ACFTU and its constituent unions neglect the latter's significant accomplishments in defending the Chinese rural and urban working class, even as major studies from the ILO and scholars within China show a remarkable capacity to organize workers in the new economy. Typically, focusing on shortcomings, these Western critics neglect the complications arising from a materialist perception of the unfolding changes which ineluctably occur in the real world. In fact, the ACFTU and its affiliate unions have continued to advance the Leninist and Maoist model of trade unionism devoted to protecting and expanding the skills and rights of the Chinese working class. In contrast to Western advanced capitalist states and most developing states, the Chinese model of trade unionism tirelessly responds to the complex needs of workers in a modernizing global economy.

Workers, Subjectivity and Holistic Trade Unions

> Changes in society are due chiefly to the development of the internal contradictions in society, that is, the contradiction between the productive forces and the relations of production, the contradiction between classes and the contradiction between the old and the new; it is the development of these contradictions that pushes society forward and gives the impetus for the suppression of the old society by the new. (Mao Zedong (1945) On Contradiction, *Selected Works*, Vol. I, 314)

1 Trade Unions and the Principal Contradiction

How do Chinese trade unions organize and represent workers to build working class power? To answer this crucial question, this chapter seeks to measure the efficacy of the All-China Federation of Trade Unions (ACFTU) through interviews with workers and stakeholders. It measures efficacy in the context of three considerations which are drawn from Mao Zedong's analysis of historical materialism, rooted in the concept of the principal contradiction (Mao Tse-Tung/Mao Zedong 1945).

To claim that the nature of capitalism, imperialism, the state and globalization are static fails to recognize dialectical materialism as the driving force in history. Mao's analysis of contradiction advances the concept of the principal contradiction which is inflected by dialectical materialism, where history always alters material conditions and class struggles.

Decidedly, under capitalism, the principal contradiction in the production process, the extraction of surplus labor, is transformed by the modification of material conditions which occur through dialectical materialism and is not temporally or spatially fixed. Modification of production directly transforms the relations of production within every phase of capitalism. Thus, for Mao:

> According to materialist dialectics, changes in nature are due chiefly to the development of the internal contradictions in nature. Changes in society are due chiefly to the development of the internal contradictions in society, that is, the contradiction between the productive forces and the relations of production, the contradiction between classes and the contradiction between the old

and the new; it is the development of these contradictions that pushes society forward and gives the impetus for the supersession of the old society by the new. (Mao Zedong 1945, 314)

Unequivocally, if new technology is integrated into the production process through the introduction of modern means of production within the labor process, the relations of production between owner and worker will also change. The subsumption of capital into the development of modern machinery, instruments and robotics will almost always increase the reserve army of labor. But it will also increase productivity and demand for skilled workers. Conversely, preserving obsolete machines to protect workers may also eventually generate unemployment and the erosion of the capacity of a state to modernize as industrial production becomes inefficient. However, it is mistaken to be certain that workers will not resist through class struggle.

For Mao, the principal contradiction is not always apparent and is conditioned by secondary contradictions, such as the opposing forces of capitalism and feudalism or owners and workers.

> [I]n capitalist society the two forces in contradiction, the proletariat and the bourgeoisie, form the principal contradiction. The other contradictions, such as those between the remnant feudal class and the bourgeoisie, between the peasant petty bourgeoisie and the bourgeoisie, between the proletariat and the peasant petty bourgeoisie, between the non-monopoly capitalists and the monopoly capitalists, between bourgeois democracy and bourgeois fascism, among the capitalist countries and between imperialism and the colonies, are all determined or influenced by this principal contradiction. ... In a semi-colonial country such as China, the relationship between the principal contradiction and the non-principal contradictions presents a complicated picture. (Mao Zedong 1945, 331)

Under Chinese market socialism today, the introduction of new machines does contribute to unemployment for those who are not trained in new skills. As redundant labor enters the labor market, they enter new jobs that do not provide equivalent wages and working conditions. But within China's socialist market economy, the ACFTU must also revise its organizing strategies to correspond to the emergence of new industries without wages and conditions equivalent to those in manufacturing. During this interregnum, the ACFTU must research and study the emerging industries to identify and apply effective strategies to improve wages, benefits and conditions.

Under the Chinese socialist market economy, the ACFTU is obligated to create conditions which strengthen the workers' state as envisioned in 1949, at the founding of the People's Republic of China (PRC) by the Communist Party of China (CPC). But how does the Chinese working class direct the policies of the state? Torkil Lauesen, echoing Mao Zedong and Xi Jinping, asserts that as a workers' state, in the final analysis, the PRC operates in the interest of the working class. Lauesen applies the principal contradiction to grasp how China remains a workers' state despite the presence of class differences between employers seeking profit and surplus value and workers:

> The changing principal contradiction has been the main reason for the shifting course of the CPC against the headwind of the capitalist world system. If capitalism is controlled, it can contribute to the development of the productive forces and better conditions for building a socialist society. But for this to happen, it is of vital importance that the working class and the peasantry retain state power. The "opening up" of China created capitalist billionaires, but as a class, they do not rule the country. (Lauesen 2024, 269)

For Mao Zedong, the principal contradiction is always subject to change within a socialist state, and while the working class may have setbacks, the long-term objective of the Communist Party and the state is to achieve socialism which represents the distinctive historical development and practices of China, or "socialism with Chinese characteristics," a concept which is misunderstood by foreigners (Boer 2022).

The principal contradiction's transformations are based on fundamental international and internal challenges. Since 1949, Chinese Communists have persistently strived to modernize and build a modern economy and have encountered opportunities and challenges. In 1978, under Deng Xiaoping, China shifted towards market socialism to modernize economically through encouraging investment in technology, a process which unfolded over nearly 50 years. This era has not been monolithic but has instead comprised contingent responses aimed at improving the country's working class conditions and standard of living. To understand the labor movement's changes, it is necessary to recognize the phases of the opening up rather than envisioning an unbroken period of continuity. Throughout, the ACFTU has had to adapt to the transformation of the material conditions and relations of production and distribution in response to modernization and technological change while ensuring that the working class persists as the dominant social force. At the outset, opening up indeed led to adversity for a preponderant rural population bonded to agriculture and subsistence. Subsequently, the ACFTU was pressed to address the challenge of a floating population migrating from rural to urban regions and it remains dutifully committed to meeting changing requirements as the economy has shifted from agrarian to manufacturing and digital labor. Today, China's heterogeneous economy remains rooted in the land, retains a large manufacturing sector, and in the last decade has branched out to the digital sector. The ACFTU must thus distinguish agrarian, industrial and digital workers with diverse needs yet collectively sharing analogous class subjectivity and interests.

The second consideration entails understanding how the ACFTU mobilizes the working class as a collective force and maintains socialist power to advance its interests. Under market socialism, the ACFTU must organize workers in the public and private sectors of the economy. The public sector controls the principal heights of the state, which reveals China's socialist nature; most of the Chinese economy is dominated by state owned enterprises (SOEs) even if most workers are employed by private enterprises. Yet, workers employed in SOEs comprise only 20 percent of all laborers in the urban economy. About 80 percent of China's workers are employed in the burgeoning private sector. Certainly, the private sector is dependent on state investment to modernize and advance technology. However, workers in private sector firms tend to have less secure jobs as technological change fashions new realities. The ACFTU must ceaselessly represent the population and improve the condition of workers, as the subjectivities of workers in China are not the same, and economic change has a direct influence on those who find themselves in different circumstances based on their training, education and status as workers with employee contracts or as third party contractors. The ACFTU must strive to hold every employer accountable for providing workers with direct contracts. However, as this is not the case, the ACFTU is permanently addressing these changes and striving to keep up with new forms of employment (NFE), as seen especially in the period from 2015 to 2025.

Finally, the archival and ethnographic research will show how Chinese workers measure up to workers throughout the world and provide an indication of how the Chinese labor movement compares to workers worldwide. The directive of the ACFTU is to mobilize workers within the context of market socialism. In this context, the research examines the holistic nature of the ACFTU and shows that it is based on bottom-up activism, top-down investigation, analysis and remedies that are consistent with the class interests of China's working class. In this way, this chapter helps demonstrate how Chinese workers organize through the ACFTU.

Chinese workers, like all other workers, organize themselves, and the ACFTU mobilizes them to build trade union power through a socialist mobilization of power resources to achieve their demands and improve wages, working conditions, social insurance and pensions through unified bottom-up and top-down power supremacy. In the West, ideas of bottom-up organizing are advanced to demonstrate that workers are engaged in self-activity. Yet, it is not sufficient to have only bottom-up organizing in the absence of a strong and vibrant trade union organization (Schmalz et al. 2019).

The research is intended to elucidate how the ACFTU and the Chinese trade union organization can effectively utilize strategic approaches to foster worker mobilization which both recognizes worker aspirations and achieves the improvement of their wages, working conditions and social insurance.

2 Holistic Trade Unions and Top-Down and Bottom-Up Organizations

In the West, notably the US, the labor movement has steadily declined from 35 percent of all workers in the 1950s to 10 percent today. In response to the decline, a multitude of strategic responses have been advanced, from rank-and-file bottom-up organizing to stem the downturn and increase membership and union density to increasing the financial resources and centralized power and discipline of the union to practically impose unionization. Others advocated mobilizing migrant workers, increasing worker democracy in unions, on-the-job collective action and striking as antidotes to increase membership or labor–management cooperation and concessionary bargaining (Ashby 2022; Milkman & Wong 2001).

From 2015 to the present, as the power-resource model has largely failed, the dominant approach to labor unions among Western leftists has centered on fostering anarchic and autonomous rank-and-file participation and jettisoning notions of building resilient and durable unions as an alternative to existing bureaucratic unionism. As attempts to construct powerful and disciplined unions through devoting resources to organizing have been unsuccessful for the first two decades of the 21st century, organized labor is on the defensive worldwide. In the US, Supreme Court rulings have eroded labor union power in the public sector, the mainstay of organized labor. In 2025, US president Donald Trump has prohibited trade unions among federal workers, a policy which has done away with collective bargaining for more than 1 million federal workers, encompassing 1 out of 15 union members in more than 12 US agencies (Glass 2025; McCartin 2025). The Trump Administration's attack against trade unions representing workers in federal agencies has further eroded working class confidence in established unions. The widespread erosion in the capacity of existing trade unions has shifted scholarly interest towards spontaneous collective action in the absence of unions. Some critics have suggested that trade unions are spent organizations which have been overtaken by insurrections, anarchistic riots and, more recently, a fetish which should be dispensed with as a defining standard of working class organization (Atzeni 2021; Clover 2016). The elevation of anarchist and spontaneous forms of worker organization reflects the breakdown of trade unions in the West. In contrast, the Chinese holistic approach to trade unions encourages democratic working class self-activity while establishing strong and effective unions.

Since 2000, as trade unions worldwide have been in free fall, Labor Studies scholars have begun to advance the concept of bottom-up mobilization as an alternative to top-down organizing. The concept is based on the belief that trade unions had not previously attended to the demands of workers in and out of unions but had advanced their own self-interest through growing their memberships. The increase in variously termed "bottom-up organizing," "whole-union organizing," and "worker-to-worker organizing" suggests that working class enthusiasm for trade unions had declined and these new methods were essential if labor was to organize into unions and improve standards of living and working conditions. Bottom-up and whole-union organizing denote that trade unions allow workers (both those in their unions and the majority of workers who remain outside them) to engage in common activities to advance their interests, and that trade unions strive to understand the daily lives of workers (Lynd & Lynd 2012; McAlevey 2018). Some scholars have asserted that on-the-job actions independent of unions and strikes exemplify the best of bottom-up organizing, implying that all significant transformation is a consequence of workers and movements rather than organizations and parties (Blanc 2025; Loomis 2018). As trade unions have continued to decline into the 2020s, Labor scholar Maurizio Atzeni maintains that the importance of trade unions is overstated and constitutes a form of "trade union fetishism" which does not reflect the interests of the working class. Thus, the organizational and ideological power should be discarded and replaced by foregrounding spontaneous working class "struggle" against capital (Atzeni 2021). This anarchistic form of organizing certainly occurs through spontaneous activity of the working class in every workplace, but the idea of abandoning trade unions is equivalent to discarding organization of any kind. This was a perspective which had been advanced by anarchists, in the early 20th century, but it was rejected by Lenin in *What Is to Be Done?* as antithetical to forming working class consciousness and effective organizations, and liable to culminate in an economism which negated the significance of the working class (Lenin [1902] 2020).

However, when bottom-up organizing or class-struggle unionism which is associated with higher levels of democracy and workers' control over their own destinies precludes strong and vigorous trade unions which direct labor in organizing trade unions in the interest of workers, considering the retrospective efforts to place worker self-activity against organizational capacity is a false construct. It evokes the altruistic yet ineffective Industrial Workers of the World (IWW), an insurgent trade union of the early 20th century as well as contemporary anarchist variants today, which encourage rank-and-file unionism in the absence of robust organization. Historian Melvyn Dubofsky shows that class struggle unionism in the absence of a strong revolutionary organization is destined to failure:

> Wobbly doctrine taught workers how to gain short-range goals indistinguishable from those sought by ordinary, nonrevolutionary trade unions. Able to rally exploited workers behind crusades to abolish specific grievances, the IWW failed to transform its followers' concrete grievances into a higher consciousness of class, ultimate purpose, and necessary revolution—to create, in short, a revolutionary working class in the Marxist sense. (Dubofsky 2000, 269)

Contrast the amorphous IWW organizational structure with the democratic and still revolutionary trade unionism of the ACFTU. On June 9, 2025, Wang Chun, chairman of the Shanxi Provincial Federation of Trade Unions, identified the key tasks of building holistic unionism through bottom-up democracy and top-down power resources and channeling the spontaneous democratic dynamism into concrete gains for the working class:

> First, we must focus on ideological and political guidance to further consolidate the common ideological foundation for the unity and struggle of industrial workers; second, we must focus on democratic management to better safeguard the status of industrial workers as masters of their own destiny; third, we must focus on skill enhancement to gradually improve the skill formation system for industrial workers; fourth, focus on growth and development to create a three-dimensional career development space for industrial workers; fifth, focus on rights protection and services to enhance the sense of achievement, gain, and happiness of industrial workers; sixth, focus on making contributions to the cause to give full play to the leading role of industrial workers; and seventh, focus on expanding the workforce to continuously consolidate the class foundation and mass foundation for the Party's long-term governance. (Li, Y. 2025)

3   Chinese Trade Unions

Chinese and socialist trade unions diverge significantly from the prevailing models in Western capitalist states. While both strive to build working class power, their doctrinal forms differ and are predicated on the distinct class natures of capitalist and socialist states. The model of trade unionism which emerged in the West in the early 20th century and continues today is established on the basis of "pure and simple unionism" and the domination of capitalists over workers. Labor economist Selig Perlman celebrates trade unionism under US capitalism as the outstanding form of union representation, viewing improved wages and working conditions on the job as the unchanging and persistent aspiration of the American worker since the formation in 1886 of the American Federation of Labor (AFL) under the leadership of Samuel Gompers. To Perlman, labor's methods, even outside the immediate vicinity of the job interest:

> show no more change than can be accounted for by the changing environment. This steadiness of labor's self-integration into the evolving American society is of significance, not only to the labor movement itself and to its theorists, but even more importantly, for its defense of democracy against totalitarianism. As labor in this country utterly rejects any idea of "class hegemony," it is thus a bulwark of the principle of "unity in diversity," upon which Western civilization rests. (Perlman 1951, 63)

The rigid and self-interested stance of labor organizations under capitalism in the US and the West foreshadows the eventual decline of trade unions from the 1980s to the present in the US and the world. Certainly, trade unions have formed as opposing models to resist the archaic "pure and simple unionism," but most have been forbidden by the state or deemed "against the law" by liberal bourgeois states, notably the United Electrical Workers in the US. In the 1970s and 1980s, activists sought to transform unions into progressive or even revolutionary organizations, but almost all these formations were suppressed by the state or by leaders advancing Perlman's "pure and simple" unionism which had predominated and defeated movements for more expansive equality. Pure and simple unionism implies that unions should place rank-and-file workers' pragmatic economic demands over more ideological social and political concerns of building working class power. However, as economic demands had become dominant from the 1920s to advance the material interests of their own members, US trade unions abandoned any pretense of class politics and working class trade union solidarity.

4   China's Holistic Trade Unionism

The general critique of bottom-up enterprise trade unionism by Labor Studies scholars who oppose China is based on a partiality to the Western model of unionism which opposes any constructive developments of the ACFTU and its affiliate unions since China's opening up and introduction of market socialism in 1978. Not one research study and interpretative article in the references originates from outside the West. Moreover, Elaine Sio-leng Hui and Chris King-chi Chan (2015) exclude the work of authoritative Chinese scholars and even US researchers who, at minimum, acknowledge the swift pace of authentic trade union organization which is initiated, on the one hand, through worker demands for higher wages, benefits and improved working conditions within public and private enterprises, and on the other hand by the organizing campaigns which originate through the ACFTU and its industrial affiliates on all geographic levels. The inherent bias can be found in the article's use of references, which value only Western sources critiquing the ACFTU.

In contrast, the holistic-union approach to organizing (bottom-up from workers and top-down from the trade unions) aims to combine building power at the workplace with the support of workers, local and regional unions, the ACFTU and the Chinese state. Western Labor Studies scholars dismiss democratic trade union elections in China, falsely contending that union elections have always been a top-down process controlled by the ACFTU and the CPC. In effect, Western Labor scholars claim that no matter what the trade union federation does to support workers, it is incapable of addressing worker demands. However, Hui and Chan (2015) found evidence of the emergence of bottom-up union elections from 2010 to 2014. This development was viewed derisively from the Western standpoint as trade unions, employers, and the Chinese state were also involved in a tripartite system which they deemed to be advancing top-down influence over the unions. This analytic perspective advanced the ideal union to be bottom-up rather than top-down, a view which has increasingly been promoted by Western scholars. Consequently, they found the Chinese model to fall short of their ideal of union democracy, a concept which had been put forward among scholars in the 1990s as trade unions were in decline in advanced capitalist countries of the West (Lynd & Lynd 2012).

In place of viewing a strong supportive union as advancing rank-and-file democracy through engaging worker demands and seeking to expand their rights, Western advocates for greater union democracy, while well-meaning, have neglected the question of building union power, or the power resources approach put forward by Schmaltz, Ludwig and Webster in their prominent intervention on building the efficacy and capacity of trade unions (2018). The power resources approach examined the reservoir of organizational influence which would contribute to successful unionization. However, bottom-up researchers have all but neglected the question of union power in an era when Western and world trade unions have been in free fall because of the weakness of unions vis-à-vis employers under neoliberal policies within increasingly rapacious capitalist states.

To critics of the ACFTU, it is impossible for the Federation to sufficiently advance the interests of labor in a state which is directed at improving the conditions of the working class. The China Labor Bulletin (CLB), an NGO supported by US and Western governments and private NGOs (1994–June 2025), is the most prominent example of the absolutist position that every ACFTU initiative is flawed. Even as the CLB acknowledged that the ACFTU and its affiliates had conducted democratic elections, it warned against the potential of possible trade union intrusion in unions, or what should be viewed as the ACFTU's facilitation of elections and commitment to union democracy at the grassroots level. Notably, the CLB was often cited as the authoritative source by Western corporate media, including the *Wall Street Journal*, the *New York Times*, the *Guardian* and others. Like anti-PRC NGOs based in Hong Kong, the media published false narratives without corroboration from actual sources in China (Wong 2021). A mark of the ACFTU's success was the closure of leading NGOs like the CLB, funded by USAID. The CLB claimed to be monitoring strikes but was based on misleading information provided by informants in China who traveled to Hong Kong for training by CLB's staff. Undeniably, funds to operate the CLB were withdrawn by USAID in spring 2025 in part because of the NGO's failure to stimulate mass strikes in China. If the CLB, the most prominent labor NGO to have monitored Chinese labor activity, had been effective, the withdrawal of funds would not have caused it to fail in its effort to motivate collective action by the working class in opposition to the ACFTU and the PRC. Instead, an effective trade union organization enjoys legitimacy among all strata of the broader Chinese working class. Most CLB and other Western Hong Kong based NGO activities had centered around unprovable critiques about unprovable ACFTU manipulation of elections, and labor disputes that were exacerbated by NGOs like the July 2018 protests disrupting production organized by the Western NGO-funded Migrant Workers Center at the Jasic Technology Co. in Shenzhen. The dispute over overtime wages and formation of a trade union came after the Pingshan District Trade Union of the ACFTU had already begun organizing an enterprise union at the firm.[1] These events were typically organized in Hong Kong through agitating a handful of workers who were given false information about labor law which did not inform them of China's extensive wage-complaint mediation and arbitration process involving the extensive system of government administrative labor courts.[2] The failure of the CLB to document any systematic and authentic violations of Chinese labor law by the ACFTU was the primary reason for CLB's decision to terminate operations (Leung 2025; RFA Cantonese 2025; Stevenson 2025).

Western NGOs apply a strictly Western perspective of trade unionism, as if all other formations of trade unionism fall short of the ideal model: a weak, independent trade union which operates within the contours of a capitalist market economy. Western labor academics engage in damning indictments of Chinese trade unions irrespective of the latter's achievements.

---

1   In July 2018, a small group of workers were pressured by an employee of a Western-funded NGO, Labor Force, to seek overtime wages and holiday pay, culminating in protests by several workers at the Jasic Technology factory in Shenzhen in July. According to reporters at the scene, the workers protested, held banners, stormed the factory and temporarily interrupted production. Subsequently, 19 members of the organization also stormed the local police station demanding the release of five organizers. All 24 were released within one or two days after receiving reprimands and warnings from authorities. But protesters returned to the police station and received extensive coverage on WeChat and other social media platforms. However, the NGO organized event gained the support of Chinese university students who had been acclaimed in the West. But the disruption by the workers organized by the Labor Force NGO was primarily designed to receive external consumption and discredit the union. The Western NGO achieved its goal in engineering an international controversy and gaining significant Chinese and Western media attention on news platforms and websites promoting opposition to the ACFTU. After the incident, Jasic workers said the NGO misinformed them about availability of an official legal dispute system which would resolve the dispute. Even before the incident, in May 2018, the Pingshan District Trade Union intervened and was resolving the worker complaints and facilitating the formation of an enterprise-level trade union at Jasic. The union also provided advice to Jasic about complying with labor law (Xinhua News Agency 2018). Predictably, the incident proved to be fodder for Western antagonists of the ACFTU, whose evidence was based on hearsay and false and distorted details of the event from the foreign news media and US government funded NGOs like Human Rights Watch and anti-China university activists.

2   As a participant observer, the author had access to NGO funded opponents of the PRC in Hong Kong who were hostile towards China. The organizations include the China Labour Bulletin, Asia Monitor Research Centre and China Globalization Monitor among others, from 2014 to 2021.

In 2010, the ACFTU advanced a position of supporting proactive trade unionism directed at forming and fortifying trade unions in the private enterprise sector of the economy comprising 75–80 percent of China's workforce.

> The ACFTU has comprehensively analyzed the actual work of enterprise trade unions and unanimously agreed that enterprise trade unions are an important organizational and working basis for our country's trade unions. With the deepening of reform and opening up and the development of the socialist market economy, our country's economic relations and labor relations are becoming more complex, and enterprise trade unions are facing many new situations and new challenges. Trade unions at all levels must further enhance their political awareness, awareness of the overall situation, awareness of potential dangers, and sense of responsibility, earnestly implement the working principle of enterprise trade of promoting enterprise development and safeguarding the rights and interests of employees, unifying their thinking, strengthening confidence, and working hard to build enterprise trade unions into a home that employees trust. (GZU Faculty and Staff Union 2010)

But proponents of the Western model of trade unionism felt this was not good enough. In 2015, Labor scholars Hui and Chan suggested that the ACFTU's decision to assist fledgling enterprise unions was tantamount to interference with bottom-up organizing and would halt the upsurge in rank-and-file unions and direct elections in the private sector which they saw as a positive development and revealing a rise in bottom-up trade unionism in China (Hui & Chan 2015).

According to Hui and Chan, the ACFTU is promoting democratic, bottom-up unionization of workers through advancing transparency, worker democracy and local control over union affairs. Notably, they seek to discredit the ACFTU's proposals to strengthen democracy and transparency through local elections and honoring the decisions of union members in enterprise unions, as well as initiatives to curb corruption by encouraging "workers' directors and workers' supervisors" to disclose it.

> Large-scale enterprises should improve the union-organization network, establish union branches, union groups and union activist teams and strengthen the construction of female employee organizations in enterprise unions. They should respect the dominant position of members, adhere to the member (representative) congress system and the permanent member representative system, promote openness of union affairs, and continuously improve the cohesion of the enterprise unions. (GZU Faculty and Staff Union 2010)

Drawing exclusively on the omnipresent Western sources critical of the PRC, Hui and Chan ignore its nature as a socialist state. They assert that the shortcomings of the ACFTU lie specifically in the effort to build an effective system of accountability within the local and regional trade unions, the ACFTU and enterprise managers and to advance training of representatives through "trade union universities." Western critics deliberately ignore the ACFTU policies [d]irected at the "construction of the socialist core value system" and "enthusiastically advanced "the great character of the working class" within enterprise unions (GZU Faculty and Staff Union 2010). The dominant literature from opponents in the West prefers to depict a spectacle of conflict within socialism over accountability, class consciousness, worker democracy codified by the ACFTU and CPC and local control of enterprise unions.

5   The Chinese Working Class Today

The *Annual Report on the Status of Chinese Workers* for 2023 shows that employed workers dropped from 51.16 percent of the labor force in 2021 to 49.89 percent in 2022, a decline which has continued from 2014 to the present. However, consideration of this decline must consider that the population in urban areas is growing (Chinese Workers 2024, 11).

It is significant that, as China's economy matures through higher productivity (in particular, with the rapid expansion of robots), average incomes have moderated within the socialist market economy. Notwithstanding this, average wages in the non-private sector continue to grow, albeit at a slower pace. Consequently, the 2022 wage gap between private sector and public sector workers has expanded from 1.70 times to 1.75 times year on year, and urban wages among urban workers are about twice as high as those of rural workers.

5.1   Social Insurance and Pension Expansion

Social insurance (including old age insurance, unemployment insurance and work related insurance) are also growing. About 80 percent of all workers are covered by old age insurance. Taken together, the expansion of benefits in China is moving towards full coverage for all retired workers in the next decade (Chinese Workers 2024). The Chinese government minimized the deleterious consequences of COVID-19 and a potential decline in pension contributions by instituting preventative plans to contain and reduce the pandemic. In addition, the government is now promoting a "multi-pillar" plan to meet the needs of an aging population and safeguard the pensions of China's expansive labor force, adjudicating cases to defend workers in economic disputes with private management.

5.2   Labor Disputes

The Chinese government is highly transparent and rigorous in reporting about labor disputes, as well as about economic downturns which impact workers, reflecting the anti-corruption initiative advanced by General Secretary Xi Jinping from 2012 to the present. These advances have been ignored by the Western media. By comparison, government reporting on economic trends from outside China is typically far less exacting. China openly records labor–management conflicts in the private sector in its annual statistical bulletins, which are reported openly in the media. The annual bulletin *Chinese Workers* documented that labor–management conflict adjudicated by the labor courts expanded from 2020 to 2022, owing to a decline in workers' median income in the private sector relative to that of workers in SOEs. Over that period, labor dispute cases handled by mediation and arbitration bodies increased to 341.3 million workers: a 20.2 percent increase from 2021 (Chinese Workers 2024, 12). Growth in adjudication of labor disputes reveals a government highly committed to resolving conflict in a state where labor laws are far more stringent than in any other country (2024, 10–13). For example, adjudicating and resolving labor disputes in the US is virtually impossible as the National Labor Relations Board (NLRB) there has a protracted dispute resolution program which favors employers. In most instances, even those workers represented by trade unions are conflict averse and wages, benefits and working conditions established by collective bargaining agreements are openly flouted by private businesses.

ACFTU encourages workers to advance claims against employers as evidenced by the dramatic growth in mediation and arbitration bodies. The government measures the success rate of labor–management dispute resolution. In 2022, national arbitration bodies closed 96.9 percent of the 3,162,000 cases filed and 72.5 percent of all arbitration cases were finalized, mostly in favor of workers, recovering ¥66.2 billion, or $US9.5 trillion (2024, 13). Having solicited public opinion on how to improve the dispute resolution process, the Ministry of Justice established an online system in 2019. Since 2023, members of the ACFTU and constituent trade unions on the grassroots level have been able to file complaints online rather than taking time off from work and establishing an independent dispute arbitration resolution mechanism (Government Gazette 2023; Ministry of Justice of the People's Republic of China 2019; Wang 2025). (See Figures 7 and 8.)

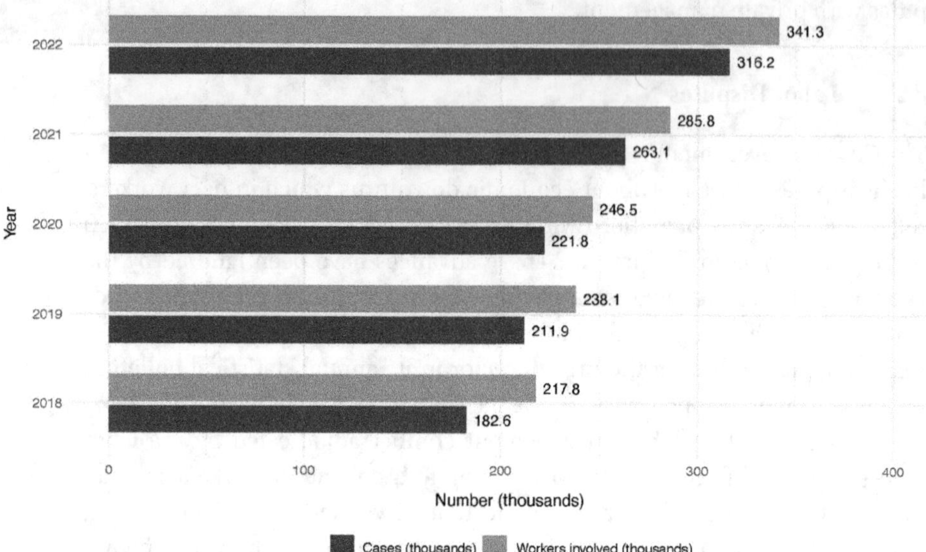

FIGURE 7   Work stoppages, 2018–22 (Source: Derived by the author from labor dispute cases and number of workers involved, 2018–2022 statistical bulletin on the development of HR and social security. Chinese Ministry of HR and Social Security)

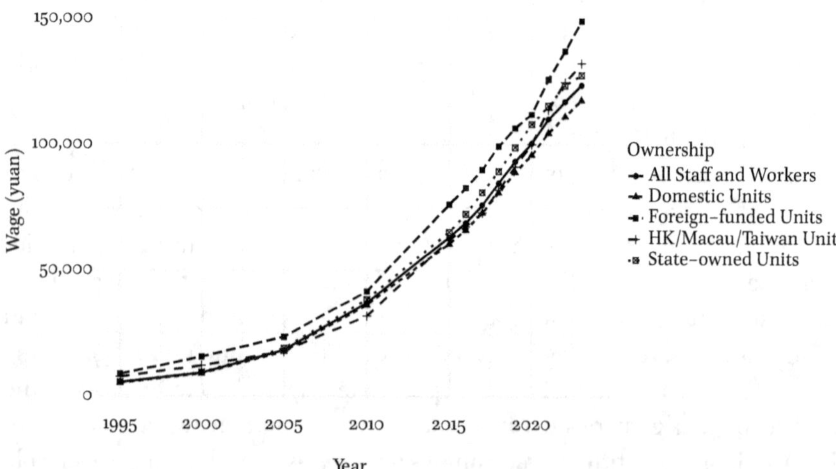

FIGURE 8   Average wages in China by ownership type, 1995–2023 (Source: Derived from labor dispute cases and number of workers involved, 2018–2022 Statistical Bulletin on the Development of HR and Social Security. Issued by the Chinese Ministry of HR and Social Security)

5.3 Shift from Manufacturing for Export to Domestic Production and Services

The Chinese government has developed advanced industries to increase domestic demand and so spur economic expansion. In this way, Chinese workers will benefit directly from state-of-the-art consumer goods and rely less on exports to generate foreign currencies. For an excessively long period since 1978, China's economy has developed through technological innovation and higher productivity. Foreign revenue has been reinvested in domestic industries. For far too long, due to unequal exchange in trade with the capitalist West, Chinese worker compensation has been devalued, notably in North America and Western Europe. From about 2010, as Chinese workers' incomes have increased, the economic policymakers have nurtured a domestic consumer market to benefit Chinese workers rather than rapacious foreign consumers in the capitalist West, who have long benefited from acquiring markedly undervalued products. Westerners, especially in the US, have taken for granted low-cost Chinese products and multinational corporations have treated China as their own backyard where they can dictate the cost of consumer goods. However, the regeneration of the ACFTU has increased Chinese worker wages as it has increased the costs of consumer goods for foreign consumers. However, Western tariffs and trade restrictions have generated a renaissance in the development of original technology in China, including digitization, information systems and artificial intelligence (AI). The commitment to developing new technology for improving wages and working conditions was a central theme of a conference commemorating the ACFTU's centenary:

> To adapt to the rapid development of new technologies, new business forms and new models, trade unions at all levels are constantly innovating their organizational forms and ways of joining and actively promoting convenient methods such as online application for membership and collective registration for membership. Employees from platform companies, small and micro enterprises, and social organizations have successively become union members and enjoy the benefits offered by the union. (Li, Z. 2025)

Industrial innovation has steadily intensified the renovation and establishment of production and service industries, increasing pressure on China's industrial labor force as manufacturing industries have closed. Rising migration to urban areas has created a flexible labor force and attendant unemployment among the urban working classes, a labor market change which has not gone unnoticed by the socialist state and the ACFTU as the number of new jobs has declined from 2018 to 2022 from 13.61 million to 12.06 million with a concomitant decline of 4.12 million in employment among workers aged between 16 and 59. Further industrial diversification through digitization has restructured the nature of work through flexibilization of labor. By 2022, 200 million workers had entered flexible jobs, stimulating the ACFTU to adapt to address the demands of workers employed on a range of digital platforms, including logistics, delivery, streaming and others (Chinese Workers 2024, 36–38; NBSC 2022).

5.4 Implications of the Expansive Growth of Labor Flexibilization

Flexible employment is rapidly expanding in China. However, significant differences exist in terms of cities, wage rates, gender and age. Zhilian, a recruitment and research agency, found that between 2019 and 2024 the proportion of all employment positions in the flexible economy climbed sharply from 8.4 percent to 15.2 percent of all jobs in China. The Institute for Economic and Social Research (IESR) at Jinan University attributes the near doubling of flexible jobs to the COVID-19 pandemic, government support for the adoption of new technology and rapid acceleration of the digital economy (IESR 2025).

In the majority of Western countries, most jobs in the digital economy pay low wages and shift the risk to the worker, whose legal status is almost that of an independent contractor or "in business for oneself." Such workers consequently lack workplace safety, must obtain health insurance on their own, lack pensions and are not entitled to unemployment insurance or social security for retirement. Platform workers include laborers contracted for single tasks, including home repairs and assembly, gardening and homecare labor: what Ursula Huws defines as "consumption work" which both exploits labor and increases consumer dependence on the commodification of common requirements for survival and subsistence through digitization of the private and public spheres (Huws 2014). Cloud work in the West is composed of crowdsourcing workers who perform tasks worldwide. The iconic Amazon Mechanical Turk performs labor in poor countries of the global South with low GDP per capita, allowing the multinational corporation and Western consumers to benefit from the low cost of labor in obtaining services for a fraction of its cost in the rich countries of the North. In addition, cloud work includes high-wage labor performing programming and other skilled information-technology development. Collectively, digital-labor demand is dominated by low-wage labor performing ride hailing, delivery and home-care work on the platform or services performed overseas, such as web design, accounting and business services.

In China, flexible labor in the digital economy is growing and consists of about one-third of the total labor force, with sharp differences between new first, second, third and fourth tier cities, where traditional employment is the norm even as the state seeks to modernize the economy through expanding digital and AI to foster higher productivity, modernization and attendant reduction of high-intensity labor. In view of government initiatives to spur technological advancement, the Institute of Economic and Social Research (IESR)[3] expects flexible employment to expand as traditional labor intensive employment declines. Location based flexible work in logistics does not require academic education and high skills, while most cloud work in China compensates employees with higher wages than they would receive in the West. In China, labor is typically not contracted to poor countries in the global South to seize on unequal exchange of trade (Emmanuel 1972/2025; IESR 2025).

IESR data analysis displays a marked trend which contradicts the mounds of research among Western Labor Studies researchers suggesting the rise of a Chinese flexible labor force correlates to lower wages. On the contrary, due to worker demands for job security and representation and the direct responsiveness of ACFTU trade unions, flexible worker membership in trade unions has expanded significantly. The IESR reports that the wages of flexible and digital worker are higher than those of workers in "traditional employment" such as manufacturing and production industries.

In general, new flexible employment positions offer higher salary levels and there are also obvious distribution differences within them. According to the IESR, 24.2 percent of traditional employment positions are in the salary range of ¥6,001–¥8,000. Among new flexible employment, location-based positions account for as much as 44.9 percent in the ¥10,001–¥15,000 range, far exceeding the 22.1 percent of traditional employment and 24.3 percent of cloud based positions. Cloud based flexible salaries are more concentrated in the ¥6,001–¥8,000 and ¥10,001–¥15,000- ranges, accounting for 24.2 percent and 24.3 percent respectively (IESR 2025).

The nostalgic yearning among US and Western policymakers, manufacturers and workers for a regression from information technology, digitization and AI to the industrial era is a conundrum even for mainstream economists. By contrast, the Chinese government supports and finances subsumption of capital into manufacturing as a means to rapidly move towards robotization of labor intensive industrial production in factories to foster the development of digital

---

3   The IESR is a leading Chinese socioeconomic labor, and policy research institute at Jinan University, in Guangzhou, PRC: https://iesr.jnu.edu.cn/2024/0426/c17699a811578/page.htm.

and AI jobs which permit workers to spend more time with their families and communities as well as engage in meaningful personal activities which enhance the quality of their lives. Our interviews with a cohort of 50 Chinese workers in four first tier cities from January through March 2025 finds that the overriding concern of many workers is for job flexibility to care for their children or furthering their own education and training. The requirement for flexibility encompasses all skill levels, geographic locations, industrial sectors and laborers with or without local residence status in urban centers. (See Chapter 5 on ACFTU recognition of the rise of digital labor and successful national, provincial, municipal and district level union campaigns to organize digital workers.)

6   Working Class Subjectivity and the ACFTU's Significance to Labor

To directly understand the concerns of workers in China, interviews were conducted among representative workers in a range of industries in the private (non-public) and public sectors in cities and regions throughout the country (see Table 4). We conducted survey interviews and ethnographic interviews to determine the attitudes and perspectives on the ACFTU. We now turn to our interviews and assessments with Chinese workers from November 2023 through April 2025 in cities across the country. The research includes interviews with more than 100 workers using a range of methods in different localities. The interviewees were all randomly selected. About 50 percent of the interviews were structured and allowed for workers to discuss their attitudes towards working in China and the role of the ACFTU. In addition, the other 50–60 interviews were unstructured ethnographic interviews with workers, union members and leaders and managers in non-public enterprises in Guangzhou, Donnguan and surrounding Guangdong Province.

The interviewees include resident workers, migrant workers and workers contracted by third party agencies, encompassing laborers who did not have formal labor contracts with the companies by which they were employed. Randomized, structured and ethnographic interviews were conducted among workers, managers and trade union representatives in the cities and provinces shown in Table 4. The interviews were intentionally conducted in distinct geographic spaces and across industrial and job categories.

The interviews represent the central theme of the research: an inquiry into working class subjectivity among workers. Open ended questions focused on worker cognition of their contribution to the labor process and the significance of the CPC and the local branch of the ACFTU in representing and defending working class interests, The interviews applied a grounded historical

TABLE 4   Geographic locations of interviews, November
            2024–April 2025

Directly controlled municipalities
                          Beijing
                          Shanghai

Province	**Cities**
Fujian	Fuzhou City
	Xiamen City
	Lianjiang County
Guangdong	Donnguan
	Guangzhou
	Shanwei
	Zhuhai
Hebei	Langfang City
Heilongjiang	Harbin City
	Shuangyashan City
Henan	Nanyang
Jilin province	Changchun City
	Yanbian/Yanji
Sichuan	Chengdu
	Yibin City
Henan	Nanyang
Shandong province	Weihai City
Zhejiang province	Hangzhou City
	Jiaxing City

Note: I am indebted to crucial support from Pan Yan, Adrian
Ortega Camara, Alex Witherspoon, Sreyashi Choudhury
and six journalists who conducted interviews with workers,
including Leah Chen, Leslie Wang, Sijia Xiao, Jia Xu, Noelle
Yi and Xinyu Zhang.

materialism advanced by Karl Marx in *Capital* (1867) and Friedrich Engels in
Socialism: Utopian and Scientific (1907). For Marx and Engels, class consciousness is a direct extension of the material being of the worker, which shapes
class subjectivity expressed by the communist party and representative union.
The party and union are the organs which reflect the material interests of the
working class, and it is through associating working class subjectivity with the
party and trade union organization that their interests in the material world

are expressed. Working class subjectivity rejects idealism, abstraction and cultural and philosophical concerns which are detached from the natural world and political economy, which are grounded in dialectical materialism and scientific socialism (Ness 2024).

The ethnographic interviews focused on worker job satisfaction and employer skills training in the manufacturing sectors as well as wages, working conditions and social insurance in all economic sectors, including among digital and logistical workers. A fundamental finding is that employers are introducing new technology within workplaces which significantly rely on higher skills to increase productivity, even among businesses with fewer than 100 workers. The nature of work in many middle-sized factories has shifted from largely unskilled labor on assembly lines to a larger share of skilled workers operating high technology means of production at higher wages. Work satisfaction is improved as employees can complete most of the tasks individually instead of working on far more alienating assembly lines. Workers in modern factories are encouraged to have high levels of creativity and can better appreciate the work process and their role in the production of tools, products and commodities.

6.1   Labor Perspectives and Outlooks in China's Socialist Market Economy

From November 2024 through March 2025, ethnographic interviews were conducted among workers in an array of industries. Most workers were laboring in NFE which have emerged in China and worldwide in the ten years from 2015 to 2025. Moreover, almost all were floating workers who had only recently migrated from the countryside or were recently unemployed workers entering the digital labor market. Among the latter, workers were seeking work in the aftermath of industrial modernization in the socialist market economy and the inescapable expansion of a reserve army of labor in search of employment. Unlike capitalist market economies, employers in the Chinese socialist market economy do not exploit workers through driving down labor costs.

Consequently, most ethnographic interviews in the survey were conducted with laborers who were primarily young and unskilled, many of whom, due to the expansion of the digital economy, had gravitated towards jobs in the industry. The significant finding is that most workers did not intend to remain in most sectors of the digital economy but planned on moving on to industries requiring training and higher skills. Nevertheless, most workers in NFE recognized the necessity to increase remuneration, dependent on gaining a larger share of revenues from the platform economy as well as improving working conditions, which were also largely uncertain in emergent labor markets. For example, food delivery workers discover that access to residential communities could sometimes be a challenge and that working conditions in increasingly frequent high summer temperatures have significant consequences. Just as workers were acclimating to NFE so too were China's trade unions. In view of the incipient nature of the digital economy it is essential to consider the distinct spatial and temporal factors to understand workers' perspectives and their material reality in the natural world as digital economy workers employed in ride hailing, delivery, other logistics, care work and additional labor markets which depend on the platform. Working class subjectivity assumes unique forms of labor which class conscious trade unions must research, analyze and absorb for workers to have agency through new strategies reflecting the unique labor process which has emerged. The nature and forms of exchange within the digital economy are categorically dissimilar from those in manufacturing, retail, services and conventional labor markets which are based on a direct exchange between the worker and the firm. In the worldwide platform economy, most workers are not employed by firms but are considered to be working for themselves. But in China, a large and growing number of digital workers are becoming direct employees of firms and negotiate their remuneration, health and safety and social security through trade unions.

Organizations can only represent the class conscious interests of the working class after recognizing the nature of an industry and the constraints which are imposed on workers. A newly formed labor market requires accountable trade unions to conduct significant research and partake in the labor process as it evolves and takes shape. A responsible trade union must develop strategies which reflect the nature of the industries and the labor process inherent to workers. Socialist trade unions have unique responsibilities absent for most capitalist trade unions, which are primarily motivated by increasing membership and defending the leadership of the organization. As a rule, trade unions under capitalism both support and fear new members who will pay dues but also have the potential to threaten the authority of leaders who are isolated from them. A genuinely effective trade union organization must operate in parallel with workers through representing their subjective interests in the creation of an agency with the capacity to unify and liberate labor (Lukács 1923/1999). And it is through agency that a trade union can grasp the dialectical understanding of the principal contradictions which workers confront through their labor.

In view of the necessity of recognizing and learning the material interests of workers, mobilization into trade unions must occur with detailed understanding of the primary practices and contradictions which emerge and are developed over time and, in due course, epitomize a new industry. Successful trade unions will emerge only after workers and trade union organizations develop a cognitive capacity through experience and research, share and perceive the contradictions and adopt an organizational form which is in harmony with workers.

In an industry which experiences a high rate of turnover among precarious workers who may move from one job to the next, any trade union seeking to organize requires extensive research and persistence as working class continuity is in a constant state of flux. A responsible trade union must not only respond to the demands of workers but also proactively advocate for the imposition of new laws and regulations governing employment status and wages and benefits. If a labor market is structured to operate with an irregular workforce where many workers do not plan to remain over the long term, trade unions must respond in a way which reflects this process and workers' highly precarious material conditions. It is insufficient to conclude that workers are simply too difficult to organize. Instead, trade unions must understand: the trajectory of workers employed in a chaotic industry with high rates of turnover; the nature of the political economy; and the plans of workers to remain or exit a specific industry. Trade unions must also consider how workers can remain in the labor market and transcend conditions of precarity. If labor turnover is high, unions must develop conditions which improve job security, the labor process and education so that workers can survive and prosper in an emerging labor market which is in high demand. Technology should not translate into precarity.

The interviews with workers reflect these significant factors and must not be separated from the underlying nature of a class conscious trade union organization, an understanding of a nascent industry and the most pivotal concern: what the principal contradictions are confronting workers. Thus, the interviews are intended to help understanding of these underlying factors and the relationship of workers to unions and of the tactics and strategy the ACFTU uses alongside socialism with Chinese characteristics.

6.2   Worker Engagement with Unions

The interviews demonstrated that most workers who do not intend to remain in their industries were less likely to engage in the activities of their trade unions. Unskilled workers are primarily focused on wages, working conditions and benefits and depend on trade unions to negotiate and ensure that employers respect and honor agreements and abide by applicable Chinese labor laws.

Participation in trade unions typically occurs when workers seek resolution of grievances over pay, working conditions and benefits. Commonly, worker participation in their trade unions occurs only after they have grievances. Otherwise, in industries with transient workers who do not plan on remaining over the long term, laborers are highly capable of addressing and amicably resolving disputes with management. If workers have individual or collective complaints which cannot be settled with employers, they are highly aware that disputes can be taken to their trade unions, which in turn commonly settle grievances directly with employers. If unions are unable to reconcile disputes with management, China maintains a significant network of administrative labor courts to address worker concerns. A frequent problem is that workers do not have direct contracts with management, an issue which has increased with the expansion of the private sector.

6.3 National Union Density Signifies Working Class Capacity

In China, most workers are directly employed by firms and represented by labor unions which can be summoned to resolve disputes. The combination of direct employment and union representation is a distinctive feature of China, not found in most other countries. Workers count on ACFTU affiliates to access additional benefits or, in the event of unresolvable disputes, to respond to their call for assistance. It is noteworthy that China is both the second largest economy in the world and has the highest trade union density rate among all countries except Iceland.[4] As the largest economy in the world, it is notable that China has the highest trade union density rate among countries with populations of 1 million or more, exhibited by the share of workers who are trade union members. In sharp contrast, trade union density rates in advanced capitalist countries are significantly lower among private sector workers.

In non-socialist states, workers are usually afraid to express concerns over employer breaches of pay rates, working conditions and benefits (in stark contrast to Chinese workers, who recognize their labor rights). But, where workers have significant individual or collective grievances, in most instances, no trade unions exist to represent them. Rarely, if ever, do workers file legal complaints against their employers in labor courts. In most instances, workers are unaware of their rights as workers and of the procedures to file labor complaints which

---

4 One of the smallest countries in the world, Iceland has a population of 300,000 and a 90 percent trade union density rate.

are adjudicated in labor courts. The interviews show that workers in China are not compelled to learn the complex intricacies of labor law but can take their unresolved grievances with management to trade unions. One interviewer reflected that, because employers are aware of the labor law and consistently abide by their obligations and because Chinese unions are ubiquitous, workers, whether members or not, do not relentlessly oppose management but instead seek out means to improve careers or their jobs. One interviewer concluded that the most significant issue for workers is career development and employment continuity:

> Most workers prioritize their own career development, income stability, and the possibility of obtaining better working conditions within the company. Their interest in unions is often limited to understanding whether they can access certain additional benefits or dispute resolution mechanisms. (Yi 2025)

A significant finding is that older workers have greater knowledge of their rights and the benefits of trade unions than younger workers who are entering the labor market for the first time or have only recently begun to work. Yet, young workers are highly conscious of their rights even if they are unaware of the significant role which the ACFTU and its affiliates play in enforcing wage rates. An essential finding emerging from the research is that the ACFTU and its affiliates have not sufficiently publicized their instrumental role in defending workers' wages and rights. Even Wang Dongming, chair of the ACFTU, has underscored the shortage of publicity of the work of the trade union federation.

> We must improve and perfect the systems and mechanisms for engaging with workers and the general public .... We must continuously improve the skills and level of cadres, especially young cadres, in engaging with the masses. We must strengthen investigation and research, conduct the Ninth National Survey on the Status of the Workforce in a thorough manner, leverage the role of trade union think tanks, assess the facts and implement practical measures. (Wang 2022)

Thus, the trade union federation's independent research shows the requirement of encouraging a "welcoming, studying, publicizing and implementing" ACFTU as a means to develop cadres among the young to educate the masses of the present and future. Dongming stresses: "We must continuously improve the skills and level of cadres, especially young cadres, in engaging with the masses" (2022).

6.4   ACFTU: Catching up with the Private Sector to Expand Formal Labor Contracts

The vast expansion of China's urban labor force over the past 40 years has presented the ACFTU with daunting challenges to absorb hundreds of millions of workers. These expose the necessity of enhancing direct contact with workers in order to support establishment of direct labor–management contracts which would lead to higher benefits among an array of private sector firms. In the past decade, the substantial expansion of the NFE has diminished the share of workers who lack labor contracts with private firms and amplified trade union recognition of the enormous task of regularizing workers as formal employees. In the absence of formal labor–management contracts, workers are unable to avail themselves of social insurance, housing provident funds and pensions. The interviews illustrate that expanding union membership must also involve private sector employers establishing direct employer–management relationships with their workers, a task which a growing number of large firms (e.g. JD.com/Meituan/Ele.Me) recognize and now address. However, the ACFTU must expand its effort to focus on small private sector firms to establish contractual relationships with their workers, who are often left behind. Yet again, rapid economic change opens new tasks for the ACFTU.

6.5   Footloose Labor and ACFTU Representations

Transformation of the Chinese political economy through the rise of floating laborers is expanding footloose labor in the burgeoning urban centers and poses new challenges for the mobilization of workers who seek improved conditions. To achieve this objective, the ACFTU must expand its presence through local district and street level unions to facilitate working class subjective interests. It creates agency through cultivating working class activism and directly safeguarding laborers' interests as they seek a greater voice at work. In many cases, this objective also requires educating inexperienced employers who are unfamiliar with Chinese labor law to protect workers through timely payment of wages and provision of occupational safety measures. Most laborers with direct employer contracts are informed of their rights on the job. Yet, as the share of employers with fewer workers grows, the ACFTU is obliged to expand its representation, especially in third and fourth tier cities with nascent and expanding economies. Most workers entering these labor markets are cognizant of the ACFTU and its charge of expanding their interests through representation. Certainly, some workers are unable or unaware of their right to form unions straightaway as employers in new businesses have not established labor contracts with workers. Once a sufficient cohort of workers employed at a single employer appears, laborers can then petition the local branches of the ACFTU for membership. But some workers undoubtedly fall through the cracks. In the interviews, we found that those workers who could not form unions were working independently without direct contracts, typically among workers in the digital economy. Branch union ACFTU representatives are attentive to the necessity to catch up in restructured labor markets in China's urban centers. The requirement to continuously recognize and identify working conditions in these new labor markets represents a significant task in a socialist state where the ACFTU is responsible for representing and protecting all workers.

Concurrently, the ACFTU's challenge has been to respond to regional, national and global crises over the past 15 years; examples include the Great Financial Recession in 2008 and the ensuing economic downturn of the global capitalist economy and the COVID-19 pandemic which began in 2019. More recently, the ACFTU has had to contend with the economic gyrations set in motion by the US government's chaotic tariff policies under Donald Trump in 2025. Consequently, workers have an array of experiences, and the ACFTU must reflect the roiling demands which workers confront. As such, the ACFTU is expanding its presence as China urbanizes.

6.6   China's Precarious Workers and ACFTU Trade Unions

Although the floating population of internal Chinese migrant workers frequently lacks job security equivalent to that of urban workers, the interviews revealed that employers did not violate wage laws even for workers without direct employment contracts. Among this cohort, the interviews suggest that most young workers employed in precarious jobs and the digital economy were seeking to improve their employment skills and job qualifications in preparation for their future careers. Still, the ACFTU was defending their economic interests in low wage jobs. Concomitantly, the workers also considered membership in the ACFTU as a means to higher wages and benefits without recognizing that the trade union federation was also defending or seeking to defend their wages, benefits and security as they were employed in lower waged jobs.

The interviews corroborate research on the extensive expansion of the digital economy in China and the challenges which workers face in gaining labor contracts and trade union representation. Clearly, those who seek utopian precision from Chinese unions eagerly critique the ACFTU without considering the necessity for it to research and organize workers. Moreover, in most cases, workers are mobilized into unions only after appealing to the ACFTU for assistance. But those who expect unionization as soon as workers join the industry are demanding the highest standard of effectiveness of the ACFTU, which can only respond to worker appeals and then afterwards plan organizing campaigns as it researches the industrial context. In fact, the ACFTU has been remarkably successful in unionizing, for example, digital workers. It has progressed in just a few short years to encourage national digital firms like JD.com and Ele.Me to directly employ workers and sign union recognition agreements with guarantees of living wages, occupational safety and benefits including social security. But, as the interviews demonstrate, where delivery drivers, couriers and cleaners often work for small and disparate firms, either directly, with third party labor dispatch agencies, or in the absence of a labor contract, the ACFTU must continuously mobilize, especially among floating workers employed in third and fourth tier cities in Sichuan and Guangdong provinces.

The ACFTU must assess and develop strategies for mobilizing workers and negotiating with management to raise wages and improve working conditions and benefits. Certainly, it is a formidable task to mobilize workers employed by different digital companies all at once. But, as the industry consolidates into major ride hailing, delivery and courier firms, the ACFTU is steadily improving working conditions and demanding employers pay social insurance. Still, a not insignificant share of digital workers do not plan on remaining in the industry but view their jobs as expedient temporary stopgaps as they gain new skills. One interviewer found that among the migrant workers interviewed, all regarded their jobs as temporary or as a means of increasing their income given the flexible working hours in the industry.

Most workers strived to gain employment contracts and trade union representation. However, the interviews demonstrate that expanded labor education is important in widening worker rights and trade union representation. Workers were cognizant of the advantages of joining unions. Unlike workers in capitalist countries, they were particularly supportive of the ACFTU and its affiliates as their representatives and did not want private union representation. One male worker adamantly opposed the Western model of private trade unions, asserting that he did not trust unions established by non-official organizations precisely because ACFTU government-run unions would be far more effective in resolving labor disputes. In particular, the worker said that the ACFTU was effective because the state was trustworthy and would not succumb to the risks of corruption or personal connections with employers, allowing workers to gain concrete benefits. Nonetheless, even in a socialist country with the world's highest trade union density rate, too many workers were not aware of their rights., too few workers were aware they had the right to join unions and that employers were prohibited from discriminating against activists. As Chapter 7 will demonstrate, workers employed in China's nascent digital labor-market economy successfully joined unions while digital workers in capitalist countries were prevented from doing so. As noted in Chapter 5, the International Labor Organization acknowledges that China stands alone in succeeding in regularizing and mobilizing the logistical (NFE) labor market into unions. By contrast, mobilization of these workers in the new economy was nil in every capitalist economy even if workers tried to form unions. In North America and Western Europe, NFE workers identify as being exploited, with no rights and little hope of joining any official union even if they are members of workers' associations (which are no more than advocacy groups). For example, Uber, the leading digital company in the US, does not recognize its drivers as workers or even contractors but as private businesses with access to the Uber app. Even though drivers for Uber are required to conform to the technology company's rules, and their performance is rated by customers (with determining algorithms which reward and punish them as individuals), they are deemed to be independent businesses, not workers. Workers in the US have no union which can represent them vis-à-vis digital technology firms and in rare instances pay dues to membership organizations which have no legal right to provide representation. The rapid increase in the number of delivery workers in the 2020s has not yielded a single representative union in the US. Likewise in Western Europe, workers sometimes form associations to share experiences, but no representative organization. Still, worker advocates pay tribute to these organizations as symbols of hope, especially because they are independent unions which emphasize individuals over class. In fact, these are nothing more than associations to share common despair. Independent and autonomous unions are extolled precisely because they have no official representatives and exemplify bottom-up unions. But if workers have legal claims, these workers typically have no representatives, and their complaints are not heard at labor courts as they are not considered employees (Però & Downey 2024; Vandaele 2020). It is puzzling that as Uber expands its power over the digital labor market, workers have no recourse but to join advocacy organizations to which they must pay dues. Some of these "unions" are even members of the US peak trade union federation AFL-CIO (e.g. Taxi Workers United), even if they have no collective bargaining agreement in the ride hailing industry. The dynamics of precarity are growing in the global North and South (Johnston & Pernicka 2021; Mathew 2005; Yasih 2025). Unions in the US have no right to enforce labor laws through the National Labor Relations Board even if these indie unions can go to court to assist drivers charged with motor vehicle violations. In New York City, the law was changed in 2025 to charge delivery workers on bicycles or motorized bicycles for violating traffic rules, like running red lights. These charges have enabled Immigration and Customs Enforcement (ICE) to arrest and deport undocumented workers (Maag 2025).

6.7   State-Owned Companies

The interviews make clear the distinctions between SOEs and private sector firms. Workers in SOEs tend to remain employed in their firms over the long term while those in private enterprises often pass from one job to another higher paying one. Some workers employed for private enterprises are transient laborers and only intend to hold their jobs temporarily. They are therefore not inclined to join unions but recognize their value in defending them while they secure higher paying jobs or are in training for higher skilled jobs. These workers may also include floating migrant workers, recent high school or college graduates, and those previously made unemployed because of technological change and declining demand. Western scholars tend to falsely conflate short term workers' disengagement with indifference when workers are traversing from short term employment to permanent jobs which better match their education, training and work preferences. Nevertheless, the ACFTU and its sectoral, geographic and enterprise unions remain committed to mobilizing low wage workers as well as those who do not have contracts with firms. If workers are performing the same tasks for a subcontractor, workers seek to gain official contracts with the lead enterprise and unionize into provincial, district and street level unions which represent them in specific industries. Ride hailing is a case in point. As digital firms search for reliable and skilled delivery workers, competition is growing and wages, conditions and benefits are improving. For example, the leading corporations in the Chinese digital economy are shifting from using workers hired through third party contractors to directly employing workers and are cooperative with ACFTU trade union representation. In 2025, labor shortages have spurred delivery courier JD.com to reclassify workers from being independent contractors to full time couriers who are provided with high wages, social security, housing funds and insurance. In turn, JD.com's competitors Meituan and Ele.me have been forced to directly employ drivers, increase wages, improve labor standards and provide social insurance to compete for workers. The ACFTU and its district union affiliates have mobilized workers and employers to codify labor standards in the delivery industry, including medical, unemployment, injury and maternity insurance cover and even a providence fund for housing (Lu 2024; Quinn 2025; Yang, C. 2025). By contrast, most trade unions outside China, including those in Western Europe and North America, have a distant relationship with digital logistics workers in the e-commerce sector, who are viewed as a potential nuisance and interloper and best sustained by labor NGOs. In the best instances, trade unions and NGOs function as watchdogs over industries they cannot organize (Ford & Gillan 2025; Frantz & Fernandes 2018).

7　Trade Unions under Chinese Market Socialism

To comprehend the Chinese labor movement and the role of the ACFTU, it is essential to grasp the nature of trade unions under socialism. Almost all detractors employ Western benchmarks of trade unionism as metrics, which distort the charge, nature and function of the ACFTU and its affiliates. If one utilizes historical and contemporary analogues drawn from the apogee of trade unionism in Western Europe, North America and advanced capitalist countries, it is highly likely that the assumptions and judgments will be based on inaccurate and misleading inferential analogies with conclusions which are irrelevant to Chinese labor history and contemporary practice. Commonly, four critiques are advanced by self-described progressive and socialist opponents of the Chinese trade unions and its labor movement:

1. Chinese trade unions reject independent trade union endeavors advanced through spontaneous activities which are unsanctioned by the ACFTU and CPC. Consequently, the ACFTU opposes industrial democracy, viewed as the embodiment of the most progressive unions.
2. Industrial democracy is anathema to the CPC and prohibited if rank-and-file leaders in trade unions seek to act in what they perceive to be the interests of the workers. In this way, the ACFTU and the Chinese state have rejected on-the-job work actions in contemporary China, notably since the 1980s. Accordingly, critics contend that the ACFTU denies members the right to self-activity and job actions to protest wages and working conditions, including work stoppages and strikes, which are the most effective weapons of the working class. During the Cultural Revolution and prior to the opening up, Chinese workers possessed a far more advanced right to participate and determine production activities in the workplace. Under market socialism, as replaceable workers, the rights of Chinese workers have been significantly reduced (Andreas 2019; Li 2023).
3. The ACFTU and the CPC forbid the formation of trade union political factions which are independent of the CPC and deprive workers the right to self-expression through advancing a partisan ideology or politics which deviates from the CPC versions. Promoters of independent politics think that Chinese workers seek to develop and expand anarchism,

social democracy or even competing communist or socialist parties (Ruckus 2023) As a result, Chinese workers are limited to operating within the ACFTU and may not develop an independent oppositional politics. This perspective is highly prevalent among NGOs which have formed after the 1980s, notably the now defunct China Labor Bulletin which developed and expanded with the support of foreign government funding (notably USAID, the AFL-CIO Solidarity Center, and the National Endowment for Democracy (NED)). Hong Kong and Taiwan-based bodies promoting US and Western notions of regime change could not operate without foreign funding. According to the former CIA agent and best-selling author William Blum, "The idea was that the NED would do somewhat overtly what the CIA had been doing covertly for decades, and thus, hopefully, eliminate the stigma associated with CIA covert activities." This is an assessment shared by the Ministry of Foreign Affairs (2024).

4. A final critique advanced by political organizations which consider themselves "non-revisionist" is that China was a socialist state under the leadership of Chairman Mao Zedong from 1949 through 1976 and reached the apogee of communism during the Cultural Revolution, or what they call the "Great Proletarian Cultural Revolution." They contend that after Mao's death, China and the CPC betrayed the Maoist socialist project through the opening up and the development of a socialist market economy. Under the leadership of the CPC, the ACFTU also abandoned the principles of Marxism-Leninism. Paradoxically, this perspective is advanced by ultra-left political parties and scholars who are devoted to Mao yet consider the market reforms a kind of capitalism in the service of the Chinese bureaucratic state which emerged in 1978.

The introduction of the socialist market economy in 1979 with the formation of four state-supported Special Enterprise Zones (SEZs) is viewed by opponents as a wholesale abandonment of the socialist ideals of the Chinese Revolution and as elements of an ineluctable transformation towards a state capitalist economy. That the Chinese state and the CPC had ultimate control over SEZs is a reality which is rarely acknowledged or considered in the context of socialist political economy and the necessity of market development as a catalyst in China's economic development, considered by CPC leaders as the principal contradiction. In the absence of development, the Chinese economy could not emerge as a socialist market economy. This notwithstanding, in the absence of a historical material analysis, Marxist ultra-leftists who viewed Chinese socialism as socialism under Maoism and unchanging rejected economic development under a socialist state which did not perfectly conform to their utopian ideals. For utopian socialists, or non-revisionist Maoists, Chinese socialism was to remain motionless in perpetuity. Most critics, chiefly among Western Marxists, did consider that the Chinese socialist state sought to develop its economy and improve living conditions, a dynamic advanced under Mao from 1949 to 1976. Ultra-left critics do not account for the continuous transformation required under socialism in China which began in 1949 and continues to the present. Political economist Tiejun Wen (2021) suggests that China has undergone a succession of economic crises from 1949 to now. In each historical conjuncture, the Chinese socialist state was compelled to adapt to the principal contradictions which the state confronted. Wen acknowledges that the transformation from 1978 to about 2002 represented an era of economic hardship for the Chinese rural working classes, just as the state encountered economic challenges under Mao. In *Ten Crises,* Wen posits that the socialist state returned to what he calls "pro people" policies from 2003 and then had to confront the global financial recession and attend to the distortions occurring under the first 25 years of market socialism. The state definitively began to adopt socialist policies under Xi Jinping, who has presided over the amplified socialization of the economy and the recognition of the ecological threat which global capitalism posed for China and the world from 2015 to the present (Wen 2021). Rather than considering socialism as an unbending dogma, the CPC responded to the changes in the political economy which the state has confronted since its origin in 1949 to the present.

8   How Do Trade Unions Form in Capitalist Countries?

To understand Chinese trade unions, one must comprehend prevailing trade unions in capitalist states, notably national trade union affiliates of the dominant International Trade Union Confederation (ITUC). Standard Western Labor research considers the Western labor–management trade union model which emerged in North America and Western Europe in the early 20th century, founded on employer dominance over the workplace, as the touchstone business model by which all workers resist through class struggle. The working class emerges victorious when employers succumb to the mobilization campaign directed by professional staff organizers and employers surrender to unionization of their firm. In the mid-20th century, employers under pressure from collective action by workers bargained with union representatives to achieve collective bargaining agreements (CBAs) with management governing wages, conditions and benefits.

Commonly, workers' movements spurring the formation of industrial unions dissipate once elites in workers' organizations gain control and curb the aspirations of the dispossessed seeking power. Piven and Cloward fault leaders for the failure to maintain militancy and for the ultimate demise of the organizations which originally formed as a result of disruptive insurgencies. "When the tumult is over, these organizations usually fade, no longer useful to those who provided the resources necessary to their survival" (Piven & Cloward 1979, xx). The view that workers and "poor-people" can only advance their interests when they maintain disruptive power reveals the weakness of working class organizational forms and the basis/explanation for their failure to maintain durable and effective power. In bourgeois liberal democracy, working class organizations are typically controlled by elites, a decisive factor in their failure to maintain continuity. Additionally, the organizations are formed under the framework of a capitalist economy.

Consequently, in the capitalist West, working class organizations acquiesced to class compromises which superficially protected them from the arbitrary repression and despotism of employers which constituted standard practice. Even non-union firms were persuaded to improve labor standards in response to mass organizing from the 1930s through 1970s, when the New Deal labor accords in the US began to disappear. Other models, which circumscribe the activities of employers through state policy and enforce labor rights through trade unions and labor courts, providing irrefutable power to labor, are not considered to be trade unions. For Western scholars of Labor Studies, the subordination of labor in every realm of the workplace is the archetype of the trade union. If employers in the West violate agreements or discriminate against workers, trade unions may file grievances, which typically fail through arbitration and are rarely taken to the courts. In the West, filing and adjudicating legal disputes are lengthy and drawn-out processes, and most dismissed workers must find new jobs out of economic necessity before a grievance is decided in court (Baichuan 2019).

The ACFTU and the Consolidation of China's Socialist Economy

The economic anarchy of capitalist society as it exists today is, in my opinion, the real source of the evil. We see before us a huge community of producers the members of which are unceasingly striving to deprive each other of the fruits of their collective labor—not by force, but on the whole in faithful compliance with legally established rules. ... I am convinced there is only one way to eliminate these grave evils, namely through the establishment of a socialist economy, accompanied by an educational system which would be oriented toward social goals. In such an economy, the means of production are owned by society itself and are utilized in a planned fashion. (Albert Einstein, 1949)

1 Why a Book on the Chinese Labor Movement?

The most prevalent accounts of China and its labor movement by Westerners are motivated by adversarial perceptions which mislead and manipulate readers with complex and challenging dynamics, seemingly unending changes in material conditions and realities, human experiences and institutional practices.

This book does not attribute motivations for conclusive yet often false narratives and analyses by Labor Studies scholars. However, popular accounts, descriptions and histories inform human cognition, perception and action, which in turn guide labor conditions and trade union activity. So, rather than presenting a familiar interpretation which confirms established opinions among Western readers without contesting them, here I strive to understand China's labor institutions relative to the goals and objectives of the All-China Federation of Trade Unions (ACFTU) and the Communist Party of China (CPC). I assert that the party, trade union federation and thousands of constituent unions operate with unalloyed commitment to advancing the socioeconomic interests of China's working class.

In 1978, China's leaders endeavored to develop a plan to dramatically improve the standard of living for the country's working class. The policy, known as "the opening up," gave rise to the emergence of market socialism, setting into motion a planned industrial economy. In this book, I have attempted to distinguish honest from misleading criticism. Certainly, the transfer of hundreds of millions of workers from the countryside to urban areas has led to transitory disruption, as Robert Weil highlighted in 1996 when he observed that China's peasantry had endured a period of social dislocation and adversity. Regrettably, Weil, who directed most of his wrath against US imperialism, did not live to see the noteworthy achievements of socialism with Chinese characteristics and the determination of its leaders to improve the conditions of its working class (Weil 1996). Indeed, market socialism eventually tackled the principal contradiction of solving poverty and delivering a high standard of living and modernizing the economy, a challenge which the PRC encountered from its origins (Wen 2021). The opening up set off investment in Special Economic Zones (SEZs) and overall efforts to make state owned enterprises more efficient. Most significantly, technological investment in the means of production has resulted in the migration of rural workers to urban areas to work in China's burgeoning industrial economy.

Today, the CPC is committed to integrating migrant workers into the mainstream of the working class. In October 2024, the party accentuated its importance in an official opinion:

> Cultivate migrant workers into high-quality modern industrial workers. Focusing on industrial transformation and upgrading, strengthen skills training for migrant workers and widely implement the "Study and Dream" program. Promote the integration of migrant workers into cities, further relax and expand urban settlement policies, and ensure equal access to basic urban public services for migrant workers. Increase public legal services to benefit migrant workers, protect their legitimate rights and interests, and promote stable employment. (Ministry of Ecology and Environment of the PRC 2024)

All forms of mobility have material and social consequences for both origin regions and destinations. China's internal migration from rural to urban areas is far and away the largest distinct population shift in human history. As such, urbanization has had ongoing impacts for the capacity of the ACFTU to respond to the reconstitution of labor markets from agrarian to urban, and then from industrial to new forms of employment among logistics and digital workers. Most opponents of China from left to right share a common view that the ACFTU is ineffective because it is affiliated with the CPC, but this view is based on specific moments when the Federation was researching and mobilizing to respond to labor market changes. The demographic shift which has refashioned China's labor market is monumental. In 1980, about 90 percent of China's population of nearly 1 billion lived in rural regions. Today, China's 956 million urban dwellers compose 67.5 percent of China's population, but the population of the country's rural areas still constitutes nearly 500 million.

Alone, China's rural inhabitants would form the third largest country in the world. Rural land represents China's safety net as it is all owned by the state, as is urban land. While all change is arduous and demanding, nearly 50 years after the institution of market socialism, every Chinese citizen continues to be entitled to return to rural areas and farm the land for sustenance. As Xinyu Lu of East China Normal University claims, China's collective economy and socialism with Chinese characteristics preserve the rights of the working class:

> Collective land ownership in rural China differs from the land tenure systems in socialist countries like the Soviet Union, which is why it may have played a crucial role in determining the success of "Chinese-style modernization." The nationalization of urban land and the collectivization of rural land form the foundation of the Chinese worker–peasant alliance. When viewed through a Marxist lens, the urban–rural dichotomy is considered an inevitable outcome of capitalist development and a challenge commonly faced by Global South countries during their developmental processes. (Lu 2024, 298)

In the context of the resiliency of Chinese socialism within a market economy, Western Labor scholars would do well to absorb the significance of Tiejun Wen's instructive lesson that economic development cannot be solved instantly by governments but necessitates study and the passage of time to effectively respond to challenges. Only utopians and non-revisionist thinkers who do not consider dialectical materialism accept as true that revolution will lead straightaway to communism.

2 The CPC and ACFTU Guide Economic Development and Shield the Working Class

Despite the formidable challenges to economic development faced by China under market socialism, Western Labor scholars remain captives to the ideology of immediate unmediated outcomes in the absence of agency or institutions. Most do not take into account the significance of organizations for achieving economic development at the same time as improving wages and conditions for China's working class. But the People's Republic of China (PRC) is not evaluated in comparison to analogous challenges for capitalist states, which typically have not considered the interests of workers. Paradoxically the weakness of organizations and institutions in the West is a fixation and commodification of superficial individualism, turmoil, the spectacle and autonomy in the absence of a genuine capacity to sustain and codify success. Lacking accountable political parties which diligently advance the interests of the working class, Labor Studies researchers in the West take solace in fleeting events of the past as trophies rather than in practical work of today which is planned methodically to survive the test of time. Western Labor research about working class institutional formations in China and the South is frequently condescending and maintains a perspective rooted in social imperialism. Economic planning under market socialism and the formation of labor organizations suitable to the political economy of China do not conform to Western archetypes; instead, they are ridiculed and dismissed as incompatible with authentic models which emerged in Western Europe and North America. However, as this book shows, Labor research in the West does not consider the reality that Chinese trade unionism emerged and affiliated with the CPC at the same time as Western industrial models in the 1920s.

Consequently, Western Labor research about the PRC and the ACFTU has been nearly universally negative. One is extremely hard pressed to find even a single article published over the last 40 years or so which provides an accurate portrait of the ACFTU and its prodigious accomplishments. Opponents engage in deductive reasoning to convey the ideal political system for trade unions as liberal-bourgeois democracy operating within an economy integrated into the world capitalist system. This incongruous perspective fails to consider material conditions in the natural world. In China's case, the shift from a rural working class to a predominantly urban working class. Yet, Western Labor scholarship which criticizes China is silent on the relentless decline of trade union membership in the West to near irrelevancy, government crackdowns on public sector trade unions, court decisions narrowing the ability of trade unions to grow strong, the absence of democracy in Western-style trade unions and the rise of right wing populism among the working class: characteristics of institutional decay. Predictably, Western Labor scholars do not consider trade union growth as an indicator of success, since it implies (in their view) that workers are forced to join trade unions. On the contrary, compulsory membership is an objective of Western trade unions which seek closed shops and funding from member dues. As noted, the ACFTU and its affiliates have never aspired to require workers to join unions to receive equivalent wages and benefits.

3   Socialism, Trade Unionism and Industrial Policy

This book also has argued that the successful development of socialism in one state requires the coordination of the communist party and trade unions to grow and meet the needs of the working classes. Even if a communist party gains power, the state must guide economic development in urban and rural regions. In the two most prominent cases, the Soviet Union and the PRC, the state, under the party's leadership, formulated socialist economic planning to advance the capacity to serve the working classes. In times of crisis, the communist parties in both countries were obligated to deviate from the course which some left opponents consider sacrosanct: the preservation and development of markets under the overarching leadership of the party. Under such conditions, the function of trade unions is to represent and advance the interests of the working class charted by the Communist Party and adhere to the principles of the dictatorship of the proletariat. V. I. Lenin and Mao Zedong both formulate a similar approach to the organization of trade unions under socialism.

To diminish the possibility of a bourgeois restoration, trade unions are required to overpower petty bourgeois influences in the trade unions. For Lenin, the primary threat to the party emerged from Socialist-Revolutionary Mensheviks and anarchists, viewed as bourgeois forces and the fount of opposition to socialism.

Only among these trends has any considerable number of people remained who defend capitalism ideologically and not from selfish class motives and continue to believe in the non-class nature of the "democracy," "equality," and "liberty" in general that they preach. It is to this socioeconomic cause and not to the role of individual groups, still less of individual persons, that we must attribute the survivals (sometimes even the revival) in our country of such petty-bourgeois ideas among the trade unions. The Communist Party, the Soviet bodies that conduct cultural and educational activities and all Communist members of trade unions must therefore devote far more attention to the ideological struggle against petty-bourgeois influences, trends and deviations among the trade unions, especially because the New Economic Policy is bound to lead to a certain strengthening of capitalism. It is urgently necessary to counteract this by intensifying the struggle against petty-bourgeois influences upon the working class (Lenin 1922/1973, 195–196).

The requirement for economic development in China was advanced by Chairman Mao Zedong in February 1948 as a decisive requirement in building socialism and economic development through advancing the productive forces. Mao considered urban trade unions duty bound to join forces with industrialists. In his directive on industry and commerce, the significance of industrial development was paramount:

> A sharp distinction should also be made between the correct policy of developing production, promoting economic prosperity, giving consideration to both public and private interests and benefiting both labour and capital, and the one-sided and narrow-minded policy of "relief", which purports to uphold the workers' welfare but in fact damages industry and commerce and impairs the cause of the people's revolution. Education should be conducted among comrades in

the trade unions and among the masses of workers to enable them to understand that they should not see merely the immediate and partial interests of the working class while forgetting its broad, long-range interests. (Mao Tse-Tung/ Mao Zedong 1977/2021, 199)

CPC General Secretary Xi Jinping's 2025 address to the ACFTU on its 100th anniversary validates Mao Zedong's 1948 directive, which had been pursued continuously by the CPC and produced concrete results for the Chinese working class over more than 75 years of unwavering struggle to realize economic modernization:

One hundred years ago, at the closing of the Second National Labour Conference, the slogan "struggle, struggle, struggle to the end" resounded throughout the venue, inspiring millions of labourers to persevere and forge ahead during the turbulent revolutionary years. Today, the Party leads over 1.4 billion people who are advancing with high spirits on the new journey of Chinese-style modernization. The times are different, missions and tasks have changed, but the spirit of arduous struggle, united struggle, and unremitting struggle will never change. Let us unite more closely around the Party Central Committee, work solidly with our feet on the ground, strive to forge ahead, struggle and dedicate ourselves, embrace the new era with creativity, forge new glory through struggle, and turn the grand blueprint of realizing the great rejuvenation of the Chinese nation into reality one step at a time! (Xi 2025)

To restate a central argument of this book, striving for economic modernization under socialism compels all government institutions to be dedicated to a common mission, which takes time and effort to achieve. Economic modernization is normally accompanied by social dislocation, as Weil makes clear. But it is irrational to expect instantaneous outcomes. Torkil Lauesen reminds us that socialist economic development is gradual and methodical and is accompanied by challenges from internal and external forces (Lauesen 2024). Just as spontaneity must be consolidated to empower the working class, economic planning is not the equivalent of realizing economic development and the improvement of living conditions for workers and peasants.

4   Western Labor Studies and Social Imperialism

Research on historical materialism and the natural world is not composed of absolutes, conclusions or the end times. Historical materialism is implanted in dialectical conflict among imperfect human beings with impurities, gradients and asynchronous predispositions. Purity and "non-revisionism" can only exist in the subjective mind: equating principles which are ethereal within nature is intolerable.

Nowhere is this more obvious than in the way that genuine evidence casting the ACFTU's achievements in a good light is unsuitable to Western Labor scholars, creating a catch-22. Both the presence and the absence of actions are always undesirable. Verifiable findings which may reveal positive attributes about the ACFTU are ensnared through incontestable truths and subjected to ad hominem attacks impugning its integrity. The occurrence or absence of labor disputes is an example of this deductive reasoning which only leads to no-win double binds. For example:

1. In times of labor tranquility and the absence of strike activity, critics argue: *The decline in strike activity in China can only be explained by the authoritarian character of the CPC and the ACFTU. The decline in strikes and the absence of mass labor disruption reveal the authoritarian nature of the Chinese state.*

2. In times of labor conflict sparked by the ACFTU and elevated labor demands, critics argue: *The rise of strikes in China suggests that the working class is opposed to the communist ACFTU as a representative of its interests. Growing labor conflict is an indicator that trade unions are unresponsive to workers.*

Accordingly, regardless of whether or not the ACFTU initiates organizing campaigns, they can never contribute to the benefit of workers.

Most Western Labor scholars do not account for the fact that unions are organized spatially and the ACFTU represents workers in millions of labor disputes every year through labor courts which typically decide swiftly. More than 95 percent of all cases are decided on behalf of workers, who are almost always accompanied by ACFTU representatives. Collectively, Western Labor scholars agree to cast China unfavorably. Most have a reflexive reaction to the CPC and ACFTU as authoritarian and repressive, or what they call "the party-state." All scholarship deriving from within the PRC is viewed with distrust. In many instances, the very concept of the working class is downplayed, and individual action is elevated.

As demonstrated in this book, Western Labor Studies is in many ways authoritarian. Irrespective of empirical research which shows the effectiveness of the ACFTU in organizing and representing workers, the conclusions must find fault in China's trade unions or conclude with hyperbolic ad hominem attacks against the ACFTU. Increasingly, Labor Studies assessments of China rely on NGO accounts and interpretations of organizations, practices, and events over those which evenhandedly and honestly evaluate the history, facts and data, which may not conform to the anti-China dogma. Many NGOs are funded by corporate foundations, via the US State Department through the National Endowment for Democracy and, up until 2025, the United States Agency for International Development.

5   Actual Labor Disputes in China

A litany of books and academic articles has been published on low wages and poor working conditions in foreign subcontractors operating in China; for example, Foxconn Technology and Yue Yuen Industrial Holdings, subcontractors for multinational electronics and athletic footwear, both headquartered in Taiwan. In the aftermath of several disputes in Shenzhen, notably suicides by Foxconn workers in 2010, the ACFTU organized workers to form an enterprise level trade union with democratically elected leaders. Likewise, the ACFTU stepped in and resolved the pension dispute at Yue Yuen when workers went on strike. In each case, conditions dramatically improved as the ACFTU organized local enterprise trade unions. Subsequently, democratically elected enterprise unions negotiated significantly improved conditions for workers. But before a trade union can act, it must learn and develop strategies to combat multinational employers and their subcontractors in Taiwan.

Notwithstanding this, the literature wholly ignores the question of unequal exchange (Emmanuel 1972/2025), which is undoubtedly the most significant cause of low wages in the global South through the depreciation of the value of workers' labor. While residents of the global North are beneficiaries of unequal exchange, the cost is shifted to those in poor countries. However, the CPC and the ACFTU counter this through increasing wages for workers producing high quality products in China. For example, in September 2023, Foxconn, the contractor for Huawei and Apple, hiked wages for workers and in turn the cost of mobile phones. The subcontractors for both Apple and Huawei's increased wages to ¥8,500–¥9,000 in 2023, or US$1,200 to US$1,300 a month. ACFTU organizing is increasing wages for workers along with competition for labor among subcontractors. Western consumers accustomed to low cost smartphones and technology are now paying more for their electronic products (Global Times 2023).

According to Jason Hickel and Dylan Sullivan, wage growth among Chinese workers and attendant higher cost products are a threat to multinational corporate profits in the US. The dramatic growth in wages is reducing wage disparities between China and the US, which have been the basis for unequal exchange and superexploitation. In August 2025, Hickel and Sullivan assessed that Chinese labor costs have risen to $8 per hour. "Capitalists in the core states are now desperate to do something to restore their access to cheap labour and resources. One option—increasingly promoted by the Western business press—is to relocate industrial production to other parts of Asia where wages are cheaper" (Hickel & Sullivan 2025).

6 Towards an Accurate and Reliable Evaluation of the Chinese Labor Movement

Most assumptions about and opinions on Chinese trade unions are formed in advance of obtaining proof, and, on occasion, entirely in the absence of evidence. Accurate assessments are not formulated on the basis of claims based on partial truths but on "realities" which are unable to be disproven. According to such confirmation bias, interpretations are only acceptable if they verify opinions. Inferences which contradict conclusions are dross which must be discarded as they challenge deductive truths. Accordingly, incontrovertible truths are advanced by adversaries of the PRC. Those who object or even contest the established tenets advanced by such hegemonic certainties are deemed to be heretics and offenders who must be isolated and purged.

To recapitulate, this concluding chapter summarizes the primary claims based on research in the foregoing chapters. Above all, the main thrust has been to understand the ACFTU on the basis of its goals and objectives, not those of Western bourgeois standards. Additionally, the ACFTU is the most salient example of holistic unionism unifying worker democracy with trade union accountability. The CPC plainly calls for workers' democracy in trade unions. In a recent statement, the PRC underscored its commitment to democratic trade unionism:

> Improve the democratic management system of enterprises. Improve the democratic management system of enterprises and institutions, with workers' congresses as the primary form. Major matters affecting the vital interests of industrial workers must be reviewed and approved by the workers' congresses in accordance with the law and the charter. Uphold and improve the system of employee directors and employee supervisors, deepen factory transparency, and actively utilize digital technology to provide more precise and convenient services for industrial workers' democratic participation. (Ministry of Ecology and Environment of the PRC 2024)

Western Labor scholars pervasively oppose the Chinese model rooted in a party–union alliance, even as it has proven effective in representing workers and improving their quality of life. The Chinese trade union model rejects the spontaneous and anarchic unionism which is gaining influence among labor analysts and is frequently found in the West in response to declining trade union density and government and corporate efforts to undermine working class power. The success of holistic socialist trade unionism under market socialism suggests that the CPC–trade union model is appropriate for countries on the periphery in search of balanced development. In coordination with the International Labour Organization, the ACFTU is assisting trade unions in Asia and the Pacific to foster trade union growth and building working class organizational power in contrast to the ineffective prototypes advocated by the International Trade Union Confederation, centered on economism and the subordination of labor to capital (ITUC 2025).

As more Western Labor Studies literature repudiates its own models of trade unions, and others contemplate syndicalist unions deprived of power, the Chinese socialist model offers a realistic and constructive alternative for the reconstitution of socialist party-trade unionism throughout the global South. At present, a growing number of unions are seeking to build socialist alliances: for instance, the National Union of Metalworkers of South Africa (NUMSA). However, in the absence of a strong and resilient vanguard party dedicated to advancing workers' long term class interests, even strong trade unions like NUMSA are limited in their capacity to develop socialism. Nor can they compel governments to invest in necessary technology to stimulate sustained socialist development. Socialist unions like NUMSA in capitalist states like South Africa are thwarted and vulnerable to capitalist investments intended to extract surplus value from their members. Consequently, it is necessary for a socialist vanguard party to lead a socialist trade union as the CPC, the ACFTU and its affiliates have done, where rank-and-file democracy is encouraged through state owned workers' unions, enterprise unions and, at the grassroots, municipal and street level branches, with the support of the central federation.

7   Party Affiliated Trade Unions

This book argues that the ACFTU is a working class organization comparable to other trade unions worldwide which affiliate with a political party to advance the interests of the working class. In May 1925, at the Second National Labor Congress in Guangzhou, 166 trade unions all over China convened to form the All-China Federation of Trade Unions, dedicated to fostering working class unity under the leadership of the Communist Party of China. At the outset, the ACFTU affiliated unions organized geographically to represent and advance the worker struggles erupting on a municipal level (China Workers' Daily 2025). The formation of trade unions in China reflected the political experiences of workers. From the outset of trade unionism in the early 20th century, political struggle was not on the national level, a pattern which continues to the present. Ching Kwan Lee and critics of the ACFTU and CPC contend that the PRC prevents nationwide strikes, which are therefore cellular and inhibited by the state. However, China's trade union structure and practice were always local, even before the Chinese Revolution and formation of the PRC (Lee 2007). Furthermore, this book contends that the aim of many trade union federations is to align with a party which seeks to advance the interests of the working class. In this manner, the ACFTU alliance with the CPC is analogous to the relationships between the Trades Union Congress and the Labour Party in Britain, the Swedish Trade Union Confederation (LO) and the Social Democratic Party in Sweden, the Central Única dos Trabalhadores (CUT) and the Partido dos Trabalhadores (Workers Party) in Brazil, and the Centre of Indian Trade Unions and the Communist Party of India (Marxist) among several other trade union–party alliances in India.

The ACFTU–CPC alliance is distinctive as it has retained power for a century. Like other socialist and communist trade union federations, the ACFTU strives to represent the entire working class rather than segments of the working class based on ethnic or confessional identity. China's ACFTU is a mass organization operating in the context of a socialist state. To comprehend the ACFTU, one must grasp how trade unions operate under socialism as opposed to capitalism. Just like the Communist Party of the Soviet Union, the CPC is designed to reflect the subjective interests of the working class and functions within the context of a dictatorship of the proletariat. Unquestionably, working classes reflect the natural world and dialectical materialism. Thus, the party and trade union must reflect the collective interests of a diverse and endlessly changing Chinese working class.

Conclusion: All-China Federation of Trade Unions—the Transitional State and the Chinese Working Class

> Communism is not a state of affairs to be established, not an ideal to which reality must adjust itself. We call communism the real movement which abolishes the present state of things. (Karl Marx, *Economic and Philosophic Manuscripts of 1844*)

In view of the extensive size of both domestic and foreign sectors of the economy and the presence of market forces in both, class conflict continues in China. However, remarkably, under the Communist Party, conflict does not take an antagonistic form, as in a society in which capital has supremacy. In a transitional state, the Communist Party can advance a socialist model through its political command over the economy. Through central planning, the PRC mediates this contradiction. Hence, the position of the Communist Party is that the current "principal contradiction" focuses on raising living standards of the Chinese people and addressing unbalanced and inadequate development.

1   The Chinese Transitional State

The PRC Constitution establishes the elements of the transitional state as it strives toward socialism. In doing so, the Chinese transitional state must pivot to respond to the principal contradictions while also serving the working class as it develops a socialist mode of production. Concomitantly, China's trade union model operates under the guidelines that Lenin and Mao specify— prioritizing the working class through the All-China Federation of Trade Unions (ACFTU). The Federation is duty bound to carry out the Communist Party's directives and respond to the demands of the working class laboring in all sectors of the economy. The CPC Constitution directly recognizes that class contradictions remain in the PRC but in 2022 they are no longer the principal contradiction.

The Communist Party Constitution declares:

> owing to both domestic factors and international influences, a certain amount of class struggle will continue to exist for a long time to come, and under certain circumstances may even grow more pronounced, however, it is no longer the principal contradiction. (The State Council 2022)

The Communist Party sets policy through adjusting the economic policy in accordance with changing domestic and global political economy. Transitional states have had to defend hard-won state power. On the other hand, it has been necessary to interact with the world capitalist system to develop their productive forces. Moreover, transitional states must endure and counter the challenges of a sequence of oppositional forces within the world capitalist system that form the principal contradictions, notably neoliberal capitalist globalization. Neoliberalism represented the fundamental adversary from the 1980s to the present, and the Chinese state and CPC were compelled to respond to global pressures to defend their development project. China, governed by a communist party, has remained relevant in a world system dominated by counter-revolutionary forces.

China's economic accomplishments have been made possible through the alliance between the CPC and the working class. This book demonstrates that the ACFTU has been more decisive in advancing the conditions of the proletariat than other countries of the periphery with "free" trade unions imposed by the legacy of the imperialist core, forcing trade unions to abide by capitalist principles.

Chinese workers are dedicated members of their trade unions and the Communist Party without seeing this as an antagonistic relationship as both CPC and ACFTU complement one another to improve the conditions of the working class. The PRC transitional state permits government and non-public enterprises, and both political forces and market forces are developing the economy. To be sure, this presents complex choices and the CPC must make difficult decisions on the path forward. For example, the dilemma of how to use generated surplus: for immediate consumption or investments in production to generate future consumption. State-owned enterprises are under the direct or indirect control of the party. In SOEs, the Communist Party represents workers through the ACFTU and sets policy through managers. Undoubtedly, conflicts of interest can occur when workers are seeking to improve their conditions by appealing to an SOE's management, which also includes representatives of the

Communist Party. But the presence of the CPC also contains the likelihood of resolving conflict for the benefit of the security and progress of the transitional state.

Western anti-communist Labor research has constructed a false binary between the era of Mao Zedong and his successors. It neglects to take account of the significant challenges that China has confronted from its foundation as an undeveloped agrarian state in 1949 till now. In *Ten Crises: The Political Economy of China's Development (1949–2010)*, Tiejun Wen disputes this perspective and contends that, throughout its history, the Chinese state has encountered crises which have challenged the state–capital–worker relationship. According to Wen (2021), China's economic crises have not been ideological or political but rooted in endogenous and exogenous factors which have no bearing on the socialist perspective of the CPC's leadership. Rather, they were genuine contestations which have concretely appeared, and which state and party leaders were compelled to address.

2 Western Critiques of the Chinese Labor Movement

The ACFTU is the largest national labor federation of unions in the world, which on the surface appears similar to other national trade union federations in structure, organization and form. The ACFTU is among the oldest labor organizations in the world, having been founded by communists more than a hundred years ago in the 1920s and subsequently outlawed by the Chinese Nationalist Government in 1927. When the CPC gained power in 1949, the ACFTU was reestablished as a trade union with limited functions though, as the country transformed from a semi-feudal peripheral economy into an industrial economy integrated into the world economy, it took on an ever-larger role in representing workers in the workplaces. China is typically viewed as a socialist economy which transformed into a neoliberal market economy following the Mao era, but it is crucial to recognize that, since 1949, the country has been industrializing in response to a succession of economic crises and the challenge to modernize. Thus, from 1953 to about 1960, China placed greater reliance on the industrialized Soviet Union for economic development. In contrast to the strict demarcation of economic policy between Mao's era (1949–76) and the post-Mao, Deng Xiaoping/Xi Jinping era (1978–present), it is far more accurate to depict the PRC as experiencing a series of ten crises, as Tiejun Wen (2021) contends.

The ACFTU maintains features similar to those of national unions across the world, representing workers in ten national industrial unions and in each of the 31 provinces of the PRC. Moreover, the ACFTU is composed of 5.3 million grassroots labor organizations throughout the country. In 2018, it claimed to represent 300 million workers across 6.4 million enterprises, far more unionized workers than in any other single nation (ACFTU 2018). Moreover, the ACFTU claims more trade union members than the two largest international labor federations: the International Trade Union Confederation (ITUC), claiming to represent 191 million workers in August 2024 (ITUC 2024); and the World Federation of Trade Unions (WFTU), claiming 105 million members in 133 countries in August 2024 (WFTU 2024b).[1] Even using ITUC and WFTU 2024 membership statistics, the ACFTU exceeds the sum total of both federations by about 500 million workers. In 2024, the International Labour Organization (ILO) found that the ACFTU has been actively encouraging workers to join unions in "new forms of employment" (NFE) including the digital economy. These are deemed

---

1   The WFTU was formed in London at the close of the Second World War in 1945 by anti-fascist and socialist unions sympathetic to the USSR and the Third International. It was initially organized by 53 national and international organizations representing some 60 million workers comprising a range of unions, from the Congress of Industrial Organizations in the US to the Trades Union Congress (TUC) in the UK. A majority of the unions were and remain sympathetic to communism and socialism, including the All-Union Central Council of Trade Unions of the USSR, the General Confederation of Labour in France, the Chinese Federation of Labour and Confederation of Labour, and the Confederation of Workers in Latin America. The onset of the Cold War in the late 1940s culminated in 1949 with the split of Western trade unions away from the WFTU into the US-dominated International Confederation of Free Trade Unions (ICFTU), as a political and labor front against communist trade unions which formed a significant part of the WFTU. After the fall of the Soviet Union in 1991, the WFTU declined to a nadir of 48 million workers in 2005 but has since relocated to Athens, Greece, as its membership has increased to 105 million, a large majority of whom are in countries of the global South (WFTU 2024a). Since the end of the Cold War, the ICFTU (now the International Trade Union Confederation (ITUC)) has deprecated the WFTU as a communist organization which failed to transform into a liberal or social-democratic international organization. Yet ITUC has maintained a Cold War ideology even after its end in 1990 through its staunch opposition to trade unions that did not join its support for Western capitalism and opposition to all existing communist states. ITUC enjoys far greater resources, in part because a large share of its membership resides in rich Western societies of the global North, has the capacity to employ representatives at high wages and enjoys an active presence through international sectoral labor federations. But the WFTU's opposition to privatization, economic inequality, informal and precarious labor and poverty has significant purchase among the rural and urban working classes of Africa, Asia, Latin America and poor countries more generally. In contrast to the ITUC, the WFTU does not support Western imperialist states of Western Europe and North America, which are viewed as engaging in extractive policies which do not contribute to development but instead foster pervasive poverty, economic imperialism and neocolonialism.

to be the most challenging sectors, which have excluded trade unions outside of China. Tu Wei and Xueyu Wang found the ACTFU had been:

> [a]ctively exploring ways to encourage the lorry drivers, online taxi drivers, couriers and riders to join trade unions. Implementing online applications for union membership, and innovative service contents and service models; (2) Initiat[ing] consultations with industry associations, head enterprises or representative organizations on piece-rate unit prices, commissions, labour quotas, labour protections, rewards and punishment systems in the industry.

In addition, the ACFTU is initiating applicable laws, regulations and policies through pilot projects to prevent occupational injuries; and implementing legal services which directly apply to platform work and to resolving disputes which may arise between management and workers in the digital sector, while providing vocational and jobs-skills training and even mental-health support services (Wei & Wang 2024, 42).

Even if workers are not organized in these challenging digital sectors of the economy, China's union density rate (measuring the share of the platform economy's workers who are in unions) is about 25 percent when in the rest of the world barely any workers in the sector are members of trade unions. In addition, the ACFTU is fostering legislative changes to improve working conditions. Workers in emergent digital sectors of the platform economy, logistics, ride hailing and so on have only recently become the object of organizational efforts by grassroots unions in major urban centers (including Guangzhou, Shenzhen and other large municipalities), but this mobilization on multiple levels is a remarkable achievement.

Western research on the ACFTU is uneven and lacks rigor and in most instances ignores statistics and data compiled by the Chinese government as well as reports by the ACFTU and its provincial, district and street-level affiliates. Most analytic and interpretative perspectives are derived from Western Labor Studies and sociology literature. Certainly, some have conducted research but there are few dependable Western sources on the Chinese labor movement available. China Labor Studies sociologist Ching Kwan Lee (2007) formulates a critique of trade union activity under market socialism through ethnographic research interviews from the late 1990s to 2003, a period of extensive change from an agrarian economy to market socialism. The conclusions, which seem predetermined, are not nuanced nor do they take into consideration the immeasurable necessity for the ACFTU to respond to social dislocation and unemployment. The primary aim is to discredit the trade union federation. Not once does the book provide evidence of positive trade union responses to technological change and industrialization. Moreover, the book does not reflect on the primary beneficiaries of the initial stages of opening up: Western multinationals who invested in Chinese manufacturing and benefit from the unequal exchange of trade between Chinese workers and Western consumers. Both Western investors and consumers profited from low wage labor at the expense of Chinese workers. It was only after Chinese wages and working conditions improved that opposition from free market capitalists emerged. Their profit margins were not as high as expected due to the ACFTU and the CPC's commitment to organizing labor and improving the conditions of the Chinese industrial working class as well as those who had entered the service and logistics sectors, which primarily serve domestic requirements rather than foreign multinationals. Lee's examination of the Chinese working class as the Chinese political economy was seeking to modernize is striking for the way it debases a genuine endeavor to modernize the economy which the PRC had strived for since its formation in 1949.

Western Sinologists are fixated with "the spectacle" of the mass demonstration and rally against the party and state rather than protests directed at foreign multinational firms, which have steadily advanced in the 21st century. To diminish working class activism in China, Lee conjures the term "cellular activism" in *Against the Law* (2007) to imply that most activism is directed at local authorities rather than the CPC and the Chinese state. To be sure, Lee is correct, but "cellular activism" may reveal support for the PRC and opposition to changing the nature of the socialist state. Directing protest against local authorities is the most effective technique to gain concessions and represents a form of "bottom-up" unionism or "organizing from below," terms applied by Western Labor scholars to identify best practices in union organization.

3   Occupational Safety: United States and China

A significant problem with Western Labor Studies is its propensity to identify shortcomings and policy concerns as they occur and not to update the research when the ACFTU responds to labor market transformations. In the real world, institutions respond upon learning and absorbing information and then afterwards enacting and implementing policies directly. Moreover, unlike in the US, the ACFTU in China implements policy which will remain unaffected by electoral shifts. Thus, in the US, when the Democratic Party holds power, the National Labor Relations Board and other government institutions may issue policy directives but often they never come to fruition due to a later shift to the Republican Party, which selects anti-labor officials and adjudicators. Five year plans are intended to prevent evading and equivocating on the implementation of labor policy precisely because of the necessity to put laws into practice. Realization of policy directives cannot occur instantaneously even in the best of circumstances. Consequently, China's five year plans account for the passage of time in improving labor conditions. In sharp contrast, US labor institutions are not held accountable for the absence of enforcement of workplace safety laws passed over 50 years ago. The Occupational Safety and Health Administration (OSHA) is notorious for its indifference to enforcing violations by private business.

The Occupational Safety and Health Act did not become a federal law until 1970, a half century after mass production industries dominated the US industrial landscape. Yet, according to most accounts, OSHA has not appreciably improved workplace safety in the US. According to Michael Felsen, in 2021, more than 50 years since the passage of OSHA:

> an average of 16 workers died each day from traumatic injuries at work, totaling 5190 in the course of the year. Add to that figure an estimated 120,000 deaths annually from occupational illnesses. In 2021, employers reported almost 3.2 million workplace-related injuries and illnesses. But because under-reporting is so common, it is believed that in private industry alone, the toll of work-related injuries and illnesses is somewhere between 5.4 million and 8.1 million each year. (Felsen 2024, 133–134)

According to the American Federation of Labor and Congress of Industrial Organizations (AFL-CIO), in 2021 (the last year a report was published, due to the absence of sufficient inspectors) it would take OSHA 190 years to inspect the 7 million workplaces under its jurisdiction in the US due to the shortage of staff. Due to hiring freezes, OSHA cannot be considered a serious workplace safety monitoring and enforcement agency (AFL-CIO 2023). Fatality rates in the US are rising, and, in most cases, OSHA is unable to document violations, especially in those industries which are most dangerous: agriculture, forestry, fishing and hunting, logistics, mining and other extractive industries. A disproportionate share of fatalities is among Black and Latino workers. Without explanation, from 1970 to 2020, only 128 criminal cases involving worker deaths have been prosecuted under the Occupational Safety and Health Act, an inexplicable average of 2.56 cases a year (Felsen 2024).

Conspicuously the US is not a signatory to the hallmark ILO resolution promoting occupational safety and health worldwide (C155, the Occupational Safety and Health Convention of 1981), a convention which has been ratified by China, Cuba, the Russian Federation, Vietnam and Laos. In contrast, the major states which have not ratified the convention along with the US are France, Germany, Indonesia and India.[2]

Undeniably, most China Labor Studies scholars in the West have a general interest in solving the perceived problems but most make blanket assertions outside the parameters of what is possible and the limitations of what is impossible. A blind spot among Western scholars is the failure to consider the shift of the working class from agrarian labor to urban industrial work. The share of Chinese urban workers has grown from about 10 percent to over 65 percent in just 35 years. Even if China Labor researchers recognize the magnitude of urbanization, most largely pay no attention to the challenge posed to the CPC and ACFTU of incorporating nearly 1 billion people into urban areas. Instead, they point to the shortcomings of the CPC and the trade unions and focus on the deficiencies of specific segments of the Chinese working class under market socialism (Solinger 2022). To a fault, practically all China Labor scholars engage in cryptic terms without explanation. For instance, the term "party-state" is used disparagingly without explaining that China is in fact a state dominated by the Communist Party and the ACFTU and must abide by directives advanced by the CPC. The inference is that China should have a multiparty system and unions with a range of political perspectives. Using a Leninist perspective, the working class party must retain authority and trade unions retain discipline in supporting the party in which they are affiliated. In most states, party and trade union discipline is a virtue as it contributes to accountability to a worker's state.

Western Labor scholars mock the sincere effort to modernize an agrarian workers' state into an urban advanced workers' state, drawing on anti-communist code that is meaningless for all but those who strive to study China. For instance, Western Labor Studies scholars like Dorothy Solinger use the term "regime" to describe the Chinese government and "strongman" in place of Chairman Mao Zedong. One can only conclude that there is both

---

2   The ILO convention regulates all forms of economic activity in the workplace, and all signatory countries are subject to penalties for non-compliance. ILO Occupational Safety and Health Convention 1981 (No. 155) calls on all member states to formulate, implement and periodically review a coherent national policy on occupational safety in the light of national conditions and practice, and in consultation with the most representative organizations of employers and workers, occupational health and the working environment, aiming to prevent accidents and injury to health arising out of, linked with or occurring in the course of work, by minimizing, so far as is reasonably practicable, the causes of hazards inherent in the working environment. The convention also protects workers from disciplinary measures because of actions properly taken by them in conformity with the policy. Employers also bear responsibility for paying all costs associated with implementing the policy (ILO 2025).

a lack of academic sincerity and a political agenda behind these and other efforts to debase the Chinese socialist state and its people. Periodizing specific moments in Chinese history since 1978, Solinger suggests that from 1949 to 1976 the Chinese were more contented and comfortable than after the opening up. Unquestionably, the Maoist era contributed to major advances in life expectancy, caloric intake and the quality of life. But how is it possible to contend in the year 2022 that the Chinese state is calculatingly seeking to devalue human lives? This double bind reveals a disingenuous effort to focus on shortcomings of the Chinese socialist project to eradicate poverty following the most arduous years of transforming the country from an agrarian to a modern urban socialist economy. Both suggesting there were better times and asserting that the Chinese working class is even more impoverished today through drawing on specific population cohorts is also incorrect. For Solinger and the expansive circle of opponents of the Chinese state, the implication is that, after Mao, poverty is expanding and the destitution of the Maoist era has been superseded by a new impoverished urban working class today (2022, 1–8). To be charitable, this pervasive position and condescending rhetoric have been pervasive in every period from the formation of the PRC in 1949 to the present. Alarmingly, the circle is expanding as academic funding for research on China expands.

The perspective contradicts numerous studies in the West showing that the Chinese workers movement was both militant and more democratic (Pringle 2011). Tim Pringle's account of the innovative experiments of the ACFTU in 2011, driven by the working class, is no longer accentuated as positive commentary on the trade union federation is *verboten* in the Labor Studies literature (Pringle 2011).

Much of the Western literature is drawn from non-governmental organizations (NGOs) or research and secondhand accounts about workers. Some researchers use official Chinese government statistical research, but the data is slanted to demonstrate an erosion of working class economic conditions over the past two decades; a view which is wholly incorrect, not just on the basis of flawed interpretations of Chinese sources but also due to a failure to acknowledge even Western accounts of a dramatic improvement in standards of living. The main narrative is to disparage China for its exploitation of the working class, though there are variations on the theme. Some scholars, who typically wish to demonstrate the erosion of the conditions of the Chinese working class and the rise of an authoritarian state under the neoliberal reforms and so forth, share a common position with the neoconservatives in the West that Chinese workers are highly exploited and that their conditions are worsening as the ACFTU fails to represent their interests. Slightly more realistic scholars are more charitable, conceding that the ACFTU has reformed itself in response to worker demands over the past two decades. Yet among this faction, the ACFTU is viewed as responding only to pressure applied by the PRC, not in response to the rising class consciousness and working class subjectivity of workers, many of whom are migrant workers or their children whose conditions have appreciably improved in the Deng years (*c.*1978–93). Taken together, opponents of the ACFTU are propagating distortions and misinformation which are drawn from most of the academic literature.

Paradoxically, the ACFTU's critics comprise a disparate patchwork of opponents, from the far right to the far left, including corporate opponents of trade unions in China and right wing economists, Labor Studies researchers in the West, NGOs, and opponents of the Chinese state more generally, including Western trade unions. A primary opponent of the ACFTU is the Western left, including anarchists, autonomists, social democrats, Trotskyists and, incongruously, those who claim to be supporters of the legacy of Mao Zedong and the Chinese Revolution, and even some who are self-described anti-imperialists.

4   Measuring the ACFTU by Western Metrics

This chapter asserts that Labor critics of the ACFTU are engaging in Western institutional metrics of and perspectives on work, labor, unions and even class which are inapplicable and superfluous to China's labor regime. Moreover, and consequentially, the ACFTU and its provincial, municipal and street (local level) affiliates are placed in a catch-22 dilemma by Western Labor Studies scholars, who mostly oppose the Chinese state and apply standards incongruous to the developing political economy which no other country even approaches. Further, most critics condemn the PRC for an erosion of conditions from the Maoist era even as, on every measure, prosperity has flourished in the aftermath of the shift to the market economy. For example, China's labor regime is castigated by some for high levels of unrest and by others for having too little. By way of illustration, in *Against the Law*, Ching Kwang Lee contends that labor militancy is expansive but is circumscribed and does not spread into a social movement which destabilizes and implicitly overthrows the Chinese socialist system (Lee 2007).

Lee's view is that work stoppages, strikes and general social upheaval necessarily contribute to improved wages and working conditions. Thus, all things being equal, higher social discontent and work stoppages are a dependent variable for higher standards of living and working conditions. Such Labor critics do not distinguish the historical practices and path dependence of state policies but apply a universal metric devoid of historical, political, organizational and economic classification. However, the short and long term historical evidence outside China reveals that, more often than not, strikes and labor unrest do not contribute to improved conditions but often to failure, with the state almost always supporting capital. Frequently, workers are not only recurrently sacked but also imprisoned and even killed by state security forces.

Neglecting how all capitalist states seek to engender business profitability, stability and social cohesion, Lee's portrait represents almost all Western Labor Studies literature in presupposing that labor militancy by definition contributes to improved conditions. However, when one examines strikes and labor unrest in the West, one finds a record of failure. For example, when the Professional Air Traffic Controllers Organization (PATCO) went on strike in August 1981, President Ronald Reagan sacked all workers involved within 48 hours, and the union was decertified 2.5 months later. Of the 13,000 PATCO workers, only 10 percent who did not go on strike remained in their jobs, despite the fact that the union had endorsed Reagan for president and most members were armed forces veterans (McCartin 2012). If Reagan could dismantle a professional union, the course was set for the erosion of unions throughout the country. By 2023, a year of labor mobilization and upsurge in the US, only 6.0 percent of all private sector workers were represented by trade unions, a decline from 6.8 percent in 2022 (BLS 2024).

An examination of three major strikes in the global South between 2005 and 2013 demonstrates that Chinese workers were not fired, imprisoned or killed for engaging in strikes, in sharp contrast to practices in most developing countries, especially India and South Africa (Ness 2015; Pun 2005).

Consequently, whether genuinely or not, Western opponents of the ACFTU are invested in demonstrating that the Federation is ineffective and lacks autonomy from the Chinese state without considering that an institutional form of class conflict was formed in 1949 and continues to this day. Certainly, low wages and conditions cause labor unrest and union responses to address the problems. Thus, the terms "party-state" and "party-union" are proffered to demonstrate the ineffectiveness of the ACFTU due to its affiliation with the CPC. Instead, an accurate assessment of Chinese labor organizing and the ACFTU is holistic, denoting bottom-up demands from workers seeking remedies and top-down outcomes and resolutions fostered by the ACFTU. In turn, the ACFTU frequently anticipates and identifies labor market changes and their impact on workers. In reality, opponents are responding to the presence of a strong and effective union which seeks to alleviate and improve workers' wages, working conditions and social insurance.

5   Labor Unions and Political Parties: a Comparative Global Analysis

To recognize the efficacy of the ACFTU, it is necessary to assess labor organizations worldwide, a question addressed in Chapter 3. Since the early 20th century, Labor scholars have recognized the significant connection of working class strength to strong labor based political parties.

While trade union–political party alliances have been considered positively, Labor Studies scholars make an exception for the significance of labor based parties in socialist countries; and, since 2000, Chinese unions have been inexplicably excluded from calculations of the organizational power of the working class, despite the fact that they have a robust labor federation which is affiliated with the labor based CCP. Rather, the ACFTU is derided and scorned by most Labor Studies scholars because it is linked to a political party, despite it far exceeding Western trade unions in promoting working class interests. While it is important to consider the ACFTU within the context of a socialist state, when one compares today's trade union federation to Western trade union models from the past, the ACFTU is decidedly more effective.

In 1900, the Labour Party in the UK was founded by the Labour Representation Committee and affiliated with the Labour Party to elect 13 of the 39 members of the Labour Party's National Executive Committee. In addition, members of labor unions today are ex officio members and often delegates of the Labour Party. The UK's TUC, the national labor federation, predated the formation of the Labor Party and, even if it is not unequivocally affiliated with the latter, has historically been the primary force exercising power and influence over Labour Governments in Britain. Its constituent unions have participated directly in the party and almost always endorse its candidates in elections (Allen 1968).

At its apogee in 1946, almost all unions in Britain were affiliated with the Labour Party. Though membership declined marginally with the party's embrace of neoliberalism under Prime Minister Tony Blair (1994–2007), taken together, British as well as European trade unions are synonymous with their labor-based parties. Irrespective of government policy and the rise of neoliberalism, UK trade unions have not broken their relationship with Labour as it drifts to the right on labor conditions but have reluctantly remained aligned with the party (Hyman & Gumbrell-McCormick 2010). Trade unions in general must not criticize and mobilize against their federations and labor-based parties. In those instances when trade unions have denounced Labour Governments, they have risked expulsion from the federation, as was the case in 2004 when the Labour Party of Britain expelled the RMT (National Union of Rail Maritime and Transport Workers) and several other trade unions for disparaging Tony Blair's opposition to renationalizing the railway system (Wring 2005).

Generally, with several exceptions, a similar pattern of loyalty despite bitterness against the trade union federation appears in Western Europe and North America, with the notable exception of the US, where the Democratic Party frequently breaks with working class positions advanced by trade unions. In the wake of the decline of trade unions and the support of the Democratic Party for neoliberal policies, the US working class have had no institutional representative. Consequently, workers are supporting populist Republicans.

The erosion of labor unions as representatives of the working class against capital in the neoliberal era has been pervasive and absolute, particularly in Western Europe and North America. In the West, labor is regarded as a casualty of the application of market reforms and the removal of constraints on capital. The attrition of labor unions here has left workers defenseless against capital flight, industrial restructuring and the closure of unions, which have endured since the foundation of mass production industries and the Fordist factory model. In the absence of established unions, scholarship has shifted to new forms of labor representation: NGOs, workers' centers and autonomous unaffiliated unions (Ness 2014). But the most significant consequences of the disappearance of unions have been poverty and inequality. Sociologists Ruth Dukes and Wolfgang Streeck assert that the loss of the state in governing labor policy and the erosion of trade union institutions has given rise to higher levels of inequality and job insecurity:

> What happened to work and workers as the state-managed capitalism of the postwar era—the postwar settlement, as it is sometimes called—was replaced by neoliberal capitalism? What are the losses, the gains if any, and how, if at all, can the losses be recovered? Are growing inequality, widespread precarity, stepped-up market pressure on wages and employment conditions, the intensification of work, declining social protection and mounting tensions between work and family life inevitable or incurable, or can they … be mitigated? In short: can remedies be found for the ailments of a neoliberal labour regime, and how exactly should they be conceived and applied? (Dukes & Streeck 2023, vi)

To diminish this challenge to social cohesion and living standards which neoliberalism has created, it is necessary to craft a form of industrial citizenship. Dukes and Streeck, who are not China scholars, dismiss the country's trade union model in a few sentences as the antithesis of industrial citizenship without even examining its state owned enterprises (SOEs) and widespread union membership, direct elections and labor participation in decisions (2023, 75). Yet, their concern is focused on the West, where unionization has disappeared, and not the global South, which has never had a modicum of viable unions outside of core sectors. This notwithstanding, the Leninist model of trade unionism is not rooted in industrial democracy as perceived by Western Labor Studies scholars but in a holistic model of bottom-up and top-down unionism wherein worker demands are typically assumed by the ACFTU, and labor's demands are transmitted to employers.

Most Labor Studies scholars evaluate trade unions exclusively from the narrow Western perspective with a preconceived notion that workers' organizations must resemble those of the US. This view fails to consider the numerous forms of labor representation present outside the West. Moreover, this defective perception does not seek to augment the power and influence of unions but maintains a constrained and inflexible notion that union democracy is synonymous with independence from political parties and the state. Paradoxically, unions with the highest rank-and-file participation are linked to parties which seek to define state policies. If one's definition of the ideal trade union is to have weak and ineffective influence and highly circumscribed capacities to bargain and negotiate with employers and influence state policy, the US model is best.

Labor historian Marcel van der Linden comprehends a world system beyond the rich countries where labor unions had become phlegmatic even before the institution of neoliberal reforms which eroded their representational and bargaining capacities and promoted a fear of challenging management and engaging in strikes and other job actions. One consequence of weak unions is that workers in the West have decreasing interest in joining them.

One of the great paradoxes of the current era is that the world's working class continues to grow, while, at the same time, many labor movements are experiencing a crisis. The absolute and relative growth of the global working class and its increasing interconnectedness might suggest that the world labor movement is growing stronger. Nothing could be further from the truth. Traditional labor movements are in trouble almost everywhere. They have been severely enfeebled by the political and economic changes of the last 40 years (van der Linden 2023, 315–316).

Still, the fact that most workers in rich Western countries are not even members of trade unions may also denote that unionization does not have significant consequences on wages and conditions. In addition, state social welfare systems which unions advocated for on behalf of the working class in the West paradoxically diminished interest in union membership. In short, though neoliberalism has produced inequality and intensifying socio-economic conflict through rising populism and xenophobia, it is also obvious that labor in Western Europe, North America and other wealthy states has transformed into a labor aristocracy benefiting from the inequality of trade between nations, inasmuch as workers in poor countries of the global South are paid a fraction of the wages for equivalent labor, a drawback to achieving global working class solidarity (see e.g. Edwards 1978; Emmanuel 1972/2025). In the last two decades, a new wave of scholars has emerged to demonstrate the long history of unequal exchange under capitalism as production at the periphery and distribution in the core intensifies (Brand & Wissen 2021; Hickel 2018; Kerswell 2018; Lauesen 2018; Ness 2015; Ricci 2019).

However, van der Linden is another scholar who shares the implicit but unsubstantiated perspective that all labor conflict in China, which must always be positive, occurs outside the ACFTU as the latter is linked with the CPC, rather than recognizing the holistic connection between rank-and-file workers and the trade union. In a footnote, he cites a British citizen who works for Multinational Monitor, an anti-CPC NGO in Hong Kong. Once more, a potentially sympathetic labor historian is subscribing to a position that all labor disputes must end in conflict, even in a socialist state. But van der Linden's predisposition to oppose the ACFTU is evident in how he views the PRC as a "capitalist economy without independent trade unions" (2023, 317) like those which formed in Europe and North America in the 19th century.[3] He is an independent historian who agrees with the monolithic anti-ACFTU position among Labor scholars and does not address the question of why a party based labor movement is supposedly ruinous for China but not for the rest of the world.

6   Strengthening Unions through Party Affiliation

Robust and disciplined trade unions affiliated with labor-based parties were the primary factor in the growth of unions in the 20th century. The decline

---

3   A principal of the organization is a Hong Kong nationalist, Au Loong-Yu, who both expresses repugnance for Chinese nationals as well as opposition to the larger and better funded China Labour Bulletin (CLB) and its leader. The latter, Han Dongfang, has a checkered and dubious political background as an operative for the US government and is a recipient of funds from the National Endowment for Democracy, an arm of the US State Department. Both organizations are now defunct as their critiques have been addressed by the ACFTU as it responded to the emergence and growth of market socialism. In June 2025, CLB officially disbanded (Yu et al. 2013). Effectively, the failure of the anti-China labor NGOs in Hong Kong to resonate with the Chinese working class played a significant part in their closure, along with the end of US government funding.

in labor based political parties is a function of two principal factors: (1) rising wages in the West and the decline in the working class as a consequence of the shift away from industrial economies; (2) unions' inability to convince members to support (even labor based) political parties which have shifted towards neoliberalism.

The scolding of China has also given rise to the dangerous rise of rhetoric which is appropriated by right wing populists and the US national security state. The main assertions are that China is a capitalist country which only claims to be socialist to mislead its working class, and that the ACFTU is not a union. The shibboleth that China is capitalist is formulated by liberals, social democrats, sectarian Trotskyists and doctrinaire non-revisionists who maintain a utopian, even religious, conviction devoid of an understanding of historical materialism. Consequently, some share the position of the US State Department on China (Friedman et al. 2024). Their bald assertion (shared by the US State Department, National Endowment for Democracy and the Central Intelligence Agency) is proffered that China is the fount of opposition to its own working class and ecological sustainability, oppresses women activists and imprisons ethnic minorities. Worse, they believe international solidarity is only advanced through opposing the Chinese imperialist enemy. Are we to believe that this diatribe is a form of balanced scholarship? This "left" position has serious repercussions which sustain military spending, support economic sanctions and economic nationalism, and contribute in Western Europe and North America to the disturbing growth of xenophobia against migrant workers there who form a significant potential demographic for unions to organize (Gumbrell-McCormick & Hyman 2013; Ness 2023b).

Most Labor scholars consider the labor based political party emerged in the 20th century to strengthen the influence and power of labor unions and their members. Political parties of the late 19th and early 20th centuries in the West were considered essential for strengthening working class power against greedy private sector businesses which had exploited workers without restraint. Consequently, socialist and communist parties in North America and Europe formed and contributed to a dramatic increase in wages, living standards and working conditions (Dubofsky & McCartin 2017; Lichtenstein 2013; Taylor 1989).

Most trade unions in Europe and beyond are directly affiliated with political parties, or what is commonly designated a labor based party. In the US, however, the AFL-CIO is considered an interest group and is not linked directly to a political party even if most of its constituent national unions endorse the Democratic Party, which itself does not view the AFL-CIO as a direct affiliate. Rarely do national unions endorse the Republican Party (viz International

Brotherhood of the Teamsters and, periodically, other unions, e.g. the United Auto Workers, which broke with the Democratic Party under Walter Reuther in opposition to its support for the US war in Vietnam). In India, almost every national trade union is directly affiliated with a political party, including communist parties. Why, then, opposition to the ACFTU? This chapter's hypothesis is that while the ACFTU represents a panoply of interests, its affiliation with the CPC, which holds state power, contributes to cynicism and derision.

Yet, the book argues that the ACFTU's connection to the CPC confers on its members superior economic and bargaining power. For the CPC, the working class not the capitalist class is the decisive and most significant constituency. Therefore, the ACFTU and its members are given precedence over capital in almost every dispute.

In 2010, the wave of labor mobilizations against primarily private capital posed a major challenge to the ACFTU and the CPC leadership, forcing it to decide whether to uphold its support for the working class or shift support to public and private capital. Most of the Western academic literature critical of China documents strikes and labor insurrections in the period from 2010 to 2013 but does not scrutinize how the Chinese state and the ACFTU responded to the actions as they were unfolding, or to the formulation of policy in reaction. Would the ACFTU, CPC and Chinese state support capital or workers?

7   Too Little Unrest or Too Much Unrest

In the aftermath of the strike wave of c.2010–13, critics of the ACFTU, the CPC and the Chinese state engaged in a contradictory debate. Like many other NGOs, the now defunct CLB thrived on distorting facts about the Chinese working class, inflating the number of strikes and job actions for the consumption of foreigners to oppose the Chinese state. In its final years of existence before it folded, the CLB did little more than encourage transparency in democratic elections for union leaders even as most unions in the US did not even hold elections, and when they did, the outcome was typically undemocratic due to manipulation of electoral procedures (Harris et al. 2007).

Labor studies scholars and NGOs share a perspective that too much labor unrest revealed a direct challenge to the Chinese Communist state: If workers engaged in strikes, they were opposed to their employers, their trade unions, the CPC and the Chinese state.

Other opponents assert that too little unrest reveals that workers are highly repressed and discouraged from striking by fear of government suppression and crackdowns, a claim which contradicts official policy encouraging workers to press wage, insurance and working condition claims against employers. Alternatively, they stress that Chinese workers lack class consciousness and are partners in their own repression, an explanation for the failure to form a labor movement. Once again, applying Western perspective to a socialist state, overlooking the nature of China as a "dictatorship of the working class" where oppositional movements are promoted by the US and the West to undermine a socialist state's efforts to resolve labor-management disputes; precisely the same goal of trade unions in the US (Lin 2020). Apart from strong evidence that workers seek to improve their wages and conditions through their unions, the ACFTU supports worker self-activity to improve their conditions. Once again, we are confronted with the attempt to apply liberal bourgeois class relations to a socialist state. Jake Lin views production center workers in secondary cities as lacking class consciousness and uninterested in striking. No consideration is offered for the possibility that, rather than lacking class consciousness, workers in the interior might have been content with their work and preferred to settle disputes through labor courts rather than job actions and mass anti-systemic social movements. By contrast, the failure of labor union organizing in the US South from the 1990s to 2020s was attributed to rapacious anti-union lawyers and corporate campaigns in opposition to trade unions, with few placing the onus on the workers themselves. Perhaps workers at foreign automobile factory transplants in the US viewed their jobs as far preferable to those with a lower capital investment in other sectors of the economy (Silvia 2023). Ironically, the current anti-union scholarship derives from Marxist research in the 1970s and 1980s which maintains that workers are apathetic about their jobs, generated primarily in production industries which consider trade unions to be uninterested in and unengaged with workers, who are in turn unmotivated by pride in their jobs or the quality of their work and only engage in necessary labor to earn their pay checks (Burawoy 1982). Harry Braverman (1974) and Stanley Aronowitz (1973) hold a corresponding view that industrial laborers are highly alienated from labor under monopoly capitalism.

Taken together, it is essential to examine the limitations of trade unions and labor movements throughout the world. However, if the US is the archetype for unions, then the Chinese labor movement is far more advanced by almost every measure: organizing and mobilization, trade union density, work actions and the orderly and rapid settlement of disputes through labor courts, which almost always favor workers over managers. Even if the ACFTU is governed by a sclerotic bureaucracy, it at least has the will to improve conditions, and, crucially, Xi Jinping and the CPC are determined to inculcate and deepen community level participation, especially in the industrial centers of Guangdong,

Zhejiang, Jiangsu, Shandong and Hebei provinces on the Chinese eastern littoral but also, increasingly, in the country's growing urban centers located inland (Xu 2025).

Applying a non-Western measure of the responsibility of trade unions, the All-China Federation of Trade Unions represents the interests of the working class under the directive of the CPC. The ACFTU is charged by the CPC to ensure that trade unions organize hundreds of millions of workers and to ensure that workers "actively participate" in advancing the goals of the workers' state. To underscore the objective goals of the CPC and ACFTU, it is important to quote at length General Secretary Xi Jinping's remarks at the 18th General Congress of the CPC on October 23, 2023:

> China's working class has played the role of the main force in the development of the Party and the country's undertakings, the cause of the labor movement has made historic achievements, and the work of trade unions has realized all-round progress. Over the past five years, the masses of workers and workers have been concentrating with the Party and struggling with it and have demonstrated an era of boldness and courage in fighting hard battles and carrying heavy burdens in major tasks such as economic construction, scientific and technological innovation, poverty alleviation, rural revitalization, epidemic prevention and control, and disaster rescue and relief. The All-China Federation of Trade Unions (ACFTU) and trade unions at all levels have strengthened the ideological and political leadership of workers, pushed forward the reform of the construction of the industrial workforce, safeguarded the rights and interests of workers, maintained political security in the field of labor, deepened the reform of the trade union system, and increased the political, advanced and mass nature of trade unions. The CPC Central Committee fully recognizes the significant contributions made by the working class and the new achievements made by trade unions. The CPC Central Committee has high expectations for the new leadership of the All-China Federation of Trade Unions.

On the subject of the relationship between the CPC and the working class, Xi Jinping calls attention to the significance of leadership, education and the centrality of the working class:

> It is necessary to strengthen ideological and political leadership, do a good job in the ideological and political work of workers, educate and guide the majority of workers to unswervingly listen to the Party and follow the Party, and ensure that the working class is always the most solid and reliable class foundation of our Party.

Xi Jinping further draws attention to the unity of the masses of workers and the CPC to advance the interests of the working class through education and training for the development of society:

> We should focus on implementing the new development concept, building a new development pattern, and promoting high-quality development, widely and deeply carry out various forms of labor and skill competitions, stimulate the enthusiasm for labor and creative potential of the majority of workers, and give full play to the role of the main force in all fields of all walks of life. We should vigorously carry forward the spirit of model workers, labor spirit and craftsmanship, give full play to the role of model workers and craftsmen as demonstrators and leaders, and inspire the vast number of workers to achieve their dreams through hard work, honesty and creativity. We should focus on the in-depth implementation of the strategy of developing the country through science and education, the strategy of strengthening the country through talents, and the strategy of innovation-driven development, deepen the reform of the construction of the industrial workforce, accelerate the construction of an army of knowledge-based, skilled and innovative industrial workers, and cultivate and create more great master craftsmen and high-skilled talents.

Insofar as the PRC is a workers' state, the objective of the trade unions is to advance the immediate and long-term interests of workers rather than oppose their class interests, which are materially advanced by the CPC.

The working class and the broad masses of working people are the main creators of social wealth, and the promotion of more visible and substantial progress in the common prosperity of all people should be reflected first and foremost in the hundreds of millions of workers. Trade unions, as the representatives and defenders of workers' interests, should earnestly fulfill their basic duties of safeguarding rights and services, focus on solving practical problems of immediate interest to the masses of workers, and pay attention to safeguarding the legitimate rights and interests of workers in new employment patterns. They should strengthen the democratic management of enterprises and public institutions, smooth the channels for workers to express their demands, guide workers to safeguard their rights and interests in accordance with the law, and promote the construction of harmonious labor relations.

Finally, the ACFTU is charged with deepening the reform of trade unions to advance the interests of the working class. The task of furthering the interests of the working class is enduring and at no point does it come to an end—just as nature and material conditions are transformed through humans, the ACFTU must adapt to changes to defend the collective interests of the working class (Xi Jinping 2023). The Western scholarship on labor is dominated by opponents of the PRC who disparage the state protections and trade union representation as well as minimize the difficult task of improving the conditions of all workers. The opposing positions are refuted by statistical evidence and empirical evidence. Briefly, the central contentions focus on the mistaken position that the CPC and ACFTU are unwilling or failing to address challenges from a burgeoning urban workforce. Even ephemeral research, corroborated by the ILO, shows the allegations are specious.

According to this narrative, the ACFTU is not a trade union in any shape or form but a repressive authoritarian organization which controls workers' wage demands and represses all forms of dissent. This position is taken by almost all Western Labor scholars who view China in absolute terms and hold the country up to a high bar. As such, they argue that China's unions lack purity and legitimacy, despite established evidence even by opponents that the ACFTU is both independent from management and that rank-and-file workers elect their own leaders. Moreover, the Western scholars ignore the existence of Chinese labor laws which protect worker rights on the job and set wage rates on a municipal basis. On June 29, 2007, at a time when Western multinational corporations had attempted to exploit the emergent Chinese working class, composed of migrants from rural areas, the Tenth National People's Congress passed the Labor Contract Law, significantly expanding labor rights through initiating a process of private sector management responsibility towards workers. This migrant population has grown significantly as the urban economy has offered greater opportunity than rural areas. The migrant population numbered almost 300 million workers in 2024 according to the National Bureau of Statistics. Even as the urban workforce grows, migrant laborers have seen their wages and working conditions improve as the ACFTU encourages labor organizing and the state compels employers to adhere to labor regulations. Over nearly two decades, the improved wages and working conditions for workers have further stimulated urban migration at a higher rate than expected. By 2024, Chinese migrant workers employed in retail, logistics and hospitality accounted for 54.6 percent of the national workforces and the proportion was growing (Xinhua 2025a).

The Chinese state and the CPC have established a labor-dispute mediation and arbitration system at workplaces and adopted the Labor Contract Law which went into effect on 1 January 2008. The provisions of the law ensure employment is monitored by state authorities and enshrine the right to leave, workplace safety, enforcement of child labor regulations and prevention of occupational diseases (Labor Contract Law 2007; Xinhua 2025b). Chinese labor laws were expanded in 2008 to provide a range of protections to a migrant workforce which had been exploited by foreign capital. Subsequently, Chinese urban workers have seen their conditions improve even as the political economy has shifted from manufacturing to tertiary services.

William Brown and Xuebing Cao (2024, 169) offer a disdainful perspective on the ACFTU, the most critical element of which is that since Chinese unions do not resemble trade unions as narrowly defined by Western scholars, labor organizations in China are simply not unions but appendages to the CPC and the Chinese state. This insolent interpretation of the Chinese trade union movement applies a European and North American craft union definition drawn from the early 20th century. It does not even reflect the composition of most trade unions in the West in the 21st century. Moreover, this interpretation mistakenly claims that the ACFTU violates the official position of the ILO, the United Nations affiliate which builds tripartite working relationships between labor, employers and the state. In this way, the remit of the ILO is to integrate unions as an equal partner with employers rather than to isolate and separate them from official activities of the state. In this context, the ACFTU serves as an active and fully integrated trade union federation which is highly effective in representing workers against private and public management. Brown and Cao misleadingly apply ILO Convention 98 (which requires unions to maintain independence from employers), but they add that since the CPC controls the ACFTU the union is not independent.

Contrary to Brown and Cao's assertions, it is the fastidious Chinese state and CPC which confer power on workers seeking to improve wages and working conditions. Why would the pretense of independence confer a higher level of democracy, even for a weak and ineffective union, if a strong employer were to reject the union's legitimacy as the collective bargaining representative of workers? Moreover, in collective bargaining, especially among state owned enterprises, workers participate directly in framing union demands under strictly enforced Chinese labor laws, a factor which is completely neglected by anti-Chinese Labor scholars. The Chinese government operates comparably to other states and adjudicates disputes between businesses and workers. Likewise, collective bargaining agreements must conform to the prevalent laws of the municipal, provincial and national governments. Jurisdictional power over labor is practiced in every state, but China critics argue that somehow the PRC has a higher bar because enterprises are owned by the state (i.e. the people).

For Brown and Cao, the ACFTU is not a union because of its ties to a party and a state. But such links are precisely what most unions seek to have: gaining traction with an effective and popular political party which takes power and influences state policy. Since the Labor Contract Law was launched in 2008, the ACFTU has increased its effectiveness in recognizing workers. Nonetheless, critics use an outmoded and inaccurate definition of a union, intending to denigrate the ACFTU in every instance without recognizing the nature of the state and the terrain on which it operates. By Western measures of successful trade unionism, the ACFTU and its affiliates are far more successful, undermining the pervasive mantra propagated by antagonists that are a caricature and misrepresentation advanced by hostile Labor scholars. For example, a characterization gives the lie to the actuality of a responsible trade union:

> The term "trade union" is misleading in the context of the People's Republic of China. The Chinese institutions described as such are unlike trade unions elsewhere in the world. ... Let us start with what Chinese trade unions definitely are not. They do not fit Webbs' classic definition of a trade union as "a continuous association of wage earners for the purpose of maintaining or improving the conditions of their working lives." ... That definition implies that the association is self-governing. Chinese trade unions are not; they are devoid of internal democratic procedures. ... Nor do they fit the International Labour Organization's (ILO) Convention 98, which specifies that trade unions must be financially independent of employers and other non-union organizations ... Chinese trade unions are wholly dependent for finance on levies of employers and on state funding. ... What makes their links with the state exceptional is that the only legal basis on which trade unions in China are permitted to operate is as part of a state agency, the All-China Federation of Trade Unions (ACFTU). (Brown & Cao 2024, 169)

The error and canard of the account is that the ACFTU is an official member of the ILO and is considered to engage in best practices of trade unionism. If the primary metric is decline and failure, then the Chinese model does not fit the Western model of trade unionism, where labor organization is in steep decline and new organization of workers is at a historic low.[4] But by any contemporary definition of a trade union and a labor federation, the ACFTU is far more effective than other national unions in defending the rights of workers who are unfairly treated and is successful in increasing wages and working conditions. By contrast, most trade unions in the West have floundered and have extensive membership decline, eroding their influence in local, state and national politics. Even in the Scandinavian region, where union density had been

---

4   Trade union membership in the US declined from 10.0 percent to 9.9 percent from 2023 to 2024. In the private sector, union membership was just 5.9 percent according to official statistics, where private sector union membership declined by 184,000 workers in 2024 (BLS 2025).

historically highest, trade union membership has declined significantly.[5] As we saw in Chapter 3, with the exception of China, the systemic decline in labor union membership is worldwide (Kjellberg 2023; SSAP 2024).

Practically all Western critics of the ACFTU deprecate China and the ACFTU as an abnormal and peculiar form denoted as a "party state", a term which is intended to represent the labor federation as an appendage of the CPC and the Chinese government, lacking autonomy and effectiveness, and bending to the will of the CPC on all matters related to the working class. In fact, as Xi Jinping stated in 2023, the trade union federation must focus on the demands of the working class as they evolve over time, improving wages and working conditions, and mobilizing members into constituent unions and improving workers' wages and living standards For them, the term "party-state" or "party-state capitalism" is code for all the undesirable elements which are attributed to the Chinese socialist market economy. Thousands of academic books and articles use the term time and again, to the extent that it has become insincere and meaningless. A recent seven page article in *Current History*, the oldest US journal of current events in continuous publication, uses the term "party-state capitalism" 31 times, as if it must be inscribed in perpetuity to inculcate a doctrine which will subjugate any other perspective (Pearson et al. 2021).

In labor relations, the term denotes: (1) the ACFTU's lack of autonomy from the CPC and the state; (2) proscription of ACFTU officials deciding on decisive internal policies and external relations with SOEs and private sector firms; (3) exclusion of local level union leaders from bargaining with management; and (4) prohibition of workers to mobilize and participate in union decisions. This is a sweeping portrayal of an authoritarian and undemocratic system of representation, but even scholars who have articulated a more balanced perspective must, for fear of being ridiculed and excluded, adhere to the obligatory disparagement of labor–management relations in China. Consequently, the accounts by the "party-state" monolith of adherents undermine all efforts to engage in constructive criticism and dialogue which might improve conditions worldwide. The anti-China academic complex in the US and the West is a propaganda behemoth established to inhibit free thinking and independent perceptions. It is so vast that one cannot draw any other conclusion than that it is deliberately intended to target the credulity and naivety of Americans.

---

5   In 2023, Anders Kjellberg documents a decline in trade union membership in each of the four Nordic states from 1990 to 2021: Sweden declined from 81 percent to 70 percent, Denmark declined from 76 percent to 63 percent, and Norway from 67 percent to 50 percent. In Finland, trade union density declined from 76 percent in 1990 to 59 percent in 2019 (Kjellberg 2023).

The "party-state" perspective is all encompassing and does not grant any institution, organization or decision making authority agency to adjudicate claims, or to determine or rule on any matter without the CPC's approval. Its adherents consider all institutions, administrative policies, judicial rulings and trade union representation to be prohibited. All authority is a direct extension of policies and calculations flowing from the CPC Politburo, which are calculated to expand and consolidate power, accumulate capital and harness dissent from below. In the estimation of Ching Kwan Lee (2007), the Chinese government has omnipresent power which suppresses any challenge by workers to protest and improve conditions. This position does not even acknowledge that Chinese workers can improve their conditions through a range of contestations between labor and management.

Lin (2020) provides a more inventive analysis by arguing that Chinese workers are not building a social movement for political change. Like Lee, however, he neglects to explain why a disruptive social movement in a socialist country committed to the improvement of working class living conditions is necessary. Lin appropriates Mao's concept of "cognition," a term which was formulated to demonstrate how human knowledge and understanding are a direct result of material practice rather than abstraction and the necessity of a discerning mass leadership. Curiously, Lin anticipates cognition to be repressed to explain the absence of a national or even regional workers' social movement. Undoubtedly, Chinese workers do not participate in collective efforts as much as many hope for, but Lin's narrative discounts the ACFTU's efforts to consolidate working class protections as well as the emergence of community unions in a growing number of Chinese cities, especially under Xi Jinping. It is possible that Lin did not anticipate that Xi would advance significant demands on the ACFTU to expand its scope of activity to the municipal and street level unions. The Chinese state's commitment to building socialism through the working class is a foundational principle which is viewed as the responsibility of the party. In 1949, 28 years after the founding of the CPC, Mao Zedong wrote that the Chinese proletariat shared a common perspective on the necessity of a vanguard party, (a view shared by Sun Yat-sen, the founder and president of the Republic of China), noting that, "We must arouse the masses of the people and unite in a common struggle with those nations of the world which treat us as equals." Sun Yat-sen, he claimed, "reached a conclusion basically the same as ours on the question of how to struggle against imperialism," continuing:

> Twenty-four years have passed since Sun Yat-sen's death and the Chinese revolution, led by the Communist Party of China, has made tremendous advances both in theory and practice and has radically changed the face of China. Up to

> now the principal and fundamental experience the Chinese people have gained
> is twofold.
>
> 1. Internally, arouse the masses of the people. That is, unite the working class, the peasantry, the urban petty bourgeoisie and the national bourgeoisie, form a domestic united front under the leadership of the working class, and advance from this to the establishment of a state which is a people's democratic dictatorship under the leadership of the working class and based on the alliance of workers and peasants.
>
> 2. Externally, unite in a common struggle with those nations in the world which treat us as equals and unite with the peoples of all countries ... and form an international united front. (Mao Tse-tung/Mao Zedong 1949, 415)

The term "party-state" is ubiquitous in the labor literature and is in keeping with the path development from the revolution. It is the state and party's responsibility to mobilize the masses. But, in the West, the term is almost always used to demonstrate that there is neither politics nor democracy in China, which is supposedly controlled by the CPC despite ample and pervasive evidence that popular participation in the state, and especially in local communities and unions, is extensive. In the past decade, more scholars have recognized the democratic nature of the Chinese state as well as its commitment to maintaining a communist system directed at advancing the interests of the Chinese working class.

The market reforms which were advanced from the 1980s to the 2000s have contributed to opposition among social democrats, expressed primarily through Western literature about the declining conditions of the working class in an economy subject to an internal and international market from its inception as a socialist state. Almost all Western socialists have condemned China in the post-Mao era in league with Western imperialists who have condemned the country from its foundation for replacing the private market with a state-dominated economy. Those who rebuke China as a party-state are now universal and run the spectrum from left to right, even though the Chinese state has consistently improved its people's standard of living since the establishment of the PRC in 1949.

One line of attack is that the Chinese labor movement is ineffective and powerless as it cannot exert power beyond the local level (as if a national strike wave is a necessary feature of worker power), overlooking the institutional structure of the state administration, where political action (such as setting wages) takes place on a local and regional rather than national level. For example, in the US, the national minimum wage is largely meaningless as it is so low that it cannot lift even wage earners without a family out of the poverty level in any state. However, in China, wage laws are set by municipal authorities, not on a national or even provincial basis. Wages directly reflect the cost of living in each district, which varies across localities, provinces and the state. Thus, wage differentials between rural and urban areas reflect actual cost-of-living differences and had eradicated poverty in China by the second decade of the 21st century (National Bureau of Statistics of China 2023).

An example of this static and unqualified reasoning, and of an absence of nuance, can be found in an "argument" advanced by Labor scholars Kuruvilla, Lee and Gallagher. In *From Iron Rice Bowl to Informalization* (2011), they wrongly infer that Chinese industrialization eroded and subverted a strong and egalitarian economy which provided economic sustenance to all its citizens. Based on previous research, the authors certainly do not regret the shift from an autarchic socialist economy to what they inaccurately refer to as a market economy in the 1970s and 1980s, as they elsewhere embrace a capitalist liberal-democratic economy analogous to those of Western Europe and North America. This is a position shared by most but not all China critics.

Within a generation, urban China has moved from a highly protected "iron rice bowl" system that guaranteed workers in state owned enterprises (SOEs) and collectively owned enterprises permanent employment, cradle-to-grave benefits, and a relatively high degree of equality to a market-determined employment system characterized by considerable variation in wages, welfare provision, labor law enforcement, and job security. The growing field of China Labor Studies offers rich documentation of this change in working conditions, enterprise and managerial reforms, systems of remuneration, patterns of labor disputes and unrest, class and gender relations, unemployment, and labor law reforms (Kuruvilla et al. 2011, 3–4).

The anti-China Labor scholars resort to scholarly misrepresentation which considers China in isolation, without comparing it to other countries. The evidence is based on selective and distorted information which gives a false idea of and manipulates Chinese government data sources through narrow interpretation of facts processed from international and even Chinese government sources, and misinterpretation of social phenomena through applying a static interpretative analysis rather than a historical and dynamic evaluation.

Even after the CPC enacted a comprehensive labor court adjudication system, Gallagher again arrives at a critique that does not take into consideration implementation of the policy. The point is that all efforts to improve the status of the working class fail or are deficient, and the motivation for the labor courts is to prevent labor unrest rather than to provide a comprehensive dispute resolution system. In Gallagher's narrative, the expansion of judicial courts to protect workers only provides protections for workers with higher levels of education who are aware of the laws. By contrast, all other workers are uninterested in the legal mediation and arbitration system, preferring to engage in workplace activities, strikes and demonstrations. The book draws on evidence marshalled by the CLB, a US NGO cutout that closed after funding was cut in 2025. CLB data lacks credibility and is based on worker remote correspondence, which is a dubious source. Gallagher is impatient and immediately forms a negative opinion as the legal system for adjudicating legal disputes is put in place. However, the CLB shows that workers are going to labor courts to resolve disputes at a high rate and winning over 95 percent of their cases. But detractors view the expansion of legal protection for workers through labor courts as a means to placate a segment of more highly educated workers rather than arising from a shared interest in worker rights as stated by Xi Jinping at the CPC meetings. Gallagher views the legal system as "dysfunctional" and failing to serve the workers. However, interviews conducted among workers across the country in a wide range of industries during 2024 and 2025 found that workers are aware of the successful outcomes of the ACFTU in defending them through labor courts. They consider the enlargement of labor courts a positive development in safeguarding their wages, social insurance and ensuring safe working conditions. For Gallagher and others, though, any effort to improve wages, working conditions and compensation of workers are concessions to workers to maintain an authoritarian system. Like so many other Western Labor scholars, without evidence, Gallagher sees an ulterior motive behind everything which the Chinese state, CPC and the ACFTU advance to benefit the working class, without grasping the nature of Socialism with Chinese Characteristics, which was in fact advanced by Mao Zedong at the origin of the PCP in 1949, when the people's dictatorship required an alliance of the working class, peasantry, petty bourgeoisie and national bourgeoisie to advance and develop. However, leading labor economists have documented the rapid expansion of labor courts as they have been established and grown in number. Even before the dramatic growth in labor dispute courts, the eminent labor economist Richard B. Freeman, of Harvard University and the National Bureau of Economic Research (NBER), noted in 2015 the dramatic rise in labor disputes, which have been documented by the Chinese government from 2000 to 2010:

> The number of labor disputes brought to the Labor Dispute Arbitration Committees (the legal entity set up to resolve disputes) sky-rocketed from 8,150 in 1992 to 135,206 in 2000 to 1,280,000 or so in 2010. Acting on their own with no help from the official unions, workers began striking in large numbers for better conditions in different parts of the country. In summer 2010 a strike by Honda workers in Guangdong made headlines around the world

when it produced a collective agreement with improved pay and benefits. (Freeman 2015, 10)

By contrast, uniformly disapproving Labor scholars in the West, who reflexively oppose the ACFTU and the Chinese state's response to industrialization, advance a sarcastic assessment of the federation as a malevolent organization resolutely opposed to improving the conditions of workers when Chinese labor was in a state of tumultuous transformation from a rural to an urban workforce. In short, at no time and place in human history has a population migrated in such great numbers as did that of modern China. If the state instructions could not keep up with this relocation, driven by a foreign private sector, opponents view this as a major transgression. But the industrialization of Britain, Western Europe and North America transpired over a period of 50 years or more and yet there is little criticism of unions there for not keeping up. According to Mingwei Liu, by 2009, for practical purposes, after little over a decade, workers in 92 percent of all Fortune 500 companies operating in China had been represented by a union affiliated with the ACFTU (Liu 2011).

The malformed union which failed to protect Foxconn workers in 2010 represents a significant failure of the ACFTU and the state to keep pace with the industrial electronics juggernaut and not a state policy to exploit workers. The ACFTU quickly responded by forming a labor union which would move swiftly to negotiate higher wages, reduce hours and enact workplace safety measures and improved living conditions for the migrant workers who produced smartphones for Foxconn. Nonetheless, fault finding Labor critics dismiss any improvements by levelling new charges. For example, China Labor scholars Jenny Chan, Mark Selden and Pun Ngai cite a *New York Times* article quoting an unnamed worker who stated in March 2015, without evidence, that: "Not many workers knew about the company union elections" at Foxconn (Chan et al. 2020, 192). Paradoxically, there is much evidence that most local union leaders in the US are not elected by a majority of rank-and-file members in the private and public sectors. Indeed, many workers do not even know they are represented by a union in the US despite the fact that they pay union dues.

Though it is true that the expansion of China as the workshop of the world and the driver of the massive rise in foreign consumption had given rise to higher levels of worker discord and direct action through strikes and dissent in the first two decades of the opening up, the antagonism and demands for improved conditions were primarily directed at foreign private firms and subcontractors which had violated workers' rights (Ness 2014). There was also a call by workers for the ACFTU to vigorously represent their interests by engaging in direct action. Opponents of the ACFTU contend that the union was motivated by a desire to quell all forms of dissent, but if this cynical position was true, why then did worker demands expand in the aftermath of the strike wave? And how does one explain the rise in November 2012 of Xi Jinping to General Secretary of the Chinese Communist Party at the 18th National Congress on a platform which emphasized the party fulfilling its responsibility and curbing all forms of corruption?

China Labor critics charge the party-state with engaging in a range of mechanisms to dodge the traditional labor–management contract, including the rise of third party contractors and the lack of direct contracts with employers, the use of interns and students as workers, and the rise of the digital economy, ridding business corporations of the obligation to provide the traditional labor–management contracts. Each critique can be addressed through the passage of time, a necessity in any study. In each instance, the Chinese government, CPC and the ACFTU have responded effectively through pressing employers to directly hire workers who form a potential bargaining unit, reducing the use of interns at workplaces; a practice which is far more pervasive in the West, where students must pay for the privilege of working without pay. In fact, a recent study of student interns found that job training was a necessary prerequisite, which often leads to offers of employment (Yang, F. 2025). Finally, the primary private platform delivery technology firms have offered direct labor contracts to workers in the digital economy who principally are employed in logistics and especially as delivery operatives. In China, the major digital platforms (Metiuan, Ele.me and JD.com) have recognized digital workers in the platform economy as workers and have directly hired them with guaranteed wages, social insurance, improved working conditions and other benefits, including maternity insurance (see Chapter 6 for an examination of Chinese digital labor).

8 Challenging China's Labor Critics

While opponents of the Chinese labor movement use scant facts which are often drawn from secondary sources to debase the labor movement, social science research among scholars based in the West and in China provides evidence of an emergent labor movement which is responding to extreme geopolitical transformations advanced through neoliberal capitalism and to the demands of mobilizing a newly proletarianized workforce in urban areas. The critique of the Chinese labor movement presented by the vast majority of Western Labor scholars is nearly unanimous; but emerging scholarship since 2013 by leading Western and Chinese political economists attributes the rapid transformations in China to the internal rural–urban migration there from the 1990s to the present. Abundant evidence is available of local and provincial success in contesting workplace power against public and private sector employers in China's urban hubs at a time when the country's working class has been dominated by first and second generation migrant workers, a factor which ordinarily inhibits the capacity of labor to wield influence and prevail in collective bargaining.

If the ACFTU and its affiliated unions are as ineffectual and impotent as Western critics would have us believe, why have Chinese workers authentically won concessions from SOEs and private sector businesses, especially in the last 15 years from 2010 to the present?

The evidence of workers organizing victories among trade unions representing workers at a single enterprise or company on the municipal level is clear, based on archival and ethnographic evidence. Lin (2022) analyses the 2020 strike wave and finds that workplace elections influenced successful collective bargaining. He demonstrates that employers' perception of workers' power resources contributes to an unambiguous capacity for workers to prevail over them in wage disputes. Lin found that authentic, workplace collective bargaining occurred when unions had a powerful array of collective resources (including mobilization capacity, negotiation skills and collective consultation) which posed a threat to managers. A key variable was collective bargaining skills, which must be learned and practiced with the support of provincial and municipal governments.

Booth et al. (2022) convincingly show that the presence of ACFTU trade unions within the workplace has significantly improved conditions (wages, workplace contracts, social insurance, working conditions, dignity and fringe benefits) for workers migrating to Chinese urban areas, and that this contributes to the willingness of workers to articulate grievances through official challenges rather than independently mobilizing to protest. Rather than basing assessments on Western sources antagonistic to the PRC, these researchers use a panel survey and quantitatively control for individual "fixed effects." They conclude:

> Relative to workers from workplaces without union presence or with inactive unions, both union-covered non-members and union members in workplaces with active unions earn higher monthly income, are more likely to have a written contract, be covered by social insurances, receive fringe benefits, express work-related grievances through official channels, feel more satisfied with their lives, and are less likely to have mental health problems. (Booth et al. 2022, 975)

Rather than taking independent or collective risks to form unions, the ACFTU has established worker organizations which are in most instances addressing the material and social requirements of workers. The authors go on to explain the remarkable improvements which the ACFTU is achieving for workers, extending from SOEs to the private sector:

> It is interesting to understand how the institutional features of the Chinese union affect workers' welfare in a largely privately owned economy. This shift to a market-oriented system has been accompanied by dramatic industrialization fueled by a strong supply of cheap labor from rural areas. (2022, 975)

As the ACFTU negotiates improved conditions for workers which have expanded to social insurance, Chinese courts are mandating social insurance and severance pay if employers failed to pay into worker accounts; decreeing that all employment contracts which omitted social insurance were rendered invalid. On August 1, 2025, the Supreme People's Court, China's highest court, mandated social insurance payments for all workers with employment contracts without exception. It also ruled that every worker who was denied social insurance throughout China would be encouraged to appeal to government authorities and lower courts to order back payments and resign with the right to severance pay. The ruling addresses non-public employers in the private sector who seek to take advantage of workers financially through dodging their responsibility to cover social insurance. According to the Supreme People's Court Ruling:

> The Supreme People's Court (SPC) issued a judicial interpretation on Aug 1, clarifying that any contractual agreement that excludes social insurance contributions is invalid. ... The SPC emphasizes that paying social insurance is a legal obligation for both employers and employees, noting that the clarification is a result of some employers evading payments and some employees opting out of the system in practice. "For example, we've found a few companies not contributing to social insurance in order to reduce labor costs, with some workers requesting employers to provide the social insurance contributions directly to them as subsidies in order to receive higher wages," said Zhang Yan, a judge in the top court's First Civil Division. She reiterated that Chinese courts should support claims by employees who request for termination of their work contract or seek compensation due to the employer's failure to contribute to social insurance. Wu Jingli, deputy chief judge of the division, also stressed the importance of paying social insurance, as legally enjoying social insurance benefits is a fundamental right for each worker, adding that

the interpretation will be effective from Sept 1 (The Supreme People's Court of the People's Republic of China 2025).

Workers did not have the right to waive their right to social insurance and could terminate their contracts if their employers did not pay and claim severance pay from the employer. The ruling, which almost immediately took effect on September 1, 2025, significantly contributes to the decline and eradication of precarious labor and non-standard employment agreements, an unprecedented achievement in the global South and rare in rich countries of the North (Qingyang & Chendi 2025; Xinyi 2025).[6] The convergence of evidence rooted in actual fact demonstrates that the conditions of the Chinese working class are improving as a collective social force which is formalized through employment relationships and the support of the ACFTU. It is worth mentioning that the ACFTU had applauded the Supreme People's Court decision, noting that the interpretation unmistakably concludes that non-payment of social insurance is prohibited even if the worker negotiated with the employer an independent agreement which excluded the benefit.

9   Conclusion

The preliminary findings of this chapter are that the Chinese state is genuinely responding to working class interests, often identifying workplace exploitation in advance and implementing strategies to reach out to the new Chinese urban working class which has emerged in the last generation. These initiatives are only growing in scale and capacity under the leadership of Xi Jinping, who in the autumn of 2014, a year after his election as general secretary of the CPC, reprimanded the ACFTU for not responding effectively to the growing demands of the internal migrants who formed the largest segment of China's working class. The evidence also shows that the Chinese state, whether or not called a "party-state," is seeking to stimulate economic growth in the aftermath of the 2008 Great Financial Crisis by developing new technology and infrastructure, and that this is contributing to higher standards of living.

---

6 According to the Chinese newspaper *Economic Observer*, "Taking urban employee pension insurance as an example, data from the Ministry of Human Resources and Social Security shows that by 2024, the number of employees participating in urban employee pension insurance will be 387 million, an increase of 7.88 million from the previous year. In contrast, the 'Ninth National Workers' Team Status Survey Report' released by the All-China Federation of Trade Unions in February 2023 shows that the total number of employees nationwide is approximately 402 million" (Economic Observer 2025).

    This chapter also asserts that even if the ACFTU is an arm of the CPC, effective trade unions seek state influence, regardless of whether the state being capitalist or socialist. The chapter builds on a position that the ACFTU would potentially be far more powerful if it more effectively established ties with its over 300 million members. Even if tens of millions are active union members, many more are also intent on gaining the benefits of workers in the union. However, the ACFTU faces a major challenge: that is, to expand its representation to those workers in the service sector, logistics and the platform economy, which are transforming rapidly. In the same way as the Federation had to respond to the expansion of financial capital and industrialization, it must now consider the changing nature of the economy and reach out to workers who are falling into the cracks between existing organizational structures. This notwithstanding, the ACFTU has been found by the ILO to represent far more workers in these contract sectors than trade unions elsewhere in the world and is seeking to broaden the safety net for all workers. Labor scholars who dominate the discourse in opposition to China are patently misleading when they assert that the CPC and the ACFTU encourage contract labor and interns as replacements for full time workers. There is no evidence to substantiate that the CPC and ACFTU seek to impoverish their own working class.

Bibliography

ACFTU (All-China Federation of Trade Unions). (2018). 6.441 million enterprises signed collective contracts, covering nearly 300 million workers. *Sina News.* http://news.sina.com.cn/o/2018-01-14/doc-ifyqptqv9149123.shtml

AFL-CIO (American Federation of Labor and Congress of Industrial Organizations). (2023). *Death on the job: The toll of neglect: A national and state-by-state profile of worker safety and health in the United States* (32nd ed.), April. Washington, DC: AFL-CIO. https://aflcio.org/reports/death-job-toll-neglect-2023

Allen, V. L. (1968). The centenary of the British Trades Union Congress, 1868–1968. *The Socialist Register 5,* 17 March, 231–252.

Amin, S. (2017). The sovereign popular project: The alternative to liberal globalization. *Journal of Labor and Society, 20*(1), 7–22.

Andreas, J. (2019). *Disenfranchised: The rise and fall of industrial citizenship in China.* New York: Oxford University Press.

Aronowitz, S. (1973). *False promises: The shaping of American working class consciousness.* New York: McGraw Hill.

Ashby, S. K. (2022). Union Democracy in Today's Labor Movement, *Labor Studies Journal, 47*(2), 109–136. https://journals.sagepub.com/doi/pdf/10.1177/0160449X211044903?casa_token=QB04gYo6MIIAAAAA:YsO3aTO2nEnpezH5Ff_zFpNhPoJ4una_85nvlMflz1Ayu71FIagGMnejzt60QN25e0YdQISA7csh

Atzeni, M. (2021). Workers' organizations and the fetishism of the trade union form: Toward new pathways for research on the labour movement? *Globalizations, 18*(8), 1349–1362. https://doi.org/10.1080/14747731.2021.1877970

Ayala-Hurtado, E. (2022). Narrative continuity/rupture: Projected professional futures amid pervasive employment precarity. *Work and Occupations, 49*(1) 45–78.

Bagchi, A. K. (2021). Imperialism from the eleventh century to the twenty-first century. *Social Scientist, 49*(3/4), 3–20. www.jstor.org/stable/27027153

Baichuan, H. (2019, April 11). Social organizations to establish trade unions – 'Ten questions and answers.' *Shanghai City Spirit.* https://mzj.sh.gov.cn/st-gzfw-bmts/20200520/MZ_shetuan383_118441.html

Bateson, G. (2000). *Steps to an ecology of mind: Collected essays in anthropology, psychiatry, evolution and epistemology.* Chicago: University of Chicago Press.

Beitsch, R. (2025). *Unions' battle for survival hits new wave with Trump termination of bargaining agreements.* The Hill. https://thehill.com/regulation/court-battles/5453207-federal-unions-trump/

Bieler, A. (2018). Agency and the power resources approach: Asserting the importance of the structuring conditions of the capitalist social relations of production. *Global Labour Journal, 9*(2), 243–248.

Bieler, A. & Lee, C. (Eds.). (2017). *Chinese labour in the global economy: Capitalist exploitation and strategies of resistance.* Abingdon, Oxon, UK: Routledge.

Bieler, A. & Nowak, J. (2022). *Conflicts in the global south.* London: Routledge.

Blanc, E. (2025). *We are the union: How worker-to-worker organizing is revitalizing labor and winning big.* Berkeley, CA: University of California Press.

BLS (Bureau of Labor Statistics, US Department of Labor). (2024). *Union Members – 2023.* January 23. www.bls.gov/news.release/pdf/union2.pdf

BLS (Bureau of Labor Statistics, US Department of Labor). (2026). *Union Members Summary*, February 18. https://www.bls.gov/news.release/pdf/union2.pdf

Bo, P. & Jin, H. (2023, July 17). Caring for workers in new employment forms, *People's Daily.* http://acftu.people.com.cn/n1/2023/0717/c392912-40037412.html

Boer, R. (2023). *Socialism in power: On the history and theory of socialist governance.* Singapore: Springer Nature.

Boer, R. (2022). *Socialism with Chinese characteristics: A guide for foreigners.* Singapore: Springer Nature.

Booth, A., Freeman, R., Meng, X., & Zhang, J. (2022). Trade unions and the welfare of rural-urban migrant workers in China. *ILR Review, 75*(4), 974–1000. https://journals-sagepub-com.brooklyn.ezproxy.cuny.edu/doi/pdf/10.1177/00197939211004440?casa_token=1hgINNb6EHMAAAAA:yaHnZtCXJn-3L6CZRNlSdo5B152q83hJreCbbEMWAHhPkuwAOvGoGr-hFtD8iiiCI4DlOowIFBmU

Brand, U. & Wissen, M. (2021). *The imperial mode of living: Everyday life and the ecological crisis of capitalism.* London: Verso.

Braverman, H. (1974). *Labor and monopoly capital: The degradation of work in the twentieth century.* New York: Monthly Review Press.

Breman, J. (2026). The delusion of decolonization. Figuring out the divide between profit and cost. *Journal of Labor and Society*, 1–30.

Breman, J. (1996). *Footloose labour: Working in India's informal economy.* Cambridge, UK: Cambridge University Press.

Brenner, K. (2026). The working class and the capitalist state: An autonomist Marxist perspective. *Critical Sociology, 52*(2), 251–267.

Brenner, A, Brenner, R. & Winslow, C. (2010). *Rebel rank and file: Labor militancy and revolt from below during the long 1970s.* London: Verso.

Brolin, J. (2007). *The bias of the world: Theories of unequal exchange in history* [Doctoral thesis, Human Ecology Division, Lund University, Sweden]. https://lup.lub.lu.se/search/ws/files/4378178/26725.pdf

Bronfenbrenner, K. (2009). *No holds barred: The intensification of employer opposition to organizing* (Briefing Paper No. 235). Economic Policy Institute, Washington, DC.

Brown, W. & Cao, X. (2024). The dynamics of labour relations and state-ancillary unionism in transition. In J. Nolan, S. Zhao, & K. Kamoche (Eds.), *Routledge Hand-*

book of Chinese Business and Management (pp. 169–184). London/New York: Routledge.

Bu, X. (2022). *Xi Jinping's historical outlook on governance for a new era* (C. Li & Y Xing, Trans.). Montreal: Royal Collins Publishing Company.

Burawoy, M. (1982). *Manufacturing consent: Changes in the labor process under monopoly capitalism.* Chicago: University of Chicago Press.

Burns, J. (2022) *Class struggle unionism.* Chicago: Haymarket Books.

Caraway, T. L., Cook, M. L., & Crowley, S. (2015). *Working through the past: Labor and authoritarian legacies in comparative perspective.* Ithaca, NY: ILR/Cornell University Press.

Chan, J., Selden, M. & Pun, N. (2020). *Dying for an iPhone: Apple, Foxconn and the lives of Chinese workers.* London: Pluto Press.

Chan, K. W. (2021). Internal migration in China: Integrating migration and hukou reform, (Policy Note No. 16). Washington, DC: World Bank.

Chan, K. W. & Zhang, L. (1999). The hukou system and rural–urban migration in China: Process and changes. *The China Quarterly, 160*, 818–855.

Chancel, L., Piketty, T., Saez, E., Zucman, G. et al. (2022). *World inequality report,* Paris: World Inequality Lab.

Chau, A. (2022). Regulating the algorithm: Platform economy workers in China. *International Union Rights, 29*(2), 19–21.

Chen, J. Y. (2018). Platform economies: The boss's old and new clothes. *Made in China Journal, 3*(3), 46–49.

Chen, Y. (2024, August 16). Didi Shanghai holds up a summer umbrella of care for online car-hailing drivers to help them have a better travel experience, *Shangguan News.*

Cheng, E. (2021). *China's economic dialectic: The original aspiration of reform.* New York: International Publishers and World Association for Political Economy.

Cheng, M. & Duan, C. (2021). The changing trends of internal migration and urbanization in China: New evidence from the seventh national population census. *China Population and Development Research, 5,* 275–295. https://doi.org/10.1007/s42379 -021-00093-7

Chibber, V. (2022). *Confronting capitalism: How the world works and how to change it.* London: Verso.

China News Service. (2018). Shanghai establishes the country's first online food delivery industry union. [上海成立全国首家网约送餐行业工会]. www-chinanews -com-cn.translate.goog/m/sh/2018/01-04/8416637.shtml?_x_tr_sl=zh-CN&_x_tr _tl=en&_x_tr_hl=en&_x_tr_pto=sc.

China Workers' Daily. (2025, April 28). Chronicle of major events in China's trade union movement. Beijing: QSTHEORY Media. www.qstheory.cn/20250428/02efb2b6e1504 42183e99e77e06647c8/c.html

Chinese Workers. (2024). *Annual report on the status of Chinese workers 2023*. Beijing: Social Sciences Academic Press. [Translated from Chinese].

Chun, J. J. (2011). *Organizing at the margins: The symbolic politics of labor in South Korea and the United States*. Ithaca: ILR Press.

Cini, L. (2025). Misbehaving for Deliveroo. How couriers' digital manipulation boosts the platform's business. *Organization*, 0(0), 1–20. https://doi.org/10.1177/13505084251334

Cini, L., Maccarrone, V., & Tassinari, A. (2021). With or without U(nions)? Understanding the diversity of gig workers' organizing practices in Italy and the UK. *European Journal of Industrial Relations*, 28(3), 341–362. https://doi.org/10.1177/09596801211052531

Clift, B. (2021). *Comparative political economy: States, markets and global capitalism* (2nd ed.). London: Red Globe Press.

Clover, J. (2016). *Riot. Strike. Riot: The new era of uprisings*. London: Verso.

Cohen, R. L. (2025). The sociology of self-employment: A typology and reconciliation. *Sociology, 59*(5), 905–924. https://doi.org/10.1177/00380385251324563

Cowie, J. (2010). *Stayin' alive: The 1970s and the last days of the working class*. New York: The New Press.

Cowie, J, Heathcott, J., & Bluestone, B. (2003). *Beyond the ruins: The meanings of deindustrialization*. Ithaca, NY: Cornell ILR Press.

Cross, H. (2021). *Migration beyond capitalism*, Cambridge: Polity.

Crowe, K. C. (1993). *Collision: How the rank and file took back the Teamsters*, New York: Charles Scribner's Sons.

Daily Worker. (2022, November 19). 20,000 Workers join the union! The birth of the first provincial-level takeaway industry union in China, *The Paper*. [Translated from Chinese.] [新刊推介 | 2万人入会！全国首个省级外卖行业工会诞生记. www-the paper-cn.translate.goog/newsDetail_forward_20807082?_x_tr_sl=zh-CN&_x_tr _tl=en&_x_tr_hl=en&_x_tr_pto=sc&_x_tr_hist=true

Davis, M. (1986). *Prisoners of the American dream: Politics and economy in the history of the U.S. working class*. London: Verso.

Davis, M. (2004/2017). *Planet of slums*. London: Verso.

della Porta, D., Chesta, R. E., & Cini, L. (2023). *Labour conflicts in the digital age: A comparative perspective*, Bristol, UK: Bristol University Press.

Deng, X. (1992). Excerpts from talks given in Wuchang, Shenzhen, Zhuhai and Shanghai. In X. Deng (1994), *Selected works of Deng Xiaoping* (Vol. 3, 1992–2002). Beijing: Foreign Languages Press. https://archive.org/details/selectedworksofdoooodeng _h7k9

Deng X. (1990). We must adhere to socialism and prevent the peaceful evolution towards Capitalism. In X. Deng (1994), *Selected works of Deng Xiaoping* (Vol. 3, 1982–2002). Beijing: Foreign Languages Press. https://archive.org/details/selectedworksofdoooodeng_h7k9

Dobb, M. (1946). *Studies in the development of capitalism.* London: Routledge & Kegan Paul.

Dobb, M., Hill, C., Hobsbawm, E., Lefebvre, G, Merrington, J., Procacci, G., Sweezy, P., & Takahashi, K. (1985). *The transition from feudalism to capitalism* (Intro., R. Hilton). London: Verso.

Dubofsky, M. (2000). We shall be all: A history of the Industrial Workers of the World (Urbana and Chicago. Champaign, IL: University of Illinois Press.

Dubofsky, M. & McCartin, J.A. (2017). *Labor in America: A history.* (10th ed.). Hoboken, NJ: Wiley).

Dubord, G. (1967/1994). *The society of the spectacle.* Brooklyn, NY: Zone Books.

Dukes, R. & Streeck, W. (2023). *Democracy at work: Contract, status and post-industrial justice.* Cambridge, UK: Polity.

Dunaway, W. & Macabuac, M. C. (2022). *Where shrimp eat better than people: Globalized fisheries, nutritional unequal exchange and Asian hunger.* Leiden, The Netherlands: Brill.

Dunford, M. & Liu, W. (2015). *The geographic transformation of China.* Abingdon, Oxon, UK and New York: Routledge.

Economic Observer. (2025, August 16). Should companies be concerned about historical arrears issues: Clarifying the ten most important questions regarding the new social insurance regulations. (Trans. from Chinese.) 企业是否要担心历史欠缴问题 … … 厘清社保" 新规" 最重要的十个问题 www.eeo.com.cn/2025/0816/745249.shtml

Edwards, H. W. (1978). *Labor aristocracy: Mass base of social democracy.* Stockholm: Aurora.

Emmanuel, A. (1972/2025). *Unequal exchange: A study of the imperialism of trade. (Updated Edition).* (Intro. by T. Lauesen, Fwd by J. B. Foster & B. Clark.) New York: Monthly Review Press.

Emmanuel, A. (1982). *Appropriate or underdeveloped technology?* Chichester, UK: John Wiley & Sons.

Engels, F. (1892/1952). *The condition of the working class in England in 1844: With a preface written in 1892.* London: George Allen & Unwin.

Engels, F. (1907). *Socialism: utopian and scientific.* Chicago: Charles H. Kerr and Company.

Fadlan, M. Damanik, I., Haviz, A., Bastian, A., Nasution, H. H. et al. (2025). Accounting profitability analysis of business combination at PT Goto Gojek Toko Pedia, Tbk. *International Journal of Economic Research and Financial Accounting, 3*(2), 318–322. https://doi.org/10.55227/ijerfa.v3i2.270

Felsen, M. (2024). Addressing worker safety and health through the lens of strategic enforcement. *New Solutions: A Journal of Environmental and Occupational Health Policy, 34*(2), 133–146. https://journals.sagepub.com/doi/pdf/10.1177/1048291124125

9874?casa_token=99iAk2eoC5AAAAAA:DhnynupDKBjAVC9-uDhgv-8VKlBzVwLH
7fArwGefhSPgr_4UGegeU8Pmc2CPDbSzHfWJyHwBXoZI

Fletcher, B. & Gapasin, F. (2009). *Solidarity divided: The crisis of organized labor and a new path toward social justice*. Berkeley, CA: University of California Press.

Ford, M. & Gillan, M. (2025). Coalition-building as a power resource: Transnational collaborations between global unions and non-union actors. *Social Movement Studies*, 1–16. https://doi.org/10.1080/14742837.2025.2530414

Foster, J. B. (2024). The new denial of imperialism on the left. *Monthly Review: An Independent Socialist Magazine*, 76(6), 1–32. https://monthlyreview.org/2024/11/01/the-new-denial-of-imperialism-on-the-left/

Frame, M. L. (2023). *Ecological imperialism, development, and the capitalist world-system: Cases from Africa and Asia*. Abingdon, Oxon, UK: Routledge.

Franceschini, I. & Sorace, C., eds. (2022). *Proletarian China: A century of Chinese labor*. London: Verso.

Frantz, C. & Fernandes, S. (2018). Whose movement is It? Strategic philanthropy and workers centers. *Critical Sociology*, 44(4–5), 645–660. https://doi.org/10.1177/0896920516661857

Freeman, R. B. (2015). A labor market with Chinese characteristics. In G. C. Chow (Ed.), *The Routledge handbook of the hinese economy*. London: Routledge. www.routledge.com/Routledge-Handbook-of-the-Chinese-Economy/Chow-Perkins/p/book/9780415643443

Freeman, R. B. & Li, X. (2013). *How does China's new labor contract law affect floating workers?* (Working Paper No. 19254). Cambridge, MA: National Bureau of Economic Research. www.nber.org/system/files/working papers/w19254/w19254.pdf

Freeman, R. B. & Medoff, J. L. (1984). *What do unions do?* New York: Basic Books.

Friedman, E. (2014). *Insurgency trap: Labor politics in postsocialist China*. Ithaca, NY: Cornell University Press.

Friedman, E. Lin, K. Smith, A. (2024). *China in global capitalism: Building international solidarity against imperial rivalry*. Chicago: Haymarket Books.

Frymer, P. & Grumbach, J. M. (2021). Labor unions and white racial politics. *American Journal of Political Science*, 65, 225–240. https://doi.org/10.1111/ajps.12537

Fukuyama, F. (1992). *The end of history and the last man*. New York: The Free Press.

Galenson, W. (1994). *Trade union growth and decline: An international study*. London: Bloomsbury Academic.

Gallagher, M. E. (2017). *Authoritarian legality in China: Law, workers, and the state*. Cambridge, UK: Cambridge University Press.

Gallagher, M. E. (2005). *Contagious capitalism: Globalization and the politics of labor in China*. Princeton, NJ: Princeton University Press.

Gerstle, G. (2022). *The rise and fall of the neoliberal order: America and the world in the free market era*. New York: Oxford University Press.

Glass, A. (2025). The Trump administration ended collective bargaining for one million federal workers, Center for American Progress, May 22. www.americanprogress.org /article/the-trump-administration-ended-collective-bargaining-for-1-million -federal-workers/

Global Times. (2023, September 24). Foxconn adds staff, hikes wages to manufacture new products for Huawei, Apple. www.globaltimes.cn/page/202309/1298822.shtml

Gold, M. E. (2014). *An introduction to labor law* (3rd ed.). Ithaca, NY: Cornell University Press.

Goodkind, D. & West, L. A. (2002). China's floating population: definitions, data and recent findings. *Urban Studies, 39*(12), 2237–2250. www.jstor.org/stable/43196823

Gould, W. R. (2022). *For labor to build upon: Wars, depression and pandemic.* Cambridge: Cambridge University Press.

Government Gazette. (2023, July 6). Beijing municipal human resources and social security bureau: Notice of Beijing Municipal Bureau of Human Resources and Social Security and other departments on issuing the implementation plan for further strengthening labor and personnel dispute consultation and mediation work. [Trans. from Chinese.] 北京市人力资源和社会保障局等部门关于印发《关于进一步加强劳动人事争议协商调解工作实施方案》的通知» 35(815). www.beijing.gov .cn/zhengce/zhengcefagui/202309/t20230922_3264176.html

Graeber, D. (2013). *The democracy project: A history, a crisis, a movement*, New York: Random House.

Gramsci, A. (1926). Letter of the Political Bureau of the PCI to the CC of the RCP. www .revolutionarydemocracy.org/rdv2on2/Gramsci2.htm

Greenhouse, S. (2020). *Beaten down, worked up: The past, present, and future of American labor*, New York: Anchor Books.

Gumbrell-McCormick, R. & Hyman, R. (2013). *Trade unions in Western Europe: Hard times, hard choices.* Oxford, UK: Oxford University Press.

GZU Faculty and Staff Union. (2010, December 16). Further strengthen the building of workplace trade unions and give them full play: Decision of the All-China Federation of Trade Unions on further strengthening the work of enterprise trade unions and giving full labor leadership to enterprise trade unions. [Trans. from Chinese.] Guiyang, Guizhou, China: ACFTU. https://lu-gzu-edu-cn.translate.goog/2010/1122 /c10520a64407/page.htm?_x_tr_sl=zh-CN&_x_tr_tl=en&_x_tr_hl=en&_x_tr_pto=sc

Hammer, A. & Ness, I. (2021). Informal and precarious work: Insights from the Global South, *Journal of Labor and Society, 24*(1) 1–15. https://doi.org/10.1163/24714607 -20212000

Lu, H. (2025). China's JD.com, Meituan to Offer Social Insurance for Food Delivery Riders. *Yicai Global,* February. www.yicaiglobal.com/news/chinas-jdcom-meituan-to -offer-social-insurance-for-food-delivery-riders

Harney, A. (2008). *The China price: The true cost of Chinese competitive advantage.* New York: Penguin Books.

Harris, J., Munro, R., & Zhang, M. (2007). Defending workers' rights in China: An interview with China Labour Bulletin. *Race & Class*, *48*(3), 83–93. https://journals.sagepub.com/doi/abs/10.1177/0306396807073861

Harvey, D. (2001). Globalization and the "spatial fix". *Geographische Revue*, 2. https://d-nb.info/1217929630/34

Harvey, D. (2005). *A brief history of neoliberalism.* Oxford, UK: Oxford University Press.

Hernández, D. (2024). Pursuant to deportation: Latinos and immigrant detention. In Torres, L. & Alicea, M. (Eds.), *Latino studies: A 20th anniversary reader* (pp. 523–559). Cham, Switzerland: Palgrave Macmillan).

Herod, A. (1998). Theorizing trade unions in transition. In Pickles, J. & Smith, A. (Eds.), *Theorizing transition: The political economy of post-communist transformations* (pp. 197–217). London: Routledge.

Hickel, J. (2021). *Less is more: How degrowth will save the world*; London: William Heineman.

Hickel, J. (2018). *The divide: Global inequality from conquest to free markets.* New York: W. W. Norton.

Hickel, J. & Sullivan, D. (2025, August 3). The real reason the west is warmongering against China. *Al Jazeeera.* www.aljazeera.com/opinions/2025/8/3/the-real-reason-the-west-is-warmongering-against-china

Hickel, J., Lemos, M. H., & Barbour, F. (2024). Unequal exchange of labour in the world economy. *Nature Communications*, *15*(1), 6298, 1–12. www.nature.com/articles/s41467-024-49687-y.pdf

Hirsch, B., Macpherson, D., & Even, W. (2024, January 16). *Union Membership and Coverage Database.* www.unionstats.com

Hobsbawm, E. (1967). *Labouring men: Studies in the history of labour.* Garden City: Anchor Books.

Hobsbawm, E. (1970). Lenin and the "aristocracy of labor," *Monthly* Review, *21*(11), 47–56. https://monthlyreviewarchives.org/mr/article/view/MR-021-11-1970-04_4

Hodges, G. R. G. (2020). *Taxi! A social history of the New York cabdriver.* Baltimore: Johns Hopkins University Press.

Holgate, J. (2021). *Arise: Power, strategy and union resurgence.* London: Pluto.

Holloway, J. (2002). *Change the world without taking power: The meaning of revolution today.* London: Pluto Press.

Hong, X. (2014, December 29). Hungry: Taobao in the field of food delivery, *Sina.* [Trans. from Chinese] 饿了么：外卖订餐领域的"淘宝]," https://tech.sina.com.cn/i/2014-12-29/doc-iawzunex8522092.shtml

Hornborg, A. (2011). *Global ecology and unequal exchange in a zero-sum world.* London: Routledge.

Hua, C. (2025, August 20). Only when sweat soaks through your clothes do you truly understand the hardships of food delivery riders. *Workers' Daily.* http://acftu.people.com.cn/n1/2025/0820/c67502-40545835.html

Huang, K. (2023). Organizing without mobilizing: The platformization of the workplace and its impact on Chinese trade unionism. (Trans. from French.) *Relations Industrielles Relations, 78*(3), 1–20.

Huang, Y. (2008). *Capitalism with Chinese characteristics: Entrepreneurship and the state.* New York: Cambridge University Press.

Hui, E. S. & Chan, C. K. (2015). Beyond the union-centred approach: A critical evaluation of recent trade union elections in China. *British Journal of Industrial Relations, 53*(3), 601–627.

Hussinger, K. & Palladini, L. (2025). Do China's special economic zones increase incentives to invest in R&D? *Industry and Innovation,* 1–27. https://doi.org/10.1080/13662 716.2025.2503283

Huws, U. (2014). *Labor in the global digital economy: The cybertariat comes of age.* New York: Monthly Review Press.

Hyman, R. (2001). *Understanding European trade unionism: Between market, class and society.* London: Sage Publications.

Hyman, R. & Gumbrell-McCormick, R. (2010). Trade unions, politics and parties: Is a new configuration possible? *Transfer–ETUI, 16*(3) 315–331. https://journals.sage pub.com/doi/pdf/10.1177/1024258910373863?casa_token=cqQK_qlOeMoAAAAA:9 sGZ4H63Ipc4LVdHKRfrVMJQSS46zseD89cEPp1vSE6gjwy2h8ANAuG4Tkssp 7kJc4B9cdcTbRzS

IESR (Institute for Economic and Social Research). (2025). *2024 China new flexible employment report: The proportion of new flexible employment demand continues to expand.* (Trans. from Chinese.) Guangzhou: Institute for Economic and Social Research, Jinan University and Zhaopin. 联合智联招聘发布2024中国新型灵活就业报告

ILO (International Labour Organization). (2024). *ILO and the All-China Federation of Trade Unions (ACFTU) forge new agreement to enhance trade union capacities in Asia and the Pacific, June 4.* www.ilo.org/resource/news/international-labour-organiza tion-ilo-and-all-china-federation-trade-unions

ILO (International Labour Organization). (2025). *Ratifications of C155 – Occupational Safety and Health Convention, 1981,* 155. https://normlex.ilo.org/dyn/nrmlx_en/f?p=1 000:11300:0::no:11300:p11300_instrument_id:312300

ILO (International Labour Organization). (2023). *History of the ILO.* www.ilo.org /global/about-the-ilo/history/lang--en/index.htm

International Commission for Labor Rights. (2013). *Merchants of menace: repressing workers in India's new industrial belt.* New York. http://www.laborcommission.org /files/uploads/2FINAL_Merchants_of_Menace_lo_res.pdf

IOM (International Organization for Migration). (2024). *World migration report 2024.* Geneva. https://worldmigrationreport.iom.int/msite/wmr-2024-interactive/

ITUC (International Trade Union Confederation). (2025). www.ituc-csi.org/

ITUC (International Trade Union Confederation). (2024). *The ITUC represents 191 million workers in 169 countries and territories and has 340 national affiliates* www.ituc-csi.org

Jacobs, K. & Reich, M. (2020, August 26). The effects of proposition 22 on driver earnings: Response to a Lyft-funded report by Dr. Christopher Thornberg, *Research Brief*. Berkeley, CA: University of California Berkeley Institute for Research on Labor and Employment. https://escholarship.org/uc/item/3m1028h9

Janus v. AFSCME. (2017). Supreme Court of the United States, Janus v. American Federation of State, County and Municipal Employees. www.supremecourt.gov/opinions/17pdf/16-1466_2b3j.pdf

Jian, J. (2015, July 7). At the central party and mass organizations work conference, Xi Jinping stressed the need to maintain and enhance the political nature, advancement and mass character of the party and mass organizations. *Xinhuanet*. https://syss.12371.cn/2015/07/07/ARTI1436278025137804.shtml

Jiang, Y. & Waley P. (2023). Keeping up with the zones(es): How competing local governments in China use development zones as back doors to urbanization. *Urban Geography*, 44(4), 752–772. https://doi.org/10.1080/02723638.2022.2041821.

Jing'an News. (2024a, September 18). You serve the passengers well and I will serve you! The Jing'an District Federation of Trade Unions provides multi-faceted services to drivers. Jing'an Government. 你服务好乘客，我服务你！上海静安区总工会多方面服务司机 (Shanghai Jing'an District Trade Union, ACFTU). https://www.jingan.gov.cn/rmtzx/003008/003008005/20240918/8d4ce01b-91a2-4378-9b91-90de54c0f086.html

Jing'an News. (2024b, December 6). Pudong new area express industry trade union was established. [Trans. from Chinese.] 浦东新区快递行业工会联合会成立], *Xinizixuun.cn*. www-xinzixun-cn.translate.goog/news/redian/2024/12/06/00048571.html?_x_tr_sl=zh-CN&_x_tr_tl=en&_x_tr_hl=en&_x_tr_pto=sc

Johnston, H. & Pernicka, S. (2021). Struggles over the power and meaning of digital labour platforms: A comparison of the Vienna, Berlin, New York and Los Angeles taxi markets. In J. Drahokoupil &. K. Vandaele (Eds.), *A Modern Guide to Labour and the Platform Economy* (pp. 308–322). Cheltenham: Edward Elgar Publishing.

Katta, S., Ferrari, F., van Doorn, N., & Graham, M. (2024). Migration, migrant workers and the gig economy. *Environment and Planning*, 56(4), 1102–1112.

Kaye, D. & O'Brien, R. D. (2025, January 30). Starbucks and union agree to mediation in quest for contract. *New York Times*. www.nytimes.com/2025/01/30/business/starbucks-workers-united-union-mediation.html

Kerswell, T. (2018). A conceptual history of the labour aristocracy: A critical review. *Socialism and Democracy*, 33(1), 70–87. https://doi.org/10.1080/08854300.2018.1512816.

Kerswell, T. & Pratap, S. (2019). *Worker cooperatives in India*. London: Palgrave Macmillan.

King, S. (2023). *Imperialism and the development myth: How rich countries dominate in the twenty-first century*. Manchester, UK: Manchester University Press.

Kjellberg, A. (2023). *The Nordic model of industrial relations: Comparing Denmark, Finland, Norway and Sweden*. Cologne, Germany: New Trends and Challenges in Nordic Industrial Relations. https://lucris.lub.lu.se/ws/portalfiles/portal/141188161/The_Nordic_model_of_industrial_relations_comparing_Denmark_Finland_Norway_and_Sweden.pdf

Kollmeyer, C. (2021). Post-industrial capitalism and trade union decline in affluent democracies. *International Journal of Comparative Sociology, 62*(6), 466–487.

Koslowski, R. & Ding, S. (2024). Selective migration policies with Chinese characteristics. *Journal on Migration and Human Society, 12*(4), 369–387. https://doi.org/10.1177/23315024241281471

Kruzel, J. (2023, June 5). Supreme court ruling could chill labor strikes. Reuters. www.reuters.com/world/us/experts-debate-how-much-us-supreme-court-ruling-chills-labor-strikes-2023-06-02/

Kumar, M., & Jha, P. (2025). India after 75 years of independence: Reflections on development and persistent challenges. *Agrarian South: Journal of Political Economy, 14*(2), 180–207.

Kuruvilla, S., Lee, C. K., Gallagher, M. (2011). *From iron rice bowl to informalization: Markets, workers and the state in a changing China*. Ithaca, NY: ILR/Cornell University Press.

Labor contract law of the People's Republic of China. (2007, June 29). www.npc.gov.cn/zgrdw/englishnpc/Law/2009-02/20/content_1471106.htm

Lapavitsas, C. (2013). *Profiting without producing: How finance exploits us all*. London: Verso.

Lauesen, T. (2024). *The long transition towards socialism and the end of capitalism*. Olympia, WA: Iskra Books.

Lauesen, T. (2018). *The global perspective: Reflections on imperialism and resistance*. Montreal: Kersplebedeb.

Lee, C. K. (2007). *Against the law: Labor protests in China's rustbelt and Sunbelt*. Berkeley: University of California Press.

Lenin, V. I. (1922/1973). The role and functions of the trade unions under the New Economic Policy. In *V.I. Lenin Collected Works* (Vol. 33, pp. 184–196). Moscow: Progress Publishers.

Lenin, V. I. (1916/1964). Imperialism and the split in socialism. In *Lenin's Collected Works* (Vol. 23). Moscow: Progress Publishers.

Lenin, V. I. (1902/1969). What is to be done? Burning questions of our movements. In *Lenin's Collected Works* (Vol. 5). New York: International Publishers.

Lenin, V. I. (1929). *What is to be done? Burning questions of our movement.* New York: International Publishers. https://archive.org/details/what-is-to-be-done/mode/1up

Leung, K. (2025, June 13). Hong Kong rights group shuts down after years of advocating for workers. Associated Press. https://apnews.com/article/china-labor-bulletin-disbands-5c36e8f2a79f27ff9646b65969a37562

Levitt, M. J. (2021). *Confessions of a union buster.* Bullard, TX: Xandland Press.

Li, S. (2019). *Rural–urban migration and policy intervention in China: Migrant workers' coping strategies.* Singapore: Palgrave Macmillan.

Li, W. (2025, July 30) Didi changsha online car-hailing drivers collectively join the union: The first cooperative union model in Hunan Province. Rednet. https://gov .rednet.cn/content/646941/74/15168270.html

Li, Y. (2025, June 7). Shanxi province holds meeting on deepening industrial worker cadre, *Workers Daily.* (Trans. from Chinese.) www.workercn.cn/c/2025-06-07/853 7425.shtml

Li, H. (2023). *The master in bondage: Factory workers in China, 1949–2019.* Stanford, CA: Stanford University Press.

Li, W. (2025) Didi changsha online car-hailing drivers collectively join the union: The first coop-erative union model in Hunan Province," Rednet July 30. https://gov.red net.cn/content/646941/74/15168270.html

Liang, Y. (2018, October 25). The reform of trade unions in non-public enterprises is moving forward. *Employee's Voice.* (Trans. from Chinese.) [非公企业工会改革阔步向前]

Lichtenstein, N. (2013). *State of the union: A century of American labor.* Princeton, NJ: Princeton University Press.

Lin, J. (2020). *Chinese politics and labor movements.* Cham, Switzerland: Palgrave Macmillan.

Lin, L. (2022). Power resources and workplace collective bargaining: Evidence from China, *Journal of Chinese Sociology, 9*(19). https://doi.org/10.1186/s40711-022-00178-x

Lindvall, J. (2013) Union density and political strikes. *World Politics, 65*(3), 539–569.

Liu, M. (2010). Union organizing in China: Still a monolithic labor movement? *Industrial and Labor Relations Review, 64*(1), 30–52. https://journals.sagepub.com/doi/pdf /10.1177/001979391006400102?casa_token=Nduc8ilVjd4AAAAA:4fCRqn7YRBQAr _991AbUPderZ9baOob8iASPbjUs2-vso2L5B7nmLrZj548Jj59xHDT7uaBPDCVN

Liu, M. (2011). Where there are workers, there should be trade unions: Union organizing in the era of growing informal employment. In S. Kuruvilla, C. K. Lee, & M. E. Gallagher (Eds.), *From the iron rice bowl to informalization of markets: Workers and the state in a changing China* (pp. 157–172). Ithaca, NY: Cornell University Press.

Longxiang, H. H. P. (2024, April 26). Yunda establishes the first trade union labor law supervision committee of the headquarters of express delivery industry. *Workers Daily.* (Trans. from Chinese.) 韻達成立快遞行業總部首家工會勞動法律監督委員會 https://acftu-people-com-cn.translate.goog/n1/2024/0426/c67502-40224531.html?_x _tr_sch=http&_x_tr_sl=zh-CN&_x_tr_tl=en&_x_tr_hl=en&_x_tr_pto=sc

Loomis, E. (2018). *A history of America in ten strikes*. New York: The New Press.

Losurdo, D. (2024). *Western Marxism: How it was born, how it died, how it can be reborn*. New York: Monthly Review Press.

Lu, H. (2025). China's JD.com, Meituan to Offer Social Insurance for Food Delivery Riders. *Yicai Global*, February. www.yicaiglobal.com/news/chinas-jdcom-meituan-to -offer-social-insurance-for-food-delivery-riders

Lu, X. (2024). *Neoliberalism or neocollective rural China: A critique and prospect*. Singapore: Palgrave Macmillan.

Lukács, G. (1923/1999). *History and class consciousness: Studies in Marxist dialectics*. Cambridge, MA: MIT Press.

Lynd, A. & Lynd, S. (2012). *Rank and file: Personal histories by working class organizers*. Chicago: Haymarket Books.

Maag, C. (2025, May 24). Drivers who run red lights get tickets. E-bike riders get court dates. *New York Times*. www.nytimes.com/2025/05/24/nyregion/ebikes-scooters -cyclists-nyc.html

Malhotra, P. & Agrawal, M. (2025). Dislike and survival: Work-related dynamics of gig platform workers in India. *New Technology, Work and Employment*, 1–17. https://doi .org/10.1111/ntwe.12337

Malm, A. (2020). *Corona, climate, chronic emergency: War communism in the twenty-first* century. London: Verso.

Mao Zedong /Mao Tse-Tung. (1963/2001). *Selected works of Mao Tse Tung* (Vol. 9). Paris: Foreign Languages Press.

Mao Zedong/Mao Tse-Tung. (1945). On contradiction, In Mao Tse-Tung. *Selected works* (Vol. 1), (pp. 311–347). Peking: Foreign Languages Press.

Mao Zedong/Mao Tse-Tung. (1977/2021). On the policy concerning industry and commerce. In *Selected Works of Mao Tse-Tung* (Vol. 4). Paris: Foreign Languages Press. https://archive.org/details/selected-works-of-mao-tse-tung-1/SELECTED WORKS OF MAO TSE–TUNG 4/page/200/mode/2up

Mao Zedong/Mao Tse-Tung. (1949). On the people's democratic dictatorship. In *Selected works of Mao Tse-Tung* (Vol. 4). June 30. www.marxists.org/reference/archive/mao /selected-works/volume-4/mswv4_65.htm

Marini, R. M. (2022). *The dialectics of dependency*. (A. Latimer & J. Osorio, Eds. & Trans). New York: Monthly Review Books.

Marx, K. (1867/1990). *Capital: A critique of political economy*. London: Penguin Books.

Marx. K. 1867/1976. *Capital: A critique of political economy* (Vol 1). London: Penguin Books.

Marx, K. (1867). *Capital, vol. 1* (S. Moore & E. Aveling, Eds.). (London: Swan Sonnenschein, Lowrey, & Co.).

Marx, K. & Engels, F. (1848/1898). *Manifesto of the Communist party*. New York: The National Executive Committee of the Socialist Labor Party. https://archive.org /details/manifestoofcommu00marx_1/page/n3/mode/2up

Marx, K. with Engels, F. (1932/1998). *The German ideology.* Amherst, NY: Prometheus Books. kalamkopi.files.wordpress.com/2017/04/karl-marx-friedrich-engels-the-german-ideology.pdf

Mathew, B. (2005). *Taxi! Cabs and capitalism in New York City.* Ithaca, NY: Cornell University Press.

McAlevey, J. (2016). *No shortcuts: Organizing for power in the new gilded age.* New York: Oxford University Press.

McAlevey, J. (2020). *A collective bargain: Unions, organizing, and the fight for democracy.* New York: Ecco/HarperCollins.

McAlevey, J. (2018). *No shortcuts: Organizing for power in the new gilded age* (2nd ed.). New York: Oxford University Press.

McCartin, J. A. (2025). Will federal workers rediscover their militancy? *Dissent, 72*(2), 84–91.

McCartin, J. A. (2012). *Collision course: Ronald Reagan, the air traffic controllers, and the strike that changed America.* New York: Oxford University Press.

McClelland, E. (2022). *Midnight in vehicle city: General Motors, Flint, and the strike that created the middle class.* Boston: Beacon Press.

Meisner, M. (1999). *Mao's China and after: A history of the People's Republic* (3rd ed.). New York: The Free Press.

Mihci, H. (2022). Precariat: A new class or a dangerous notion for the class struggle, *Efil Journal, 5*(3), 10–29. https://shop.efilyayinevi.com/wp-content/uploads/woocommerce_uploads/2022/09/EfilJournal-5.3-lst34k.pdf#page=12

Milkman, R. & Wong, K. (2001). Organizing immigrant workers: Case studies from Southern California. In L Turner, H. C. Katz, & R. Hurd (Eds.), *Rekindling the movement: Labor's quest for relevance in the 21st Century* (pp. 99–128). Ithaca, NY: Cornell University Press/ILR Press.

Ministry of Ecology and Environment of the PRC. (2024, October 22). *Opinions of the CPC Central Committee and the State Council on deepening the reform of the construction of the industrial workforce development.* (Trans. from Chinese.) www.mee.gov.cn/zcwj/zyygwj/202410/t20241022_1089908.shtml

Ministry of Foreign Affairs, People's Republic of China. (2024, August 9). *The National Endowment for Democracy: What it is and what It does.* www.fmprc.gov.cn/eng/xw/wjbxw/202408/t20240809_11468618.html

Ministry of Justice of the People's Republic of China. (2019, November 25). *Government Information Disclosure: The Ministry of Justice's reply to proposal no. 5984 of the second session of the 13th National People's Congress.* (Trans. from Chinese.) 关于建立劳动人事纠纷在线争议解决机制的公告（法办[2022]第3号）

Moody, K. (1988). *An injury to all: The decline of American unionism.* London: Verso.

Moody, K. (2017). *On new terrain: How capital is reshaping the battleground of class war.* Chicago: Haymarket Books.

Moussaly, O. (2022). Domenico Losurdo's historical interpretation of class struggles. *Marxism & Science*, *1*(2), 131–156. https://marxismandsciences.org/wp-content /uploads/2022/08/5.-Domenico-Losurdos-Historical-Interpretation_print.pdf

Murthy, V. (2023). *Pan-Asianism and the legacy of the Chinese revolution*. Chicago: University of Chicago Press.

Naughton, B. (2017). Is China socialist? *Journal of Economic Perspectives, 3*(1), 3–24. https://pubs.aeaweb.org/doi/pdf/10.1257/jep.31.1.3

NBSC (National Bureau of Statistics of China). (2021a). *China national population survey, 2020*. China statistical yearbook. Beijing: China Statistics Press.

NBSC (National Bureau of Statistics of China). (2021b). *Main data of the seventh national population census*. Beijing: China Statistics Press. www.stats.gov.cn/eng lish/PressRelease/202105/t20210510_1817185.html

NSBC (National Bureau of Statistics of China). (2022, January 17). *The Director of the National Bureau of Statistics answers questions from reporters on the operation of the national economy in 2021*. (Trans. from Chinese.) 国家统计局局长就2021年国民经济运行情况答记者问

NSBC (National Bureau of Statistics of China). (2023). *China statistical yearbook, 2022*. Beijing: China Statistics Press. www.stats.gov.cn/sj/ndsj/2022/indexeh.htm

Neilson, B. & Rossiter, N. (2017). *Logistical worlds: Infrastructure, software, labour, no. 2 Kolkata*. London: Open Humanities Press. https://openhumanitiespress.org/books /download/Neilson-Rossiter_2017_Logistical-Worlds-Kolkata.pdf

Ness, I. (2015). *Southern insurgency: The coming of the global working class*. London: Pluto Press.

Ness, I. (2023a). The chimera of new forms of worker organisation: Why trade unions matter in rebuilding national and global labour movements. *Work in the Global Economy, 3*(2), 225–242.

Ness, I. (2023b). *Migration as economic imperialism: How international labour mobility undermines economic development in poor countries*. Cambridge, UK: Polity.

Ness, I. (Ed.) (2023c). *The Routledge handbook of the gig economy* Abingdon, Oxon, UK: Routledge.

Ness, I. (2024). Western Marxism, anti-communism and imperialism. *International Critical Thought, 14*(4), 493–518. https://doi.org/10.1080/21598282.2024.2431960

Ness, I. (2014) *New forms of worker organization: The syndicalist and autonomist restoration of class struggle unionism*. Oakland: PM Press.

O'Brady, S., Bamber, G. J., & Cooper, B. (2025). Academic capitalism and precarity in the neoliberal university: Job insecurity and stress in two liberal market economies. *Industrial Relations Journal*, 1–10. https://onlinelibrary.wiley.com/doi/pdf/10.1111 /irj.12466

Öcalan, A. (2023). *Beyond state, power, and violence*. Oakland: CA: PM Press.

OECD Data Explorer. (2023). *Trade union density*. Paris: OECD. https://data-explo rer.oecd.org/vis?df[ds]=DisseminateFinalDMZ&df[id]=DSD_TUD_CBC%40DF _TUD&df[ag]=OECD.ELS.SAE&dq=..&pd=2000%2C&to[TIME_PERIOD]=false& vw=tb

Osorio, J. & Reyes, C. (Eds.). (2023). *Labour super-exploitation, unequal exchange and capital reproduction: Writings on Marxist dependency theory*. Stuttgart & Hanover, Germany: ibidem Press.

Østbø, H. & Speelman, T. (2022, January 28). China's rapid development has transformed Its migration trends. *Migration Policy Initiative*. https://cepr.org/voxeu/col umns/trade-unionism-and-welfare-rural-urban-migrant-workers-china

Pankaj, A. K., Manish, K., & Jha, M. K. (2024). Gig workers in precarious life: The trajectory of exploitation, insecurity, and resistance. *The American Journal of Economics and Sociology*, *83*(5), 935–946. https://onlinelibrary.wiley.com/doi/abs/10.1111 /ajes.12563?casa_token=4IaMCPYs7J8AAAAA%3AMCKPBpS4AESHnYyH3oUb -ZHzKl5gXcj_6B30GwK7DtUiPXZIrLDlIc9RcwDa-IfcxxtvZpP9HoJ96w

Pearson, M., Rithmire, M., & Tsai, K. S. (2021). Party-state capitalism in China *Current History*, *120*(827), 207–213. www-jstor-org.brooklyn.ezproxy.cuny.edu/stable/48637 954?seq=1

People's Daily Online. (2003, September 13). Effort hopes to place migrant workers under unions' umbrella. https://en.people.cn/200309/13/eng20030913_124220.shtml

Perlman, S. (1951). The basic philosophy of the American labor movement, *The Annals of the American Academy* (274)(1) March 57–63.

Però, D. & Downey, J. (2024). Advancing workers' rights in the gig economy through discursive power: The communicative strategies of indie unions. *Work, Employment and Society*, *38*(1), 140–160.

Piven, F. F. & Cloward, R. (1979). *Poor people's movements: Why they succeed, how they fail*. New York: Random House.

Pringle, T. (2011). *Trade unions in China: The challenge of labour unrest*. Abingdon, Oxon: UK: Routledge.

Pun, N. (2005). *Made in China: Women factory workers in a global workplace*. Durham, NC: Duke University Press.

Pun, N. & Chan, J. (2012). Global capital, the state, and Chinese workers: The Foxconn experience. *Modern China*, *38*(4), 383–410.

Putnam, R. D. (2001). *Bowling alone: The collapse and revival of American community*. New York: Simon & Schuster.

Qian, P. (2018). Deliverymen, your "family' is here to protect you from the wind and rain. *China Workers Daily*. [Trans. from Chinese.]

Qingyang, R. G. & Chendi, B. (2025, August 1). The supreme court made It clear that any agreement not to pay social security is invalid, *People's Daily Online*. (Trans. from

Chinese.) 最高法明确：任何"不缴社保"的约定均无效 – 社会·法治- 人民网 www
.allbrightlaw.com/CN/10475/389b81fd04e42970.aspx

Quinn, T. (2025, April 21.). JD.com's food delivery gambit: A threat to monopolies or
a risky gamble? *Ainvest*. www.ainvest.com/news/jd-food-delivery-gambit-threat
-monopolies-risky-gamble-2504/

Raffer, K. (2023). Analyzing inequality, dependence, and poverty in the world system.
In G. Segell (Ed.), *Development, globalization, global values, and security* (pp. 41–49).
Cham, Switzerland: Springer.

Rani, U. & Gobel, N. (2023). Job instability, precarity, informality, and inequality: Labour
in the gig economy. In I. Ness (Ed.), *The Routledge handbook of the gig economy*
(pp. 15–32). Abingdon, UK & New York: Routledge.

Ray, A. (2024). Coping with crisis and precarity in the gig economy: "Digitally organised
informality," migration and socio-spatial networks among platform drivers in India.
Environment and Planning A, 56(4), 1227–1244.

Refslund, B. & Arnholtz, J. (2021). Power resource theory revisited: The perils and
promises for understanding contemporary labour politics. *Economic and Industrial
Democracy, 43*(4), 1958–1979. https://doi.org/10.1177/0143831X211053379 https://jour
nals.sagepub.com/doi/epub/10.1177/0143831X211053379

Reid, A., Rhonda-Perez E., Schenker M.B. (2021). Migrant workers, essential work, and
COVID-19. *American Journal of Industrial Medicine, 64*(2), 73–77.

Renaldi, V. (2025). Examining China's recent economic transformation: The state's role
and structural challenges. *Asia Pacific Business Review*, 1–6. https://doi.org/10.1080
/13602381.2025.2546614

RFA Cantonese. (2025, June 13). *China labor rights group shuts down in latest setback for
civil society in Hong Kong*, Radio Free Asia. www.rfa.org/english/china/2025/06/13
/china-labor-bulletin-shutdown-hong-kong/

Ricci, A. (2022). Global locational inequality: Assessing unequal exchange effects. *EPA
Economy and Space, 54*(7), 1323–1340.

Ricci, A. (2023). Ecologically unequal exchange and the value of money. *Capitalism
Nature Socialism, 34*(3), 22–42. https://doi.org/10.1080/10455752.2023.2195673

Ricci, A. (2021a). *Value and unequal exchange: The geography of global capitalist exploitation*. London: Routledge.

Ricci, A. (2021b). Unequal exchange and global value chains. In R. Herrera (Ed.), *Imperialism and transitions to socialism*. Bingley, UK: Emerald Publishing, Ltd, 59–76.

Ricci, A. (2019). Unequal exchange in the age of globalization. *Review of Radical Political Economics, 51*(2), 225–245. https://journals-sagepub-com.brooklyn.ezproxy
.cuny.edu/doi/epub/10.1177/0486613418773753c

Robinson, W. I. (2014). *Global capitalism and the crisis of humanity*. New York: Cambridge University Press.

Rothstein, S. A. (2025). Solidarity across the platform: Mobilizing high-wage and low-wage workers in the tech sector. *Work in the Global Economy*, 5(2), 167–189. https://doi.org/10.1332/27324176Y2025D000000036

Ruckus, R. (2023). *The left in China: A political cartography*. London: Pluto Press.

Ruckus, R. (2021). *The communist road to capitalism: How unrest and containment have pushed China's revolution since 1949*. Oakland, CA: PM Press.

Sainato, M. (2025a, August 22). White House cancels union contracts for hundreds of thousands of federal workers. *The Guardian*. www.theguardian.com/us-news/2025/aug/22/trump-federal-workers-union-rights

Sainato, M. (2025b, January 14). A bargaining breakdown and strikes: The bitter union fight at Starbucks. *The Guardian*. www.theguardian.com/business/2025/jan/14/starbucks-union-fight

Schmaltz, S., Ludwig, C., & Webster, E. (2018). The power resources approach: Developments and challenges. *Global Labour Journal*, 9(2), 113–134.

Schmalz, S., Sommer, B., & Xu, H. (2016). The Yue Yuen strike: Industrial transformation and labour unrest in the Pearl River Delta. *Globalizations*, 14(2), 285–297. https://doi.org/10.1080/14747731.2016.1203188

Schmalz, S., Ludwig, C., & Webster, E. (2019). Power resources and global capitalism. *Global Labour Journal*, 10(1) 84–90.

Scholz, T. (2017). *Uberworked and underpaid: How workers are disrupting the digital economy*. Cambridge, UK: Polity.

Schumpeter, J. A. (1911/1934). *The theory of economic development*, Cambridge, MA: Harvard University Press.

SCIO (State Council Information Office). (2025, April 28). Singing the song of workers embarking on a new journey of struggle and progress. *People's Daily*. www.scio.gov.cn/live/2025/35870/xgbd/202504/t20250428_893388.html

Scully, B. (2016). Precarity north and south: A southern critique of Guy Standing. *Global Labour Journal*, 7(2) 160–172. https://doi.org/10.15173/glj.v7i2.2521

Sears, J. B. (2019). *The electrical unions and the Cold War: Generation of resistance*. New York: International Publishers.

Seidman, G. W. (1994). *Manufacturing militance: Workers' movements in Brazil and South Africa, 1970–1985*. Berkeley: University of California Press.

Shanghai City Spirit. (2024, April 24). The first online car-hailing industry trade union federation in the region was established, and more than 2,000 online car-hailing drivers now have a "home." (Trans. from Chinese.) 全区首个网约车行业工会联合会成立，2000多名网约车司机有"娘家". Shanghai: Shanghai Putuo District People's Government. www.shpt.gov.cn/tzdt-ys/20240424/942614.html

Shanghai Municipal Transportation Commission. (2022). White paper on transportation development in Shanghai (上海市交通发展白皮书), October 2022. https://jtw.sh.gov.cn/cmsres/od/0dab6b1c127f4d00811a424d9b25ffa5/b2b13f70451641f211145db4c14353891.pdf

Silver, B. J. (2003). *Forces of labor: Workers' movements and globalization since 1870.* Cambridge, UK: Cambridge University Press.

Silvia, S. J. (2023). *The UAW's southern gamble: Organizing workers at foreign-owned vehicle plants.* Ithaca, NY: Cornell/ILR Press.

Slobodian, Q. (2023). *Crack-up capitalism: Market radicals and the dream of a world without democracy.* New York: Metropolitan Books.

Smith, C. (2024, December 13). Didi statistics and user count for 2024, *DMR.* https://expandedramblings.com/index.php/didi-chuxing-facts-statistics/

Solinger, D. J. (1999). *Contesting citizenship in urban China: Peasant migrants, the state, and the logic of the market.* Berkeley: University of California Press.

Solinger, D. J. (2022). *Poverty and pacification: The Chinese state abandons the old working* class. Lanham, MD: Rowman & Littlefield.

SSAP (Social Sciences Academic Press). (2024). *Chinese workers: Annual report on the status of Chinese workers 2023.* Beijing: Social Sciences Academic Press.

Standing, G. (2011). *The precariat: The new dangerous class.* London: Bloomsbury Academic.

The State Council. The People's Republic of China. (2022). *The Constitution of the Communist Party of China.* Beijing: Xinhua. https://english.www.gov.cn/news/topnews/202210/26/content_WS635921cdc6d0a757729e1cd4.html

The Supreme People's Court of the People's Republic of China. (2025). SPC clarifies mandatoiry social insurance payment obligation. August 8. https://english.court.gov.cn/2025-08/08/c_1116506.htm

Stevenson, A. (2025). Chinese labor rights group led by former Tiananmen protest leader closes, *New York Times,* June 12. www.nytimes.com/2025/06/12/business/hong-kong-labor-rights-nonprofit-closes.html

Sugrue, T. (2014). *The origins of the urban crisis: Race and inequality in postwar Detroit.* (Updated ed.). Princeton: Princeton University Press.

Sun, W. (2022). *Population and labour market policies in China's reform process.* Abingdon, Oxon: UK).

Tassinari, A. & Maccarrone, V. (2020). Riders on the storm: Workplace solidarity among gig economy couriers in Italy and the UK. *Work Employment & Society,* (34) 35–54.

Tattersall, A. (2010) *Power in coalition: Strategies for strong unions and social change.* Ithaca, NY: Cornell University Press.

Taylor, A. J. (1989). *Trade unions and politics: A comparative introduction.* London: Palgrave.

Taylor, B. & Li, Q. (2007). Is the ACFTU a union and does It matter? *Journal of Industrial Relations,* 49(5) 701–715. https://doi.org/10.1177/0022185607082217

Teelucksingh, J. (2015). *Labour and the decolonization struggle in Trinidad and Tobago.* London: Palgrave Macmillan.

Thomas, A., Kochan, T. A., Fine, J., Bronfenbrenner, K., Naidu, S., Barnes, J., Diaz-Linhart, Y., Kallas, J., Kim, J., Minster, A., Tong, D., Townsend, P., & Twiss, D. (2023). An overview of US workers' current organizing efforts and collective actions. *Work and Occupations, 50*(3), 335–350.

Trappmann, V., Bessa, I., Joyce, S. Neumann, D. et al. (2020). *Labour unrest on platforms: The case of food delivery workers.* Berlin: Friedrich Ebert Stiftung. https://library.fes .de/pdf-files/iez/16880.pdf

Traub-Merz, R. R. (2011). *All China Federation of Trade Unions: Structure, functions and the challenge of collective bargaining* (International Labour Office Working Paper Series No. 13). Berlin: Global Labour University.

Tu, W. & Wang, X. (2024) *New forms of employment and labour protection in China* (ILO Working Paper No. 103). Geneva: International Labour Organization.

Tuñón, M. (2006). *Internal labour migration in China: Features and responses.* (Beijing: International Labour Organization).

Vandaele, K. (2018) *Will trade unions survive in the platform economy? Emerging patterns of platform workers' collective voice in Europe* (Working Paper 2018.05). Brussels: European Trade Union Institute. www.etui.org/sites/default/files/Working %20Paper%202018.05%20Vandaele%20Trade%20unions%20Platform%20econ omy%20Web.pdf

Vandaele, K. (2020). *From street protest to improvisational unionism: Platform-based food delivery couriers in Belgium and the Netherlands.* Bonn: Friedrich Ebert Stiftung.

Vandaele, K., Piasna, A., & Zwysen, W. (2024). *Are platform workers willing to unionize? Exploring survey evidence from 14 European countries* (ILO Working Paper No. 106). Geneva: ILO. https://doi.org/10.54394/QWUL5553

van der Linden, M. (2021). Why the global labor movement is in crisis. *Journal of Labor and Society, 24*(3) 375–400.

van der Linden, M. (2023). *The world wide web of work: A history in the making.* London: UCL Press.

van Doorn, N. (2023). Liminal precarity and compromised agency: Migrant experiences of gig work in Amsterdam, Berlin, and New York City. In I. Ness (Ed.), *The Routledge handbook of the gig economy* (pp. 158–179). London: Routledge.

van Doorn, N. Ferrari, F., & Graham, M. (2022). Migration and migrant labour in the gig economy: An intervention. *Work, Employment and Society, 37*(4), 1099–1111. https:// doi.org/10.1177/09500170221096581

Visser, J. (2024). Will they rise again? Four scenarios for the future of trade unions. *Economic and Industrial Democracy, 45*(3), 629–652.

Wang, D. (2022, February 11). Speech at the fifth executive committee meeting of the seventeenth All-China Federation of Trade Unions, January 29, 2022. *Workers' Daily.* http://acftu.people.com.cn/n1/2022/0211/c67502-32350304.html

Wang, H. & Liang, J. (2022, December 27). Shanghai Federation of Trade Unions promotes the occupational welfare of workers in new industries (上海工会促增新业态劳动者的职业福祉), *Sina,* China Workers Network.

Wang, S. & Young. S. (2023). *Unionization, employer opposition, and establishment closure*. Washington, DC: US Census Bureau, Center for Economic Studies.

Wang, Z., Lin, L., Tang, S., & Xiao Y. (2023). Migration and migrants in Chinese cities: New trends, challenges and opportunities to theorise with urban China. *Transactions in Planning and Urban Research*, 24(4), 317–331.

Wang, Z., Wang, S., Wang, J., & Wang, Y. (2022). Development zones and urban economic performance in China: Direct impact and channel effects. *Growth and Change: A Journal of Urban and Regional Policy*, 53(4) 1762–1782.

Weber, I. M. (2021). *How China escaped shock therapy: The market reform debate*. London & New York: Routledge.

Wei, T. & Wang, X. (2024). *New forms of employment and labor protection in China* (ILO Working Paper No. 103. Geneva: ILO.

Weil, R. (1996). *White cat, red cat: China and the contradictions of "market socialism."* New York: Monthly Review Press. www.ilo.org/sites/default/files/wcmsp5/groups /public/%40asia/%40ro-bangkok/%40ilo-beijing/documents/publication/wcms _913322.pdf

Wen, T. (2021). *Ten crises: The political economy of China's development, 1949–2020.* Singapore: Palgrave Macmillan. https://archive.org/details/wen-tiejun-ten-crises -online-pdf-20210619-revised-1

Wang, W. (2025, April 15). *Establishing an independent labor dispute resolution mechanism, China Social Sciences Network*. (Trans. from Chinese.) 建立独立的劳动争议解决机制, www.cssn.cn/skgz/bwyc/202504/t20250415_5869178.shtml

Wetzel, T. (2022). *Overcoming capitalism: Strategy for the working class in the 21st century*. Chico, CA: AK Press.

WFTU (World Federation of Trade Unions). (2024a). *History*. www.wftucentral.org/history/

WFTU (World Federation of Trade Unions). (2024b). WFTU Program of activities in the 113th ILC, Geneva, 2–13 June 2025. https://www.wftucentral.org/wftu-program -of-activities-in-the-113th-ilc-geneva-02-13-june-2025/

Wie, T. & Wang, X. (2024). *New forms of employment and labour protection in China* (ILO Working Paper No. 103). Geneva: ILO.

Womack, J. (2023). *Labor power and strategy* (P. Olney & G. Perusek, Eds.). Oakland: PM Press.

Wong, C. H. (2021, March 7). Xi Jinping's eager-to-Please bureaucrats snarl his China plans *Wall Street Journal.* www.wsj.com/world/china/xi-jinpings-eager-to-please -minions-snarl-his-china-plans-1161514119

Woodcock, J. & Graham, M. (2019). *The gig economy: A critical introduction*. Cambridge, UK: Polity.

Wring, D. (2005). The labour campaign. *Parliamentary Affairs*, 58(4), 712–724.

Wu, J (2025, July 28). My country's truck drivers' union has 5.9 million members, *Xinhuanet*. (Trans from Chinese.] www.scio.gov.cn/live/2025/35870/xgbd/202504 /t20250428_893388.html

Wu, W., Yang., Y. Leyan S., Sun, Y., & Liu, T. (2024). Internal migrants, skill complementarity and wage premiums for local workers: A micro econometric analysis of Chinese households. *Journal of the Asia Pacific Economy*, 1–24. https://doi.org/10.1080/13547860.2024.2344237

Xi, F. (2018, January 17). The total number of employees in China reached 391 million. *Xinhuanet.* www.xinhuanet.com/politics/2018-01/17/c_1122274062.htm

Xi, J. (2025). *Xi's speech marking 100th anniversary of trade union federation.* Beijing: People's Publishing House. https://english.www.gov.cn/news/202505/07/content_WS681b40c5c6d0868f4e8f2527.html

Xi, M., Zhou, L., Zhang, X., & Zhao, S. (2021). Labor relations conflict in China: An analysis of conflict measure, conflict solution and conflict outcomes. *The International Journal of Human Resource Management, 33*(17), 3414–3450.

Xiang, B. 2007. How far are the left-behind left behind? A preliminary study in rural China. *Population, Space and Place, 13*(3) 179–191.

Xie, Z. (2022). The legislative progress of labor rights protection for platform workers. (Trans. from Chinese.) (Beijing: China Law Network) 中国法学网 首页.

Xinhua. (2025a, June 27). China sees increasing number of private sector entities. https://search.english.www.gov.cn/en/search.shtml?code=17dbe3acd9d&codes=&configCode=&searchWord=privatesector&dataTypeId=57&sign=6d94bbeb-0957-4c4f-9ddb-d8493527eec0

Xinhua. (2025b, April 30). China's migrant workers see steady income rise in 2024. The State Council of the People's Republic of China. https://english.www.gov.cn/archive/statistics/202504/30/content_WS6812249ac6d0868f4e8f2395.html

Xinhua News Agency. (2018, August 24). Behind the Jasic workers' rights protection incident. *Xinhuanet.* (Trans. from Chinese.) www.mps.gov.cn/n2254098/n4904352/c6207393/content.html

Xinyi, J. (2025, August 13). Skip social insurance, pay severance: China's top court tells employers. *Sixth Tone.* www.sixthtone.com/news/1017475

Xu, Y. (2025, March 7). General Secretary Xi Jinping visits groups at the two sessions: Social work must be strengthened. *People's Daily.* https://www-12371-cn.translate.goog/2025/03/07/ARTI1741334890505295.shtml?_x_tr_sl=zh-CN&_x_tr_tl=en&_x_tr_hl=en&_x_tr_pto=schttps://www.12371.cn/2025/03/07/ARTI1741334890505295.shtml

Xu, Z. (2023). The gig economy in China. In I. Ness (ed.), *The Routledge handbook of the gig economy* (pp. 392–400). Abingdon, UK: Routledge.

Yang, C. (2025, February 20). China's food-delivery platforms vow welfare coverage for armies of riders. *South China Morning Post.* www.scmp.com/economy/china-economy/article/3299473/chinas-eleme-joins-meituan-jdcom-vowing-welfare-coverage-armies-riders

Yang, F. (2025). Empowering college student employment through community cultural wealth: A case study of human resource management students in China. *Frontiers in Education,* 10:1538054, 1–15. https://doi.org/10.3389/feduc.2025.1538054

Yasih, D. W. P. (2025). *Workers' solidarity in an age of precarity, Precarious workers in the gig economy. Contestations in contemporary Southeast Asia.* Singapore: Singer Nature.

Young, M. (2017). *Union power: The United Electrical Workers in Erie, Pennsylvania.* New York: Monthly Review Press.

Yu X. (2021, March 8). Black hands wear "White gloves" again! This NGO spends $10 million to slander China." *Beijing Daily Client.* (Transl. from Chinese.) https://xin wen.bjd.com.cn/content/s6045f99ce4b0063e4e72f95e.html

Yu, A.-L., Xue, B. R., & Jetin, B. (2013). *China's rise: Strength and fragility* (A.-L. Xue, Ed.). London: Merlin Press.

Yuan, J. E. & Zhang, L. (2025). From platform capitalism to digital China: The path, governance and geopolitics, *Social Media + Society, 11*(1). https://journals.sagepub .com/doi/full/10.1177/20563051251323030

Zeng, Y. Cheong, T. S., Wojewodzki, M., & Shi, X. (2024). Mapping the dynamics of FDI in China: Convergence, divergence and policy insights within free trade zones and beyond. *The Journal of International Trade & Economic Development, 34*(4), 894–912. https://doi.org/10.1080/09638199.2024.2339465

Zhang, W., Qi., H. & Li, L. Z. (2023). "Control of the platform reserve army: The roles of the state and capital in China's platform economy," *Science & Society* 87(4) 502–530. https://guilfordjournals.com/doi/pdf/10.1521/siso.2023.87.4.502

Zhang, L. (2024). Labour process theory and research on the changing nature of work and employment in China. *Work in the Global Economy, 4*(2), 193–214.

Zhang, Z. (2025). *Maoist and classical Chinese roots of Chinese experiments in eco-socialism.* Unpublished manuscript. Lanzhou University Marxism Department.

Zhou, I. (2020). *Digital labour platforms and labour protection in China* (ILO Working Paper No. 11). Geneva; ILO. www.ilo.org/sites/default/files/wcmsp5/groups /public/%40asia/%40ro-bangkok/%40ilo-beijing/documents/publication/wcms _757923.pdf

Zhou J. & Hui, E. C. (2022). The hukou system and selective internal migration in China. *Papers in Regional Science, 101*(2), 461–483. https://doi.org/10.1111/pirs.12651

Zhu, Y. (2004). Workers, unions and the state: Migrant workers in China's labour-intensive foreign enterprises. *Development and Change, 35*(5), 1011–1036.

Zuo, M. (2024, December 20). Migration from China's countryside to cities to be a key factor in resource allocation. *South China Morning Post.* www.scmp.com/economy /china-economy/article/3291707/migration-chinas-countryside-cities-be-key-factor -resource-allocation

Epilogue and Acknowledgements

Most Western observers of trade unions stereotypically disparage or ignore the achievements of the All-China Federation of Trade Unions (ACFTU) and all its elected leaders, organizers and members as captured by a party system. This book is intended to generate debate and discussion about the condition of the Chinese working class from a socialist perspective. The book avoids ideals and superlatives. It takes seriously the work of Marx, Engels, Lenin, Mao and Xi through applying their analysis to Chinese workers in the context of revolutionary transformation and consolidation. A motivating force of this book is the necessity to respond monolithic and uncompromising interpretations and studies among scholars of China.

From the left to the right, almost all Labor scholars maintain an inflexible unyielding perspective and are unlikely to examine the People's Republic of China, the Communist Party of China and ACFTU and its members without blinders. This book is intended to assess the CPC and ACFTU for how their claims are proven or unproven through a dialectical and grounded analysis. How did the founders of the PRC envision the dictatorship of the working class under the ACFTU trade union at the formation of the socialist state and how do theory and practice today conform or deviate from them? I have found that there are no unalloyed truths but only positions which emerge out of material and confessional vantage points—notably a common opposition to the People's Republic of China. In contrast, I adopt Mao Zedong's concept of the principal contradiction which a fledgling socialist state must confront as it fends off imperialists and counterrevolutionaries and perceptions and constructs typically advanced by one and the same.

First and foremost, I acknowledge the generous support of diverse people for making this project possible and to whom I owe a large debt of gratitude. I garnered information and interpretation from synthesizing the multifaceted views of people who were open to sharing their opinions about the trade union movement in China. Make no mistake, this account recognizes the party–trade union alliance which prevails in China and recognizes the necessity that opposing worker organizations are proscribed. Yet, this admonition is endorsed by socialists, from Marx and Engels to Lenin and Mao. This lineage of revolutionary theorists, practitioners and workers recognized that the bourgeoisie would remain a threat to the emergent socialist transitional state after socialist revolutions. To prevent this, Marx and his successors unambiguously recognized that just as capitalism requires a dictatorship of the bourgeoisie, the transition from capitalism to socialism also required an equivalent dictatorship of the proletariat to prevent the restoration of capitalism. All unambiguously grasped the embryonic transitional state as exposed to bourgeois intrusion through infiltrating state institutions and trade unions.

By keeping their identities anonymous, I have taken special caution to protect all those who lent their time to discuss their viewpoints from the maelstrom of criticism and scorn that inevitably could flow from this study. However, trade unionists and workers have openly discussed how the ACFTU is responsible for rapidly improving their standard of living and has given them a critical voice to openly express their opposition to rapacious employers who have violated labor law. The PRC has established labor courts to mediate or arbitrate disputes quickly, unlike anywhere else in the world.

My acknowledgements are spare. Foremost, I thank anonymous scholars, trade unionists, workers and small-business owners who have shared their time and ideas through engaging this project and offered critical opinions that shaped the manuscript. A contentious book is intended to elicit positive and negative feedback. I thank all those who seriously engaged with this project. I do not expect agreement, but critical and serious comments.

Special thanks go to Torkil Lauesen, who has been instrumental in commenting on the framing of the concept of the transitional state. Ali Kadri introduced me to students and faculty in China who served as interlocutors that got this project off the ground.

I received sage insight and critiques from Michael Pelias, a Marxist philosopher who has provided thoughtful comments on multiple drafts of the manuscript. Many others have read and commented and corrected the manuscript, including Zhun Xu, a prodigious political economist whose vision I share.

I express gratitude to Pan Yan, Adrian Ortega Camara and Alex Witherspoon for their extraordinary critical comradely support. Thanks go to Leah Chen for assisting in many ways. Notably, Leah recruited six journalists who conducted ethnographic interviews with workers in diverse jobs across China. Thanks go to Sreyashi Choudhury for advice and encouragement and to Alesandro D'Angelo for elucidating the rise of an authentic trade union center in Hong Kong. I extend special thanks to Michael Crook for helping me to situate the Chinese and international working class.

I am grateful to Yan Hairong of the Tsinghua Institute for Advanced Study in Humanities and Social Sciences for hosting a seminar for a paper on Western Marxism and for sharing her astute knowledge of migration in China and sharing her ethnographic research on how the Uyghur people prosper in rural Xinjiang Province.

Among many in South Africa, I thank Pragna Ragunanan, Malehoko Tshoaedi, Luke Sinwell and Eddie Cottle who have shaped my understanding of migration, trade unions, labor and imperialism.

Over the past 15 years, I benefited from discussions with Renate Bridenthal, Matteo Capasso, Mateo Crossa, Essam Elkorghli, Jeannette Graulau, Jennifer Holdaway, Timothy Kerswell, Max Lane, Lefeng, Nemanja Lukić, Corinna Mullin, Viren Murthy, Alejandro Pedregal, Richard Freeman and many others who contributed to my understanding Kay yew Koh provided sage advice and encouragement. In November 2023, on a visit to Shanghai, Roger Harris asked vital but difficult questions about the nature of China's working class.

I appreciate Wilma Dunaway and Honghui Park for perceptive advice that sustained this research project and manuscript.

I owe a large debt of gratitude to Alan McIntosh for poring over the text, editing and proofing the manuscript. I am grateful to Christine Hededam and Simona Casadio, my editors at De Gruyter Brill. Many thanks go to illustrator Jovana Joković, in Belgrade, for a vivid imagination. I also thank project manager Madhan Kumar D.

Research support was generously provided from the South Africa Department of Higher Education and Training, City University of New York Research Foundation, and a PSC/CUNY grant.

Finally, I alone bear all responsibility for the substance, claims and opinions of this book. In the final instance, correspondence and friendship do not translate into shared positions, and vice versa. There are no absolutes and we must learn to differ without rancor.

www.ingramcontent.com/pod-product-compliance
Lightning Source LLC
Chambersburg PA
CBHW051736250726
48659CB00001B/97